David Macritchie

The Testmony Of Tradition

David Macritchie

The Testmony Of Tradition

ISBN/EAN: 9783742830111

Manufactured in Europe, USA, Canada, Australia, Japa

Cover: Foto ©Andreas Hilbeck / pixelio.de

Manufactured and distributed by brebook publishing software (www.brebook.com)

David Macritchie

The Testmony Of Tradition

THE RUINS OF THE ROUND TOWER, CONEY ISLAND
(View in 1907)

THE
TESTIMONY OF TRADITION

BY

DAVID MacRITCHIE
AUTHOR OF "ANCIENT AND MODERN BRITONS"

WITH TWENTY ILLUSTRATIONS

LONDON
KEGAN PAUL, TRENCH, TRÜBNER & CO., LIMITED
1890

PREFACE.

A LARGE portion of this work has already appeared in the form of a series of articles contributed to the *Archæological Review* (Aug.-Oct., 1889, and Jan., 1890), but these have here undergone some alteration and have been supplemented to a considerable extent.

With regard to the correctness of the deductions drawn in the following pages from the facts and traditions there stated, there may easily be a difference of opinion. And indeed one writer, Mr. Alfred Nutt, in the course of a very learned dissertation on the Development of the Fenian or Ossianic Saga,[1] has expressed his dissent from the theories advanced in the articles referred to. It would be out of place to enter here into a consideration of the grounds of Mr. Nutt's objections, even if that did not demand an undue amount of space; but it may be pointed out that the articles upon which his criticism is based only state very partially the case which even the following more enlarged version is far from presenting fully. But what is of much greater importance is, that the theory which I have here endeavoured to set forth has the peculiar advantage of

---

[1] Appended to the collection of "Folk and Hero Tales from Argyllshire" which forms the second volume of the series entitled "Waifs and Strays of Celtic Tradition" (London, 1890; published by the Folk-Lore Society).

possessing a tangible test of its worth. What that test is will be readily seen by every reader. If the result of future archæological excavations should be to confirm tradition (as it is needless to say the writer of these pages believes will be the case), the question then will be one, not of interpreting tradition so that it may square with current beliefs, but of modifying or altering these beliefs, where they are distinctly in disagreement with tradition.

CONTENTS.

PREFACE . . . . PAGE v

CHAPTER I.
Shetland Finns—Orkney Finnmen—Finn Localities—Kayaks and Kayak-men—An Orkney Kayak of 1696 1-11

CHAPTER II.
"Zee-Wooers"—Piratical Mer-folk—Landsmen and Mermen—Iberian Skin-boats—Boats made by Norway Finns—"Marine People" of the Hebrides—Probable Finns in Galloway . 12-25

CHAPTER III.
"Inhabitants of the Isles of this Kingdom"—The Isles in the Seventeenth Century—"Barbarous Men" . . . 26-32

CHAPTER IV.
Homes of the Finns—Norwegian Suzerainty . . . 33-38

CHAPTER V.
Finnish Influence in Norway 39-42

CHAPTER VI.
The Feinne—The Battle of Gawra—The Feenic Confederacy 43-50

CHAPTER VII.
Feens or Cruithne—Fin in the Kingdom of the Big Men—Dwarfish Tyrants 51-57

CHAPTER VIII.

Pechts or Dwarfs—Pechts' Houses—Earth-Houses in Greenland—
"Interlude of the Droichs" 58-65

CHAPTER IX.

How the Pechts Built—Pecht-lands—The Builders of Corstorphine
Church—"Unco wee bodies, but terrible strang" . . 66-74

CHAPTER X.

Strongholds of the Feens—The *Howe* and the *Sith-Khrog* 75-79

CHAPTER XI.

Finns and Fairies—Tenth-Century Fairies—Continental Finns and
Fairies—Finn and his Dwarf in Sylt 80-88

CHAPTER XII.

Witchcraft of the Trollmen—The King of the Sidhfir of Munster—
The "Great-Bosomed Deer" of the Feens—Reindeer in Scotland in the Twelfth Century—Pechts and Fairies . . 89-100

CHAPTER XIII.

Hollow Hillocks—The Settler and the Mound-Dwellers—"Hog-Boys"—Maes-How—Interior of the Chambered Mound—A
Dwarf's House in Sylt—The Little People in Scotland—Fairy
Mounds 101-118

CHAPTER XIV.

The Brugh of the Boyne—The Brugh as Described in 1724—Cineh
tuatha Dananna—Dananns, Fir Sidhe, or Fairies—Cruithne
Palace—Inmates of the Brugh—Plunder of the Boyne Hillocks
in 861—Sidh Eamhna—Tales of Adventures in "Weems"—
The Dowth Mound 119-140

CHAPTER XV.

Goblin Halls—The Castle Hill of Clurie—Tomnahurich, Inverness
—The Palace of the King of the Pechts—Pecht Localities—
The Fairy Knowe of Aberfoyle—Chambered Mounds 141-155

CHAPTER XVI.

Scott's "Rob Roy"—Shaggy Men—Red Fairies of Wales—Brownies and Forest-Men—The Ainos—A Hairy Race—Modern "Pechts"—Cave-Men—Dwarf-Tribes and Reindeer—*Pygmæi Vulgo Screilinger Dicti* . . . 156–175

CHAPTER XVII.

Platycnemic Men—*Ur-uisg an Naillnachan* . . 176–180

Appendix A.—*The Brugh of the Boyne* . . 181–189

Appendix B.—*The Skrællings* . . . 190–193

Index 195–205

LIST OF ILLUSTRATIONS.

The Brugh of the Boyne, New Grange, County Meath
Frontispiece.
Kayakers in High Sea . . . . . *To face page* 12
Wigwams of the Jura Islanders in 1772 . . „ „ 24
Maes-How, Orkney . . . . . . „ „ 108
Sectional View and Ground Plan of Maes-How . „ 108
The Interior of the "How" . . . . „ 109
Sectional View of the Brugh of the Boyne . „ „ 120
Doorway of the Brugh . . . . „ 121
Enlarged Sectional View of Passage and Chamber, Brugh of the Boyne . . . „ „ 122
Ground Plans of Passage and Chamber, Brugh of the Boyne. (From Drawings of 1724 and 1889) „ „ 124
Eastern Recess of Central Chamber, Brugh of the Boyne . . . . . . „ „ 126
Dowth (*Island Point Barken at Dubath*), County Meath . . . . „ „ 136
Plan of Dowth . . . . . . „ 137
Plan of Passage and Chamber at Dowth . . „ 138
Bee-Hive Chamber, Dowth . . . . „ 139
Knowth (*Island Cnoghbha*), County Meath . „ „ 140
The Dwarfs of German Folk-Lore . . „ „ 164
An Aino Patriarch . . . . . . „ 168
Aino of 1804 . . . . „ 170
A "Good Fairy" of Tradition . . . . „ 173

THE TESTIMONY OF TRADITION.

CHAPTER I.

In one of an interesting series of papers on "Scottish, Shetlandic, and Germanic Water Tales,"[1] Dr. Karl Blind remarks as follows:—

It is in the Shetland Tales that we hear a great deal of creatures partly more than human, partly less so, which appear in the interchangeable shape of men and seals. They are said to have often married ordinary mortals, so that there are, even now, some alleged descendants of them, who look upon themselves as superior to common people.

In Shetland, and elsewhere in the North, the sometimes animal-shaped creatures of this myth, but who in reality are human in a higher sense, are called *Finns*. Their transfiguration into seals seems to be more a kind of deception they practise. For the males are described as most daring boatmen, with powerful sweep of the oar, who chase foreign vessels on the sea. At the same time they are held to be deeply versed in magic spells and in the healing art, as well as in soothsaying. By means of a "skin" which they possess, the men and the women among them are able to change themselves into seals. But on shore, after having taken off their wrappage, they are, and behave like, real human beings. Anyone who gets hold of their protecting garment has the Finns in his power. Only by means of the skin can they go back to the water. Many a Finn woman has got into the power of a Shetlander and borne children to him; but if a Finn woman succeeded in reobtaining her sea-skin, or seal-skin, she escaped across the water. Among the older generation in the Northern Isles persons are still sometimes

[1] Contributed to *The Contemporary Review* of 1881, and *The Gentleman's Magazine* of 1882.

heard of who boast of hailing from Finns; and they attribute to themselves a peculiar luckiness on account of that higher descent.

* * * * * * *

Tales of the descent of certain families from water beings of a magic character are very frequent in the . . . . North. In Ireland such myths also occur sporadically. In Wales . . . . the origin from mermen or mermaids is often charged as a reproach upon unhappy people; and rows originate from such assertions. In Shetland the reverse is, or was, the case. There the descendants of Finns have been wont to boast of their origin; regarding themselves as favourites of Fortune. . . .

* * * * * * *

But who are the Finns of the Shetlandic story? Are they simply a poetical transfiguration of finny forms of the flood? Or can the Ugrian race of the Finns, which dwells in Finland, in the high north of Norway, and in parts of Russia, have something to do with those tales in which a Viking-like character is unmistakable?

* * * * * * *

Repeated investigations have gradually brought me to the conviction that the Finn or Seal stories contain a combination of the mermaid myth with a strong historical element—that the Finns are nothing else than a fabulous transmogrification of those Norse "sea-dogs," who from old have penetrated into the islands round Scotland, into Scotland itself, as well as into Ireland. "Old sea-dog" is even now a favourite expression for a weather-beaten, storm-tossed skipper—a perfect equal among the wild waves.

The assertion of a "higher" origin of still living persons from Finns . . . . would thus explain itself as a wildly legendary remembrance of the descent from the blood of Germanic conquerors. The "skin" wherewith the Finns change themselves magically into sea-beings I hold to be their armour, or coat of mail. Perhaps that coat itself was often made of seal-skin, and then covered with metal rings, or scales, as we see it in Norman pictures; for instance, on the Bayeux tapestry. The designation of Norwegian and Danish conquerors, in Old Irish history, as "scaly monsters," certainly fits in with this hypothesis.

* * * * * * *

But however the Finn name may be explained etymologically, at all events Norway appears in the Shetland tales, and in the recollection of the people there, as the home of the "Finns." And this home—as I see from an interesting bit of folk-lore before me—is evidently in the south of Norway. . . .

"Before coming to this important point, I may mention a Shetlandic spell-song. . . . [which] refers to the cure of the toothache; the Finn appearing therein as a magic medicine-man:—

A Finn came ow't to Norroway,
Fu ta pit teeth-ache away—

> Oot o' da flesh an' oot o' da bane;
> Oot o' da sinew an' oot o' da skane;
> Oot o' da skane an' into da stane;
> As dare may do remain!
> As dare may do remain!
> As dare may do remain!

In this, though not strictly and correctly, alliterative song, the Finn is not an animal-shaped creature of the deep, but a man, a charm-working doctor from Norway. . . . Presently we will, however, see that the Finns of the Shetlandic stories are martial pursuers of ships, to whom ransom must be paid in order to get free from them. This cannot apply. . . . to a mere marine animal or sea monster: for what should such a creature do with ransom money? . . . . As to their animal form, Mr. George Sinclair writes:—

"Sea monsters are for most part called 'Finns' in Shetland. They have the power to take any shape of any marine animal, as also that of human beings. They were wont to *pursue boats at sea*, and it was dangerous in the extreme *to say anything against them*. I have heard that *silver money was thrown overboard to them* to prevent their doing any damage to the boat. In the seal-form they came ashore every ninth night to dance on the sands. They would then cast off their skins, and act *just like men and women*. They could not, however, return to the sea without their skins—they were *simply human beings*, as an old song says:

> "'I am a man upo' da land;
> I am a selkie i' da sea.
> An' whin I'm far fa every strand,
> My dwelling is in Shool Skerry.'"

* * * * * * * *

There are many such folk-tales in the northern Thule. A man, we learn, always gets possession of the Finn woman by seizing the skin she has put off. One of these stories says that the captured Finn woman would often leave her husband to enjoy his slumber alone, and go down amongst the rocks to converse with her Finn one: but the inquisitive people who listened could not understand a single word of the conversation. She would, it is said, return after such interviews with briny and swollen eyes.

The human family of this Finn were human in all points except in hands, which resembled web feet. Had the foolish man who was her husband burnt or destroyed the skin, the Finn woman could never have escaped. But the man had the skin hidden, and it was found by one of the bairns, who gave it to his mother. Thereupon she fled; and it is said that she cried at parting with her family very bitterly. The little ones were the only human beings she cared for. When the father came home, he found the children in tears, and on learning what had happened, bounded through the standing corn to the shore, where he only arrived in time to see, to his grief, his good wife shaking flippers and embracing an ugly brute of a seal. She cried:—

> "Blissin' be wi' de,
> Baith de and da bairns!
> Bit do kens, da first love
> Is aye da best!"

whereupon she disappeared with her Finn husband and lover.

* * * * * * * *

.... I here give what Mr. Robert Sinclair says of the capture of Finn brides by Shetlanders:

"Each district, almost, has its own version of a case where a young Shetlander had married a female Finn. They were generally caught at their toilet in the tide-mark, having doffed the charmed covering, and being engaged in dressing their flowing locks while the enamoured youth, by some lucky stroke, secured the skin, rendering the owner a captive victim of his passion. Thus it was that whole families of a mongrel race sprang up, according to tradition. The Finn women were said to make good housewives. Yet there was generally a longing after some previous attachment; if ever a chance occurred of recovering the essential dress, no newly formed ties of kindred could prevent escape and return to former pleasures. This was assiduously guarded against on the one side, and watched on the other; but, as the story goes, female curiosity and cunning were always more than a match for male care and caution; and the Finn woman always got the skin. One or two of these female Finns were said to have the power to conjure up from the deep a superior breed of horned cattle; and these always throve well. I have seen some pointed out to me as the offspring of these 'sea-kye.'"

In answer to my question, the Shetland friend lays great stress on the fact of the Finn woman being wholly distinct from the Mermaid ....

* * * * * * * *

Of the Finn man my informant says:—

"Stories of the Norway Finns were rife in my younger days. These were said to be a race of creatures of human origin no doubt, but possessed of some power of enchantment by which they could, with the use of a charmed seal-skin, become in every way, to all appearance, a veritable seal; only retaining their human intelligence. It seems that any seal-skin could not do; each must have their specially prepared skin before they could assume the aquatic life. But then they could live for years in the sea. Yet they were not reckoned as belonging to the natural class of 'amphibia.' As man or seal they were simply Finns, and could play their part well in either element. Their feats were marvellous. It was told me as sheer truth that they could pull across to Bergen—nearly 300 miles—in a few hours, and that, while ordinary mortals were asleep, they could make the return voyage. Nine miles for every warp (stroke of the oar) was the traditional speed...."

Here, then, the Finns are men of human origin; remaining intelligent men in their sea-dog raiment; coming from Norway; not swimming like marine animals, but rowing between Shetland and Norway—namely, to the town of Bergen, which lies in the southern .... part of Norway. As strong men at sea, they row with magic quickness. . . . Each one of them .... must have his specially prepared skin. . . . There is nothing here of the swimming and dipping down of a seal.

We have followed Dr. Karl Blind so far. But, while recognizing the value of his statements and comments up to this point, it is necessary to give only a modified assent to some of his subsequent deductions, and to flatly deny the correctness of others; because his researches in "Shetlandic folk-lore" have clearly been too limited in their extent, or rather, he has omitted to check those traditions by any possible contemporary records. Some of those tales were received from a Shetland woman "who strongly believed in the Finns, and declared herself to be a descendant of them. . . . . She was, she said, the 'fifth from the Finns,' and she attributed great luckiness to herself, although she was as poor as poor could be." One of her stories is of her father's great-grandfather; and as this ancestor of the woman's is not spoken of as a "Finn," it would seem that she was "fifth from the Finns" through another branch of her lineage. But, at any rate, this progenitor in the fourth degree cannot have belonged to a much later period than the middle of the eighteenth century. However, we shall see these Shetland Finns more plainly described if we turn to the latter part of the seventeenth century.

In "A Description of the Isles of Orkney," written by the Rev. James Wallace, A.M., Minister of Kirkwall, about the year 1688, one reads as follows:—

Sometime about this Country (Orkney) are seen these Men which are called *Finnmen;* In the year 1682 one was seen sometime sailing, sometime Rowing up and down in his little Boat at the south end of the Isle of *Eda*, most of the people of the Isle flocked to see him, and when they adventured to put out a Boat with men to see if they could apprehend him, he presently fled away most swiftly: And in the Year 1684, another was seen from *Westra*, and for a while after they got few or no Fishes, for they have this Remark here, that these *Finnmen* drive away the fishes from the place to which they come.

Again, in Brand's "Brief Description of Orkney, Zetland, etc." (1701), it is stated:—

> There are frequently *Fin-men* seen here upon the Coasts, as one about a year ago on *Stronsa*, and another within these few Months on *Westra*, a gentleman with many others in the Isle looking on him nigh to the shore, but when any endeavour to apprehend them they flee away most swiftly; Which is very strange, that one man sitting in his little Boat, should come some hundred of Leagues, from their own Coasts, as they reckon *Finland* to be from *Orkney*; It may be thought wonderfull how they live all that time, and are able to keep the Sea so long. His Boat is made of Seal-skins, or some kind of leather, he also hath a Coat of Leather upon him, and he sitteth in the middle of his Boat, with a little Oar in his hand, Fishing with his Lines: And when in a storm he seeth the high surge of a wave approaching, he hath a way of sinking his Boat, till the wave pass over, lest thereby he should be overturned. The Fishers here observe that these *Finmen* or *Finland-men*, by their coming drive away the Fishes from the Coasts. One of their Boats is kept as a Rarity in the *Physicians Hall at Edinburgh*.

This last fact was first stated by Wallace (1688; previously quoted), who remarks:

> One of their Boats sent from Orkney to Edinburgh is to be seen in the Physicians hall with the Oar and the Dart he makes use of for killing Fish, [and it is stated by Mr. John Small, M.A., &c., in his edition¹ of this book that the boat spoken of was "afterwards presented to the University Museum, now incorporated with the Museum of Science and Art, Edinburgh"; and a note appended to the second edition also states that "there is another of their boats in the Church of Burra in Orkney."]

Wallace's book has also a note ascribed to the author's son, to the following effect:

> I must acknowledge it seems a little unaccountable how these *Fin-men* should come on this coast, but they must probably be driven by storms from home, and cannot tell, when they are any way at sea, how to make their way home again; they have this advantage, that be the Seas never so boisterous, their boats being made of Fish Skins, are so contrived that he can never sink, but is like a Sea-gull swimming on the top of the water. His shirt he has is so fastned to the Boat, that no water can come into his Boat to do him damage, except when he pleases to untye it. . . . .

There is, it will be seen, some difference of opinion as to

---

[1] A reprint of 1883: William Brown, Edinburgh.

the place whence these Finn-men came. The Shetlandic folk-lore indicates Bergen, on the south-western coast of Norway; Brand regards Finland as their home; while Wallace takes a still wider range. This last writer (who is the first in point of time) says this of them:—" These *Finn-men* seem to be some of those people that dwell about the *Fretum Davis* [Davis Straits], a full account of whom may be seen in the natural and moral History of the *Antilles*, Chap. 18." At first sight, and according to modern nomenclature, the connection between the Antilles and Davis Straits seems very remote. But it must be remembered that the traditional country of "Antilla," or the "Antilles," probably included the modern Atlantic seaboard of North America; and that, when that territory was invaded by the Norsemen of the tenth century, it was found to contain a population of exactly the same description as those "Finn" races—people of dwarfish stature, who traversed their bays and seas in skin-covered skiffs.[1] However, Wallace's theory is obviously untenable. It is most improbable that any Eskimo of Davis Straits would attempt the trans-Atlantic passage in his tiny *kayak*, supporting life on the voyage by eating raw such fish as he might catch. Indeed, the feat is almost an impossibility. Moreover, it is quite clear that those Finn-men were voluntary and frequent visitors to the Orkneys, and (more especially) to the Shetlands; and the "Fin-land" from which they came is stated by the Shetlanders to have been no further off than Bergen, on the Norwegian coast.[2]

It is quite evident that "the Finns of the Shetlandic story" formed a branch of the "Ugrian race of the Finns"; and that some of them "came ow'r fa Norraway"—whether as "wizards," or as fishermen, or as pirates (for they figure in

---

[1] *Antiquitates Americana.* See Appendix B.
[2] It may be from them that an inlet at Bergen is called "Finn Fiord." Bergen is so much associated with the "Finns" of Shetlandic tradition that it is at least worthy of notice that a special caste, known as *Stril* (pronounced "Streeb"), who are very primitive in character, and who are regarded by the neighbouring Norwegians as of a different stock from their own, still inhabit the numerous islands that protect Bergen from the ocean. "They speak Norwegian after a fashion of their own, but it is very difficult to understand them, and there is reason to suppose that their idioms have a Samoyedic root." ("Bergen," by Lieut. G. T. Temple, R.N., in *Good Words*, 1880, p. 707 *et seq.*)

all these characters). The description of their skin-covered canoes is of itself quite sufficient to show that those "Finns" of Orkney and Shetland were of the Eskimo races. So that those "sea-skins," without which the captive Finn women could not make their escape, were simply their canoes. And the exaggerated stories of the speed with which the Finns could cross from Shetland to Bergen have their foundation in the fact that those little skiffs can be propelled through the water at such a rate that the hunted Finn was enabled to "flee away most swiftly" from the clumsier boats of his pursuers. The speed of the kayak is very clearly illustrated in an account of the doings of one of "these people that dwell about the *Fretum Davis*," who was brought to this country in 1816, and who, in that year, showed the great superiority of his skiff in a contest with a six-oared whale-boat at Leith. "He paddled his canoe from the inner harbour," says the *Scots Magazine* of that year (p. 656), 'round the Martello Tower and back in sixteen minutes, against a whale-boat with six stout rowers, and evidently showed his ability to outsail his opponents by the advantages he frequently gave them, and which he redeemed as often as he chose." This, it will be seen, was simply a repetition of the scenes described a hundred and twenty years earlier, in the Orkney and Shetland groups; the chief difference being that those earlier Eskimos had their home in Europe, and not in any part of the western hemisphere. Of course, the Shetland belief that the Finns could " pull across to Bergen in a few hours," and that " nine miles for every warp (stroke of the oar) was the traditional speed," is obviously an exaggeration. But the distance (which is nearer 200 than "300" miles) might almost be traversed in the course of the long midsummer day of those northern latitudes—by such seafarers, and in such craft.[1]

[1] A recent visitor to the Greenland branch of that family states that "a skilled Eskimo can, in his kayak, go even eighty miles in one day." The length of the day is, of course, an important matter. Dr. Nansen, the traveller referred to (who made the above statement in his paper read before the Scottish Geographical Society at Edinburgh on 1st July, 1889) gained his experience of kayaks during winter, when the Greenland day is very short. If the eighty miles were done then, the speed is marvellous. It is so, indeed, in any case. When Dr. Nansen reached Godthaab in October, the nearest Europe-bound ship was lying at a place

But, while the "seal-skin" of the traditional Finn was primarily his skin kayak, it is likely enough that he is also remembered as the wearer of a seal-skin garment; and that from this has arisen the confusion of ideas regarding this magic "skin." "His boat is made of seal-skins, or some kind of leather," says Brand, in describing the Finn-man; but he adds that "*he* also hath a coat of leather upon him." And Dr. Wallace tells us that the Finns "have this advantage, that be the seas never so boisterous, their boats being made of fish skins, are so contrived that he can never sink, but is like a sea-gull swimming on the top of the water." And he continues: "His shirt he has is so fastened to the boat that no water can come into his boat to do him damage, except when he pleases to untie it." Dr. Rink, in referring to the kayaks of those "Finn-men" who inhabit the regions surrounding the Fretum Davis, uses similar terms: "The deck alone was not sufficient; the sea washing over it would soon fill the kayak through the hole, in which its occupant is sitting, if his clothing did not at the same time close the opening around him. This adaptation of the clothing is tried by degrees in various ways throughout the Eskimo countries, but it does not attain its perfection except in Greenland, where it forms in connection with the kayak itself a watertight cover for the whole body excepting the face."[1] But, in making this last statement, Dr. Rink is speaking of the nineteenth-century representatives of this race; and in ignorance of the fact that the "Eskimos" of the North Sea had long ago realized the necessity for this waterproof covering.[2]

This waterproof "shirt" is also specially mentioned in

250 miles to the south, and a "kayaker" was despatched thither to try and detain the vessel, which was to sail in the middle of the month. Though unsuccessful in his mission, he reached the vessel in plenty of time. The dates of his journey are not given. But the mere fact of the man being thus sent as an express messenger argues that a very high rate of speed was relied upon.

[1] "The Eskimo Tribes," Copenhagen, 1887, p. 6.
[2] It may be mentioned that the variety worn by the Alaskan Kabana is not of seal-skin. It is described as a "peculiar waterproof coat called a camulinkte, made from the entrails of the seal, and is nearly as fine as tissue paper, almost every inch of it being quilted, to strengthen it. The Aleut wears this costume garment when seated in his canoe." ("Seal Hunting in Behring Sea"; contributed to the *Scotsman* of Sep. 20, 1895, by Edward C. Richards.)

connection with the Finn kayak that the two Scotch writers of the seventeenth century refer to. Wallace, it will be remembered, says of the Orkney Finn-men that "one of their boats sent from Orkney to Edinburgh is to be seen in the Physicians' Hall, with the oar and the dart he makes use of for killing fish." At the time when Wallace wrote, in or about the year 1688, there is no doubt that the boat was so deposited. But, although the second writer, Brand, makes the same statement, it is evident that he only did so on the authority of his predecessor. Because, four or five years before Brand's book appeared, the Finnman's kayak had been presented by the Royal College of Physicians to the University of Edinburgh. The way in which the Physicians' College had obtained the boat was through the president of the college, Sir Andrew Balfour, eminent as a physician, botanist and naturalist, and a great collector of all sorts of curiosities. At his death in 1694, his collection passed to the University of Edinburgh, by bequest. But, for one reason or another, the Finn-man's boat still remained in the Physicians' College. This will be seen from the following extract from the Minute Book of that College, which records the transfer of the boat to the University of Edinburgh, two years after Sir Andrew Balfour's death. The date of the Minute is 24th September, 1696.[1] "The qlk [whilk] day ye colledge considering y^t dr Balfour's curiositys are all in ye Colledge of Edr & amongst them ye oars of ye boat & ye Shirt of ye barbarous man y^t was in ye boat belonging to ye Colledge of physitians & y^t the same boat is likly to be lost they having noe convenient place to keep it in doe give the s^d boat to ye colledge of Edr ther to be preserved & y^t it be insert there y^t its gifted by ye royall Colledge."

From this extract we gain the additional information that the "Shirt" or "Coat of Leather" of the "barbarous man" himself had also found its way to the University Museum of Edinburgh; presumably through Sir Andrew Balfour also, or perhaps through his friend and colleague, Sir Robert

---

[1] For this extract I am indebted to the courtesy of the President and Council of the Royal College of Physicians of Edinburgh.

Sibbald (known as the author,[1] *inter alia*, of a "Description" of the Orkney and Shetland Isles).[2]

[1] More correctly, the editor and publisher of a previous MS.

[2] It is an unfortunate circumstance that, owing to the lamentable indifference of the controllers of the Finnman's canoe subsequent to the year 1696, it seems impossible to say whether or not that vessel is still preserved. In 1865 the Edinburgh Museum of Science and Art became possessed of the collection of the University, and in that collection were two kayaks, with regard to which nothing definite was known at the time of transference. If the University "preserved" the Finnman's kayak, as the College of Physicians expected, then it must be one of those two, as these were the only kayaks in the University Museum in 1865. (In the hope of obtaining a definite solution of this question, I have given a description of that kayak which appears to be the most likely to be the Finnman's, in a paper read before the Society of Antiquaries of Scotland on 10th February, 1890.)

CHAPTER II.

ANYONE familiar with the shape of the long, narrow, skin-covered skiff of the Eskimo (which, as has just been pointed out, is completely "decked," with the exception of the round aperture in the middle, where the rower sits—his legs being thrust in front of him, underneath the "deck,") will see that when the Finn had fastened his seal-skin garment to the sides of the aperture, he and his boat were one. Thus not only could "no water come into his Boat to do him damage," but he appeared (to people unacquainted with his anatomy) as some amphibious seal-man—"a selkie i' da sea," as the Shetland rhyme goes. This resemblance is even further borne out by the ability of the kayaker to overset himself and his kayak, and then to re-appear on the surface of the water, without either himself or his skiff suffering any injury, as both were impervious to water. This feat is evidently a delight to the kayaker, and the Eskimo already referred to as having displayed his skill at Leith in the year 1816, performed this manœuvre many times, to the great astonishment of the onlookers. Thus the Finnman of the North Sea, who presumably indulged in this amusement, like his representatives in Greenland to-day, was thereby rendered still more like a creature of the deep, "a perfect seal among the wild waves," as Dr. Karl Blind remarks.[1] It is to the

[1] This peculiar feat is mentioned by Drs. Rink and Nansen, as well as in connection with the Greenlander of 1816. Another "kayak" custom may here be noticed. Brand stated of the Orkney Finn-man, that "when is a storm he seeth the high surge of a wave approaching, he hath a way of sinking his Boat, till the wave pass over, least thereby he should be overturned." This manifestly does not refer to the deliberate overturning for amusement, in calm weather. But Hans Egede, in describing the Eskimo kayakers of Greenland, during the eighteenth century, is evidently speaking of the usage referred to by Brand, when he says: "They do not fear venturing out to sea in these boats in the greatest storms; because they can swim as light upon the largest waves as a bird can fly: and when the waves come upon them with all their fury, they only turn the side of the boat towards them, to let them pass, without

apparently amphibious nature of this peculiar people, that one may trace much—if not all—that has been recorded of mermen and mermaids; who, in other words, were seamen and seamaids. The conventional mer-man is portrayed as visible above water from the waist upward. And that the kayaker presents a similar appearance may be seen from a description given of an Eskimo flotilla by one who has had personal experience of the Hudson's Bay regions,[1] wherein it is stated that, at some distance from the land, "the low kayaks" of the Eskimos, being almost quite flush with the water, "it seemed as if their occupants were actually seated on the water." The accompanying spirited sketch by Mr. A. R. Carstensen of a modern Eskimo, as he appears "when the waves come upon him with all their fury," helps much to make one realize the appearance of the Orkney Finnman, whether in storm or in calm.[2] It is easy to see how a race of "*sea-nwners*" such as these could gradually become remembered as an actually amphibious people.

Those legendary mermaids who are described as using combs and mirrors were plainly allied to these Finn-women. It is manifest that no amphibious woman (the possibility of whose existence is not here denied) would carry a mirror and a comb about with her; or that she—whose chief element was the water—would be for ever engaged in the mad task of arranging hair which every plunge in the sea would disarrange most effectually. But those female Finns, whom the amorous Shetlanders captured before they could regain their skin-canoes are described as "engaged in dressing their flowing locks" at the eventful moment: a most natural proceeding on the part of any woman who has just landed from a sea-voyage (whether these particular women had come all the way from Bergen, or which is likely—from some outlying island of the Northern groups). The *reality* of those merwomen of Shetland is manifest throughout the tales relating to them. They bear children to their Shetland lovers;

---

the least danger of being seen." (Quoted in the *Scots Magazine* of 1816, p. 654.)

[1] Mr. R. M. Ballantyne; "Ungava," chap. 22.

[2] This illustration appears in Mr. Carstensen's "Two Summers in Greenland." London, Chapman & Hall, 1890.

they "were said to make good housewives;" and their descendants in the Shetland Islands to-day are, presumably, as "real" and human as any of Her Majesty's subjects. That most of those unwillingly-wedded Finn-women tried to regain their liberty at the first opportunity is seen from the repeated statement that the Shetland husband was always careful to hide the "sea-skin" of his Finn wife. But, in many cases the Finn-woman appears to have decided to throw in her lot with her Shetland husband and people.

Although Bergen was latterly the home of those Finns who came to Shetland, it is most probable that many of the stories regarding them related to a time when they still retained possession of certain districts in the Shetland islands. When they were "frequently" seen off the Orkney coast, quietly fishing, it is most improbable that their homes were among the Fiords of Norway—more than two hundred miles away. It seems clear that they retained their hold upon Shetland longer than Orkney; but even in some parts of the latter archipelago they were apparently pretty much at home in the year 1700. This was the date of the Rev. Mr. Brand's tour, and a remark of his leads one to such a conclusion. It must be remembered that those Finns were regarded as wizards and witches by the more ignorant classes; "the belief that witches and wizards came from the coast of Norway disguised as seals was entertained by many of the Shetland peasantry even so late as the beginning of the present century." And they were regarded as, in some sense, supernatural beings. Now Dr. Blind, in suggesting that the "skins" of the Finns may have been (as in one aspect they actually were) their outward garments, "made of seal-skins, and then covered with metal rings or scales"—in assuming this, Dr. Blind is quite in agreement with a statement made by Brand in 1700; which is to this effect, that "supernatural" beings were, at the date of his visit, "frequently seen in several of the Isles (the Orkneys) dancing and making merry *and sometimes seen in Armour*." It ought not to be forgotten that although the Finn fisherman "fled away most swiftly," when chased by a considerable party of his foes, yet "it is worthy of note that the supposed object of [the Finn invaders] ... was *plunder*;[1] that "they were wont to pursue boats at sea;" that "*silver money was thrown to them* to prevent their doing any damage to the boat; and that "it was dangerous in the extreme to say anything against them."[2] Whether such attacks were made in their small skin-canoes, or whether they used larger vessels, it is evident that they were formidable marauders; and that, as Dr. Blind suggests, and as the Rev. Mr. Brand records, those Finn pirates were "sometimes seen in Armour."

But neither the belief in Mer-men, nor the existence of traditionary pedigrees deduced from such people, forms a distinctive characteristic of the Shetland Islands. Just as there are Shetlanders who trace their lineage to one or more ancestors of Finn blood, so are there similar family traditions in many parts of the British Islands. "It is believed that there are several old Welsh families who are the descendants" of Mer-folk; and similar examples are found "in the traditions of the O'Flaherty, O'Sullivan, and Macnamara families."[3] "The inhabitants of the Isle of Man have a number of such stories, which may be found in Waldron;"[4] and the tale of Macphail of Colonsay and "The Mermaid of Corryvreckan" is not the only Hebridean illustration of this feature. The references that are made to mermaids in the prefatory remarks to Leyden's version of the Corryvreckan story are quite in keeping with the Shetland traditions. That is, there are certain attributes ascribed to those mer-women which, on the surface, are incredible; but which the knowledge that is given to us by Brand and Wallace renders quite intelligible. The "train" or "tail" of the mermaid has only to be translated "canoe" or "kayak," and what was formerly nonsense becomes sense. For example,

---

[1] *Gentleman's Magazine*, March 1, 1882.
[2] *Contemporary Review*, September, 1881.
[3] *Contemporary Review*, August, 1881. In the *Archaeological Review* (June, 1889, pp. 219-220) Mr. G. L. Gomme gives various references of this kind, Irish and Shetlandic. One instance describes the "Morrow" ancestress as "half fish and half woman," which corresponds with the Shetlandic "selkie-wife," or sealwoman. More extreme still is the tradition that the Irish clan of Conneely, like the natives of Burra Firth, in Unst, are actually descended from "seals."
[4] Preface to Leyden's "Mermaid," in "The Minstrelsy of the Scottish Border."

the statement that "the mermaid of Corrivrekin possessed the power of occasionally resigning her scaly train," is only a jumbled reminiscence of the fact referred to by Dr. Wallace who, when speaking of the mer-men, says: "His [seal-skin] shirt has been so fastened to the Boat, that no water can come into his Boat to do him damage, except when he pleases to untye it, which he does . . . when he comes ashore." In the other phraseology, he "possessed the power of occasionally resigning his scaly train."

In the remarks prefacing Leyden's "Mermaid" (in The Minstrelsy) it is stated that "mermaids were sometimes supposed to be possessed of supernatural power." The Shetland peasantry, also, believe (or did believe) that "*witches* . . . came from the coast of Norway disguised as seals." And "Ranulph Higden says 'that the *witches* in the Isle of Man anciently sold winds to mariners, and delivered them in knots, tied upon a thread, *exactly as the Laplanders did.*"[1] At one time—if not now, Lapland was regarded as a stronghold of "magic." Butler in referring to one of the things "in which the Lapland Magi deal" makes selection of this practice of "selling winds" to sailors;[2] the "Magi" being (in this detail) feminine. But the British Islanders have practised many "Lapp" mysteries: and there is a distinct "Ugrian" element among the British people; neither of which facts are at all at variance with the traditions that derive the descent of many modern Britons from sea-faring tribes of "Finns" and other Mer-folk.

One account[3] states, with regard to the mer-woman, that "the sailors pretend to guess what chance they had of saving their lives in the tempests, which always followed her appearance." Apparently, this refers more particularly to Norway. In the Channel Islands a similar belief exists regarding the mer-man, who is styled "the King of the *Auxcriniers*." "*Il est le baladin lugubre de la tempête*," says M. Victor Hugo, in describing this mer-man of the Channel.[4] The probable

---

[1] "Letters from the Isle of Man." London 1847; p. 59.
[2] The allusion in "Hudibras" bears more specially on the custom of selling the winds in bags or "bottled;" which is a variation of the Manx practice.
[3] The preface to Leyden's "Mermaid."
[4] "Les Travailleurs de la Mer."

explanation of this belief is that, when a tempest was
threatening, those solitary rovers—knowing that their fragile
"sea-skins" could never outride a heavy storm—made hastily
for the nearest coast. Indeed, when one looks at those deli-
cate little vessels, wholly dependent upon the thoroughness
of the stitching that unites the various pieces of skin together,
one can only wonder at the daring of the people who ventured in them a hundred miles and more from any land.
"Nothing but a plank between one and Eternity" is not so
dangerous as it sounds; for planks can float one when the
worst happens. But what is to be made of half-a-dozen bits
of whalebone or wood, with one thin covering of seal-skin
stretched over them? The giving of a stitch, or the smallest
fracture in the skin—and both skiff and skiff-man are under
the water.

To point out the various characteristics of the traditional
mer-men and mer-women, and to suggest an explanation of
each, is more than need be attempted here. But it is
enough to remark that the mere fact that marriages between
"men" and the mer-folk were possible and frequent, is quite
sufficient to prove that there was no radical difference
between the two races. When one reads of mer-women
bearing children to land-men, and "making good housewives" to them; or, when one learns that the mer-men
were given to "deceiving women," then one may feel pretty
certain of their humanity.

It has been noticed that one of their skin-boats, or kayaks,
was "kept as a Rarity" in the Museum at Edinburgh, and
that another was preserved "in the Church of Burra in
Orkney."[1] There are many British traditions of such boats
in connection with such people; although the names by
which those skiffs are popularly remembered are as unreason-
able as the "scaly train" of the Finn-woman of Corryvreckan.
In Sutherland it is said that those people used to cross the
Dornoch Firth in "cockle-shells;"[2] while one man records
having seen them quitting the coasts of the Isle of Man "in
empty rum puncheons," in which vessels he "saw them

---

[1] This boat, and all memory of it, seems quite to have vanished from Burra.
(See "The Orkneys and Shetland," by J. R. Tudor, London, 1883, p. 341.)
[2] Mr. J. F. Campbell's "West Highland Tales," vol. ii. p. 64.

C

scudding away as far as the eye could reach."¹ It is very likely that those traditional "witches" who went to sea in "sieves" were also identical with those who came from the coast of Norway "disguised as seals;" and that the *sieve* was nothing else than the *kayak*.

That the Finns of Orkney and Shetland used the long, narrow *kayaks* of the modern Esquimaux and Samoyeds is unmistakable: and the same shape of skiff has probably been employed by British and other European "mer-men" for an immemorial period. But other varieties of this kind of boat have been used. For example, the natives of those islands and promontories which form "the Rosses" of Donegal are described (in the years 1753 and 1754) as using seal-skin boats; but their shape does not seem to have been identical with that of the kayak. "Their boats" (says a visitor to the "Rosses" at that date²), "called curraghs, were oval baskets, covered with seal-skins; and in such weak and tottering vessels they ventured so far out as was necessary to get fish enough for their families."

These *curraghs*, it would seem, were nearer those still used in Wales (and also by the Mandans of the Upper Missouri) than the long, covered-in skiff of the Arctic tribes. Or, perhaps, they resemble those *curraghs* now used in Ireland, which differ chiefly from ordinary "boats" in their frames being covered with skins in place of planks. In his Gaelic dictionary, Armstrong states that "the *curack*, or boat of leather and wicker," was "much in use in the Western Isles (Hebrides), even long after the art of building boats of wood was introduced." As he says that Islemen "fearlessly committed themselves, in these slight pinnaces, to the mercy of the most violent weather," it seems most likely that the "decked" kayak is the kind of which he is speaking, and when he gives a diminutive form of *curack* (*curachan*), and defines it "a little skiff; a canoe," it is almost certain that he has in view the "kayak" of the Finn-man.

Whichever of these two terms may be assumed to indicate the kayak, it is scarcely conceivable that the Hebrideans

---
¹ "Letters from the Isle of Man." London, 1847, p. 63.
² Quoted in the "Annual Register" of 1756; "Manners of Nations," pp. 77–80.

would "fearlessly commit themselves to the mercy of the most violent weather," in an *open* skin-boat. But this is what the *kayakers* do. "They do not fear venturing out to sea in these boats in the greatest storms," says Hans Egede, referring to the Eskimos of the eighteenth century, "because they can swim as light upon the largest waves as a bird can fly; and when the waves come upon them with all their fury, they only turn the side of the boat towards them to let them pass, without the least danger of being sunk."[1] Referring to the same usage of the Orkney Finnman, Brand says that he does this, "when *in a storm* he seeth the high surge of a wave approaching." And Wallace's annotator has the same remark: "They [the Finnmen] have this advantage, that *be the Seas never so boistrous*, their boats being made of Fish Skins, are so contrived that he can never sink, but is like a Sea-gull swimming on the top of the watter."

It appears impossible to ascertain a time when skin-boats were *not* used in Europe. In speaking of the Oestrymnic Isles and their inhabitants, Dr. Skene quotes the following account of their vessels, as given by Rufus Festus Avienus, a writer of the fourth century:—

> "They knew not to fit with pine
> Their keels, nor with fir, as use is,
> They shape their boats; but, strange to say,
> They fit their vessels with united hides,
> And often traverse the deep in a hide."

As Dr. Skene points out, these Oestrymnic Isles were identical with the *Cassiterides*, (*i.e.*, "Tin Islands,") and, under either name, were famous for their tin mines. But, in identifying them with the Scilly Isles, Dr. Skene is manifestly in error; as all evidence on this point tends to show that the Oestrymnides, or Cassiterides, formed a group of islands lying off the Spanish coast, which, at some period during the Christian era, became submerged. The fourth-century writer quoted "says that the northern promontory of Spain was called Oestrymnis, and adds, 'Below the summit of this promontory the Oestrymnic bay spreads out before the inhabitants, in which the Oestrymnic Isles show themselves.'"

---

[1] See foot-note, pp. 12-13, *antr.* The expressions of Egede and Armstrong, however, are obviously exaggerated, as no kayak could weather a really violent gale.

The testimony of Diodorus is to the same effect: "Above the country of the Lusitanians, there are many mines of tin in the little islands called Cassiterides from this circumstance, lying off Iberia, in the ocean." So also Strabo, who states that "the Cassiterides are ten in number, and lie near each other in the ocean, towards the north from the haven of the Artabri."[1] All this is consistently borne out by the map of Spain ("from the Latin Ptolemy, 1478") which Mr. Elton, who calls Dr. Skene's deduction in question, appends to his "Origins of English History."[2] In that map, it will be seen that, according to Ptolemy, the Cassiterides—ten in number—lay off the Spanish coast, north-west of Cape Finisterre, and that that portion of the mainland was inhabited by the Artabri. Among all these writers and geographers, therefore, there is entire agreement; and none of their statements have any reference to the neighbourhood of the English coast.[3] That these islanders did not know the art of building vessels of wood, and were accustomed to cross the sea in skin-boats, is regarded by Dr. Skene as corroborative of his belief that they were British and not Iberian islanders. "But the Iberian coracles were as well known as those of the Britons," says Mr. Elton;[4] and of this we ought perhaps to see a survival in the "*curo*, a small boat used on the Garonne," which Armstrong compares with the Gaelic *curach*.

Of the presence of the skin-boat in British waters there

[1] These citations from Avienus, Diodorus, and Strabo are taken from Skene's *Celtic Scotland*, I., 165-168.
[2] London, 1882 (Plate I.)
[3] In assuming the Oestrymnides, or Cassiterides, to be the same as the Hesperides, Dr. Skene again shows that the locality referred to is the Iberian coast. For the writers of the second and sixth century whom he quotes state that the Hesperides are inhabited by Iberians, and are situated "near the sacred promontory where they say is the end of Europe." Now, in Ptolemy's map, above referred to, "the sacred promontory" (*Sacrum Promontorium*) is Cape St. Vincent; which would place the Hesperides at even a greater distance from England than the Oestrymnic Isles. The islands called *Londobris* and *Deorum Insulæ* on Ptolemy's map may be those referred to. Neither they nor the Oestrymnic Isles exist at the present day; but in questions of ancient history the fact ought never to be overlooked that the surface of the earth is constantly undergoing changes,—at one place the sea encroaching upon the land, at another retiring from it.
[4] *Op. cit.*, p. 20, note.

is ample evidence, and it would be superfluous to enlarge upon this. There is, moreover, evidence that certain "transmarine nations" came *to* Britain in such craft, in early times. And, half-way between the opening centuries of the Christian era and the period of the Orkney Finnmen, there is a reference which suggests the skin-boat among the Finns of Norway, although it does nothing more than suggest. In the *Heimskringla* (Saga xiv) it is stated that Sigurd Slembe and his followers passed the winter of 1139 in a cave at Tialdasund, the sound which separates the Lofoten Isles from the Norwegian mainland, and that on that occasion the Finns (or Lapps, as they are indifferently called) constructed two large boats for them. These boats were of fir, but the peculiarity about them was that not a nail was used in their construction. Like the framework of the modern kayak, the various parts of these boats were fastened together by *sinews*,[1] a method which, as the saga shows, was certainly not that of Sigurd and his people, who remark upon the absence of nails. Thus, although this incident shows that those Finns of the twelfth century were able to build boats of wood, yet their method of joining the timbers suggests the affinity which they otherwise bear to the Eskimos. But, while their own boats may have differed from those they built for their visitors, there is nothing in the passage to support this assumption.[2]

That the round *curach* or *coracle*, covered with skin, and similar to that still seen in Wales, was in use in the north of Scotland in the early part of the last century, is testified to by a letter quoted in the *Proceedings of the Society of*

[1] Dr. Rasmus B. Anderson says "deer sinews," while Dr. Joseph Anderson states that the original word may either denote "sinews," or "sea-grass."

[2] Misled in some measure by Mr. Laing's too free translation, wherein the expression "skin-sewed Fin-boats" is used, I had assumed that these two vessels were really large open skin-boats, like those of the British Islanders and the Eskimos. But I am indebted to Dr. Joseph Anderson for pointing out that the passage distinctly states that the boats were of wood, and that the allusion is to the "sewing" alone. As an article contributed by me to the *Archaeological Review* (Vol. IV., Aug. 1889) contains this erroneous assumption, I take this opportunity of stating that my inference is contradicted by the original passage, with which I was not then acquainted. Additional references, however, supporting the belief that skin-boats were then and subsequently used in Norway, will be found in Appendix B.

Antiquaries of Scotland, 1880-81, p. 179-80, from which it will be seen that the tradition already referred to—that the dwellers on the shores of the Dornoch Firth used to employ "cockle-shells" as ferry-boats—is nothing but a fanciful and imperfect resemblance of this particular kind of *curack*. The *curacks*, however, in which the Western Islanders "fearlessly committed themselves .... to the mercy of the most violent weather" cannot have been of this shape. But either variety of skin-boat was undoubtedly the property of the one race of people. Among the Eskimos, also, there is considerable variety. We are told, for example, in a description of the Aleutian Islanders during last century, that "their vessels consist of two sorts," of which one is the *kayak*, propelled by the double-bladed paddle, while the other is large enough to hold thirty or forty people, and has "oars on both sides." But both kinds are skin-covered. The Eskimo tribes have also the smaller open skin-boat, capable of holding eight or ten people. And this, like the similar skin-boat of the British Isles, has sometimes sails. These facts are therefore quite consistent with the belief that the European tribes using this variety of Eskimo boat used also the slender, decked canoe or "kayak."

Enough, then, has been said to indicate the presence of those skiff-people in various parts of the British Islands, and in various parts of Europe. It may be that the latest *authentic* records of British Esquimaux are those given by Brand and Wallace, in the end of the seventeenth century.[1] True, the Shetlandic (and perhaps other) traditions bring us down to later dates. But traditions are necessarily uncertain. However, we do know that the waters surrounding the Orcadian and Shetland groups were fished in by Esquimaux tribes so recently as the year 1700[2]; and we also know from tradition, that these same "Finns" or "Finn-men" "were wont to pursue boats at sea," and to demand a money-tribute from the fishermen whom they chased. (In turn, they themselves were pursued by the islanders, when they

[1] I am informed by Professor Kaarle Krohn of Helsingfors that the modern Lapps employ light skiffs, which they propel with a double-bladed paddle. But this vessel, which is so light that one man can carry it on his head, is made of wood, not skin, and is, moreover, open—not decked, like the kayak.

[2] Brand.

made their appearance singly, near their coasts.) That they were feared by the islanders is evident from the Shetlandic legends; and it will be noticed that those Shetlanders who are understood to have Finn blood in their veins "look upon themselves as superior to common people." All this suggests that those straggling "Finn-men" of the year 1700 were really the representatives of a decayed caste of conquerors. The fact that they are remembered as wearing armour places them before us as a distinctly military race; and "the Darts they make use of for killing Fish" were probably the least important of their weapons.

The non-Finnish Shetlanders who overheard the captive woman talking with her friends "could not understand a single word of the conversation." It is not necessary to assume that this denoted more than a mere dialectic difference; accent being a wonderfully important consideration in cases of this sort. That Finn settlements were often conterminous with districts occupied by those who regarded the Finns as enemies is suggested by the existence of a "Finns' Town" in Orkney, and a "Finn Town" in Donegal.[1]

Of course, these Finns must have one or many historical names. It is probable that they constituted a large proportion of the population of the Outer Hebrides. One of the stories relating to such people is of a mer-woman who "fell in love with a young shepherd, who kept his flocks beside a creek *much frequented by these marine people*"—the locality being somewhere on the Manx coast. "She frequently caressed him" (the account continues—somewhat superfluously), "and brought him presents of coral, fine pearls, and every valuable production of the ocean."[2] Now, this woman may easily have been one of those "marine people" who inhabited various parts of the Hebrides, and who used the skin-skiff of the Esquimaux "even long after the art of building boats of wood was introduced." The coral and "fine pearls" which this mer-woman brought to her Manx lover may have come from no greater distance than the Island of Skye: since Martin tells us that the

---

[1] And perhaps by many other names of like nature—such as *Finsbury, Findon, Finhaven, Finnarth*, etc.

[2] This is quoted from "Waldron's Works," p. 178.

people of that island used to adorn their garments with "fine stones" and "pieces of red coral"—the latter article being found in "great quantity" on the shores of the Lewis. At that time the islanders of Jura dwelt in turf-covered wigwams identical with those used by modern Lapps; as may be seen from the illustration here copied from Pennant's second "Tour." And the people of Harris were described in the following terms, in the early part of this century[1]:—"In general the natives are of small stature, ... Scarcely any attain the height of 6 feet, and many of the males are not higher than 5 feet 3 or 4 inches." "The Harrisian physiognomy" is thus detailed: "The cheek bones

WIGWAMS OF THE JURA ISLANDERS IN 1772.
(*From Pennant's Second Tour.*)

are rather prominent, and the nose is invariably short, the space between it and the chin being disproportionately long. The complexion is of all tints. Many individuals are as dark as mulattoes. ..." The population thus described was greatly mingled at the period when these latter observations were made; but there is nevertheless strong evidence of the possession of Ugrian blood in the people thus portrayed. And their boats and dwellings do nothing to contradict this theoretical connection with the races we now know by such names as Lapp, Finn, Samoyed, and Eskimo.

[1] This description is given at p. 550 of Dawson's "Statistical History of Scotland."

The author of the "Gallovidian Encyclopædia" gives also a hint of the existence of such a population in Galloway: when (under the name "cutty glies") he refers to "a class of females," whom he describes as "little" and "squat-made," and to whom he assigns (without exception) the amorous nature of the Manx mer-woman just spoken of. And, as the Gallovidian chronicler lived near the inlet known as "the Manxman's Lake," it is not improbable that this also was "a creek much frequented by these marine people"; and that, in short, Mactaggart's "little, squat-made females" were of the same stock as the Mer-women of the Isle of Man and the Hebrides, and the Finn-women of the Northern Isles.

NOTE.—For additional information on the subject of skin-boats, and the races connected with them, see pp. 174, 178–9, *post*, and Appendix B.

CHAPTER III.

It is clear that those popular traditions and records, as well as the indisputable statements of Brand and Wallace, indicate two very different kinds of people, who, sometimes fighting, sometimes inter-marrying, occupied territories that were, in many cases, conterminous. That they were often enemies is evident. The Finn-man, when alone, was hunted from the non-Finnish islands by the natives: and, on the other hand, he was "wont to pursue boats at sea," and to demand tribute from the fishermen—when his superior arms, or the number of his comrades, warranted him to do so.

Now, there is documentary evidence of this state of things during the seventeenth century; though the localities therein referred to are the Northern Hebrides, rather than the Orkney and Shetland Isles. But the description corresponds, in everything else, with that given by the Islesmen of the North-East. We are told[1] that, in the year 1635, certain sections of the Hebridean Islanders "comes in troupes and companeis out of the Yles where they dwell to the Yles and Lochs where the fishes ar tane and there violentlie spoyles his Majesteis subjects of their fisches and sometimes of their victualls and other furniture and persewes thame of their lyffes, breakes the schooles of thair herring and comitts manie moe insolenceis upoun thame to the great hinder and disappointing of the fishing, hurt of his Majesteis subjects, to the contempt of his Majesteis auctoritte and lawes," etc. This—even to the detail that they "by their coming drive away the Fishes from the Coasts"—is an exactly similar account to that given, in the same century, to Brand and Wallace, and in the present century (but relating to about the same period) to Dr. Karl Blind. In the one case, the scene is the North-Western coasts of Scotland: in the

[1] In a "Proclamation by the Privy Council of Scotland regarding the Fishing in the Isles"; given at p. 111 of "Collectanea de Rebus Albanicis."

other it is the North-Eastern. But the kind of people described are pretty evidently alike.

In either case, too, the Mer-folk or Finn-men are not spoken of as subjects of the Modern-British kingdom. The Proclamation of 1635, quoted above, does not regard "some of the inhabitants of the Yles of this kingdome," as being "his Majesteis subjects." The phrase, "Yles *of this kingdome*," does, indeed, imply something of a common nationality; but, as a matter of fact, certain portions of North-Western Scotland were not strictly under the rule of Charles the First, at that period. That this was so may be seen (if nowhere else) in the papers relating to those territories, of dates ranging from 1574 to 1635, which are quoted in the *Collectanea de Rebus Albanicis* (pp. 100-121). One of these is a letter written by Charles I. "to the Privy Council of Scotland directing an inquiry into the exactions by the Heritors of the [Hebridean] Isles from those engaged in the Fisheries; and the bringing in of Foreigners by the Heritors." And this letter runs as follows: "Whereas it is not unknown to you with what care we have intendit the good of the Association of the Fischings within thess our Kingdomes *for the use of our subjects*[1] and that we will be provident to protect *them* from the exaction of *the heritours in the Yles*, who as we are informed without warrant exact sundrie dewteis from them to their great prejudice, bringing in strangers and loading the vessells with fisches and other native commoditeis contrair to our lawis," etc. The letter then commands the Scotch Privy Council to learn "upon what warrant they [" the landislordis of the Yles wher the fisching is "] tak thess dewteis." In the Report made, six months later, by the Commissioners appointed by the Privy Council, regarding "the duteis exacted be the Ylanders frome his Majesteis subjects of the associatioun resorting in these parts," it is stated: "*that it was the ancient customs*[2] ... to everie ane of thame in whose boundis the herring fishing fell oute, *to exact of*[2] everie barke and ship resorting thereto" such-and-such a tribute, in money and in kind: "Being demandit by what warrand they uplift the saids exactions and

[1] Not italicised in the original.
[2] In this instance the italics occur in the original.

dewteis foresaids, they answer that they ar heretours of the ground and so may lawfully take up satisfactioun for ground leave and ankerage; it being ane ancient custome and in use to be done past memorie of man."

Through all these documents of this period there runs a feeling (not distinctly formulated) that "his Majesteis subjects"—"his Majesteis frie liegis"—"the haill inhabitantis of The Burrowis of this Realme"—were terms that did not strictly apply to "the heritours in the Yles." And that these latter—though nominally the subjects of the British monarch—still exercised a kind of semi-sovereignty in their own territories; enforcing tribute from "his Majesty's free lieges," and carrying on commercial relations with "foreigners," contrary to the wishes of Charles himself. That these independent rights were to some extent recognized by Charles may be gathered from his own expressions in the documents referred to. And the existence of this antagonism to British law was quite distinctly acknowledged by Charles' father (James) when, in the year 1608, he issued his instructions to a Commission "appointed for the Improvement of the Isles;" wherein he states his "desire to remove all suche scandalous reproches aganis that state, in suffering a pairt of it to be possessed with suche wild savageis voide of Godis feare and our obedience."[1]

Nor was this independence confined to the mere exacting of a tribute, according to "ancient custom," from those fishermen who, themselves coming under the denomination of "his Majesty's subjects," resorted occasionally to the coasts of the North-Western Isles. The Report of 1634 showed that this tax was rigorously levied by those Island kings when the alien fishermen arrived within the "bounds" of certain islands. But they did not content themselves with this. The Proclamation of the Scotch Privy Council of the following year (1635) begins by stating that "the Lords of Privy Council ar informed that of lait ther hes been manie great insolenceis committit be some of the inhabitants of the Yles of this kingdome not onlie upoun his Majesteis subjects hanting the trade of fisching in the Yles but upon the Lords

---

[1] "Collectanea de Rebus Albanicis," p. 115.

and others of the Association[1] of the Royall Fishing of Great Britane and Ireland; whiche Ylanders comes in troupes and companeis *out of the Yles where they dwell* to the Yles and Loches where the fishes ar tane and there violentlie spoyles his Majesteis subjects of their fisches and sometimes of their victualls and other furniture and persewes thame of their lyffes," etc. This statement reveals quite plainly a condition of enmity between "his Majesty's subjects," and certain sections of the Hebridean population. And the traveller, Pennant, furnishes additional proof of this state of things, in describing the condition of society in the Island of Skye (or its vicinity) at about the period under consideration. "Each chieftain (he tells us—and the "chieftains" of whom he speaks were presumably "his Majesty's subjects")—each chieftain had his armour-bearer, who preceded his master in time of war, and, by my author's account in time of peace; for they went armed even to church, in the manner the North-Americans [the colonists] do at present in the frontier settlement, and for the same reason, *the dread of savages.*" Of which "savages" there are many traditions still extant in the legendary lore of the West Highlands.

Of more historical nature is the evidence of Buchanan, who, in describing the Inner Hebrides during the seventeenth century, states that the Island of Pabbay, close to the Skye coast, was then "infamous for robberies, where the thieves, from their lurking-places in the woods, with which it is covered, intercept the unwary travellers." Of the island of Rona, lying a little to the northward of Pabbay, and, at that time, "covered with wood and heath," he says: "In a deep bay it has a harbour, dangerous for voyagers, as it affords a covert for pirates, whence to surprise the passengers." To the west of Skye, and in the Outer Hebrides, there was the island of Uist, containing "numerous caves covered with heath, the lurking-places of robbers." Off the mainland coast to the north-east of Skye, lay "the island Eu, almost wholly covered with wood, and of service only to the robbers, who lurk there to surprise travellers;" while

[1] In a letter to the Privy Council of Scotland, of 19th July, 1632, Charles refers to this Association as "of new erected by us."

"more to the north lies Gruinort (says the same writer), also darkened with wood, and infested with robbers." That is to say, all of these districts *belonged* to certain races who waged war against other populations in that archipelago; and who, in all probability, were the "savages" referred to by the traveller Pennant.

It is not only this latter writer and James VI. of Scotland who refer to certain North British populations in the seventeenth century as "savages." Nor are such people only visible in the Hebrides at that date. "In a curious old book called 'Northern Memoirs; calculated for the Meridian of Scotland,' written in the year 1658,"[1] the following short description occurs with reference to the district of Strath Navar, in the north of the county of Sutherland :—

"The next curiosity to entertain you with, is the county of Southerland, which we enter by crossing a small arm of the ocean from Tain to Dornoch. So from thence we travel into Cathness and the county of Stranavar, where a rude sort of inhabitants dwell (almost as barbarous as Cannibals), who, when they kill a beast, boil him in his hide, make a caldron of his skin, browis of his bowels, drink of his blood, and bread and meat of his carcase. Since few or none amongst them hitherto have as yet understood any better rules or methods of eating."

Here, then, is a community of people, "almost as barbarous as Cannibals," in the estimation of a civilized writer of 1658. But none of the expressions of this kind, used by writers of the seventeenth century, will strike modern men more strongly than that applied to the Finn-men of Orkney in the Minute Book of the Edinburgh College of Physicians. To the civilized Scotch of two centuries ago those Finn-men were simply savages,—"barbarous men." The term "savage" is always a relative one; and what one civilization regards as savagery is really the fag-end of an earlier civilization. Nevertheless, the seventeenth-century Finn-man represented what must necessarily appear to us as a "savage" state of society, if that word is to have any meaning at all. And the predominant castes of Orkney and Shetland and the mainland of Scotland were quite in unison upon this point.

[1] See *Blackwood's Magazine*, 1818, p. 674, whence the above paragraph is taken.

The Edinburgh physicians, as a matter of course, regarded those kayakers as "barbarous men," just as we regard their Arctic kindred to-day. The same view was taken by the predominant castes in the Inner Hebrides, at the same period, and apparently with regard to the same race of people. At that period, therefore, the seventeenth century, we see the higher castes of Scotland asserting themselves against an "Eskimo" race that threatened the safety of the more civilized populations all along the northern and western fringe of the country.

Even last century, something that modern nomenclature calls "savage" was visible in these north-western localities. On one occasion, when Dr. Johnson and his irrepressible biographer were exploring those north-western islands, the natives who rowed their boat seemed, to Boswell, "so like wild Indians that a very little imagination was necessary to give one an impression of being upon an American river." One of them, he tells us, was "a robust, black-haired fellow, half-naked, and bare-headed, something between a wild Indian and an English tar" (of the eighteenth century). And some of the McRaas of the mainland he describes as being "as black and wild in their appearance as any American savages whatever."[1]

Other tokens of "savage" customs might easily be adduced. For example, decaying specimens of the rude "dug-out," the most primitive of all canoes—a mere hollowed log—are now and then found in the depths of some Highland loch, or peat-bog; and are rashly pronounced to be "pre-historic;" whereas these very canoes were in common use in the north and west of Scotland less than two centuries ago.[2] However, neither this species of canoe, nor the vague references of

---

[1] Others of the same tribe were "as comely as Sappho;" and the inference is that, ethnologically regarded, these were totally different from the others. It must be remembered that the mere surname, borne by all the members of a Highland clan, did not imply kinship. The word "clan" was originally used to denote only the blood-relations of the chief; but latterly it was applied to the whole community. And that the community was frequently composed of men of a wholly different stock from their chiefs may be seen from the fact that the former are specially distinguished as "the native men" (i.e., aborigines) in several clan documents.

[2] See Armstrong's "Gaelic Dictionary," s.v. *Biorlinn*; also "Proceedings of the Society of Antiquaries of Scotland," 1880-81, pp. 179-80.

Boswell, point unmistakably to the Ugrian or Mongoloid castes whom we are here considering; although it is not unlikely that these latter were one and the same as the "wild Indians" and the owners of the "dug-outs."

What is certain is that, when, in the October of 1599, one of the ships belonging to the Fifeshire colonists of the Lewis was about to start on its homeward trip, it was surrounded by "a fleet of small vessels peculiar to those islands," and the natives, swarming on board, put to death all except the captain.[1] Now (although the act was simply a legitimate incident in the warfare of the time and locality), these islanders were the people whom King James spoke of as "wild savages." And it is tolerably certain that their "small vessels" were those "slight pinnaces" of skin that Armstrong says were "much in use in the Western Isles"—in other words, the *kayaks* of the Eskimos or Finn-men. It is not unlikely that the resemblance to the modern Eskimo was very close in many details. For example, the West Highland traditions tell of "savages" who played the game of chess; which fact in itself argues decidedly a form of civilization. Now, although the art of carving chessmen is extinct among modern Hebrideans, the traditional accounts were quite borne out by the discovery, in this century, of the now famous Lewis chessmen, "in all fifty-eight pieces, ingeniously and elaborately carved from the walrus tooth."[2] Consequently, it would appear that the Finn-man occasionally hunted the walrus, in which pursuit he no doubt employed "the Dart he makes use of for killing Fish:" exactly like a modern Eskimo.

[1] Anderson's "Scottish Nation," vol. iii. p. 49.
[2] Dr. Daniel Wilson's "Old Edinburgh," vol. i. p. 29.

CHAPTER IV.

BUT, admitting the existence, at so recent a date, of a visibly "Eskimo" caste in some parts of the Hebrides, what evidence is there that any of these people found their way to Shetland? One writer, we have seen, brings the Shetland Finns all the way from Davis Straits, another draws them from Finland, and the Shetlanders themselves say that they "came ow'r fa Norraway," especially from the neighbourhood of Bergen. The correctness of this last belief need not be questioned, as regards some of that caste. But it has been suggested in the foregoing pages that many of those "Finns" who persecuted the Shetland fishermen were those kayak-using Hebrideans who avowed their ancient right to despoil and to exact tribute from others, not only when fishing among "the Isles where they dwell," but in other waters.

We read[1] of raids made in the Orkneys and Shetland, during the latter part of the fifteenth century, by "bands of Islemen" (*i.e.*, Hebrideans), "Irish, and Scots, from the woods"; which last term strongly suggests the "robber" denizens of the thickly-wooded islands spoken of by Buchanan two centuries later. The raiders were, no doubt, heterogeneous. But the piratical kayak-men were surely among them. There are many traditions extant in some parts of the north-eastern archipelagos regarding these raids —In the island of Westray, in Orkney, for instance, where, at a certain "Fitty Hill," there was once a great fight between the Westray people and the invading Lewismen, all of whom were slain. Now, this Fitty Hill is associated strongly with the people recognizable as "Finns," or at least was so in the year 1701, according to a writer previously quoted (Brand, p. 57), and both he and Wallace (who wrote in 1688) mention the frequent visits of Finn-men to the

[1] *See* pp. 372, 378, and 483 of "The Orkneys and Shetland," by J. R. Tudor; London, 1883.

Westray fishing-grounds. Indeed, the *kayak* preserved in Edinburgh seems, according to the latter writer, to have been one of those secured by the Orkneymen; who probably made sure that the Finn himself should have no further use for it.

Thus, it is a simple historical fact that certain castes of the Hebrideans, whose practice of despoiling and exacting tribute from others was a thing beyond question, were very frequent visitors to the Orkney and Shetland groups, whose natives they did their utmost to overawe. And, as the skin skiffs of the Hebrideans were of such a description that the skiffmen "fearlessly committed themselves in these slight pinnaces to the mercy of the most violent weather," they were well qualified to sing the song of the Finn-man:

> I am a man upo' da land,
> I am a selkie i da sea.

Indeed, the concluding lines of that verse are peculiarly appropriate to the Hebridean. For the "shool skerry," which is the rocky islet of *Sule* or *Sula*, lying about forty miles N.N.E. of Cape Wrath, formed a very convenient refuge for him when "far from every strand," during his voyages between Shetland or Orkney and the Hebrides.[1]

And it is in this aspect, as tyrannical sea-rovers, that the "Finns" are often remembered in Shetlandic tradition. It was their custom to pursue the boats of the Shetland fishermen, and to exact from them a tribute in "silver money." So much were they dreaded that "it was dangerous in the extreme to say anything against them." The original feeling of respect must have been very strong, since it has survived into the present century.

This, of course, relates to the Finns considered as men and as fighters. The other side of the question shows us the Finn-women, and also the Finn-men in peaceful guise. And here, too, it is evident that those people were by no means

---

[1] The ballad of "The Great Silkie (*i.e.*, Seal) of Sule Skerry" is given by the late Captain Thomas, on pp. 86-89 of the "Proceedings of the Society of Antiquaries of Scotland," vol. i. (First series). This "great seal" figures in the song as the father of a Shetland woman's child. It may be added that this islet lies about thirty-five miles in a northerly direction from the Strath Naver referred to on a previous page.

regarded as an *inferior* race by the non-Finnish section of the Shetlanders (whatever that non-Finnish element may have been composed of), for those who claim a "Finn descent" at the present day regard this line of their ancestry as wholly superior to that which, for want of a better word, may be called "Shetlandic."

The Finn-women, we are told, very frequently became the wives of the islanders: and, consequently, they became the mothers of "half-breed" families—that is, in those cases where the husband himself was of a wholly different stock. In some instances, owing to a Finn connection in the previous generation, such children may have been more Finnish than anything else. Many of the Finn wives seem to have cast in their lot altogether with their Shetland husbands, to whom they brought dowries of cattle which—according to the peasant tradition—they "conjured up from the deep," of which the probable interpretation is that they caused them to be sent across from Bergen. Peaceful memories of the Finn-men may also be traced in such things as the rhyme of the medicine-man who "came ow'r fa Norraway" to conjure the toothache out of some unhappy Shetlander.

But these references, and apparently all the more recent of the Shetlandic traditions, point to Norway, and not to the Hebrides, as the home of the Finns; and it seems quite clear that the Bergen neighbourhood was a stronghold of this Mongoloid people within recent times.

Mr. H. Howorth,[1] in discussing these Mongoloid, or Ugrian people, remarks: "The Finns and Laps have been pushed back in Scandinavia to a very small portion of their ancient holding. In Livonia, in Esthonia, and in three-fourths of European Russia the Ugrians were, even in the eleventh century, the preponderating population"; that is, Esthonia and Livonia then formed a part of "Finland," and the Gulf of Riga was a Finnish sea. We are not given a date as to their "preponderance" in Scandinavia; but, if they were so numerous in the east Baltic districts during the eleventh century, it may be assumed that they were also of considerable importance in the Scandinavian peninsula at the same time, and even much later.

[1] In the Ethnological Society's *Journal*, vol. ii. No. 4.

There is, at any rate, a very interesting reference to Finns of Swedish nationality, made in connection with these Finns of Orkney. A last-century reader of Wallace's "Description of Orkney" (whose occasional comments upon that book are included in the reprint of 1883) gives, as his opinion, that the "Finnmen" of Orkney, in the years 1682-4, belonged to "the Finns, or inhabitants of Finland, part of the kingdom of Sweden." Whether this writer meant the Finns of Esthonia and Livonia, or of Finland proper—for all these provinces were under Swedish rule in the seventeenth century—it is evident that he went too far afield for his "Finnmen." But what really is important is the statement which he goes on to make, incidentally, with regard to the Finns of Sweden. "They had," he says, " a settlement in Pennsylvania, near the freshes of the river Delaware, in the neighbourhood of the Dutch, who were the first planters here" (and he gives as his authority "The British Empire in America," vol. i. p. 309).

Now, this colony of Swedish *Finns* is clearly that which is otherwise spoken of as a colony of *Swedes*. When William Penn took possession, in the year 1683, of the territory which has ever since been associated with his memory those "Swedes" were already settled there. "'He was hailed there with acclamation by the Swedes and Dutch,' says one authority, who informs us that the Swedes were living in log cabins and clay huts. The men dressed in 'leather breeches, jerkins, and match coats,' the women in 'skin jackets and linsey petticoats.'"[1] Those *Swedes*, then, of 1682, are identified by an eighteenth-century writer with the Swedish *Finns* of that period, and at the same time with the contemporary Finns of Orkney: who, also, according to Brand, wore "coats of leather." And their "log cabins and clay huts" were probably very much like the sod-covered dwellings of modern Lapps.

It is an interesting picture. Because this is plainly an infusion of unadulterated "Eskimo" blood, among the Pennsylvanians of that date, which is quite independent of the representatives of that family at present occupying Greenland

[1] This is taken from an article on the Founding of Philadelphia; contributed by the Rev. Dr. Stoughton to *The Sunday at Home*, 1882.

and the northern parts of British North America. It is "Eskimo" blood that was "European" only two or three centuries ago. And it is quite likely that many modern Americans whose descent is drawn from those seventeenth-century colonists of Pennsylvania, referred to as "Swedes," have some of this blood in their veins. That they may have inherited a further share of it through other channels—"British," and perhaps also "Dutch"—is quite probable.

There is something very suggestive in the Shetland accounts that, several generations ago, Shetland fishermen were frequently terrorized into paying "silver money" as tribute to people who are said to have come across from Bergen. Many portions of the north-eastern corner of Scotland appear to have been within the diocese of Bergen, and to have owned the authority of that province up to very modern times. Of this there is ample evidence in title-deeds and other documents. This, of course, was a survival of the Scandinavian suzerainty over the extreme north and west of Scotland, which in the fifteenth century was actual sovereignty, as regards Orkney and Shetland; while, for the Hebrides, the Scottish monarchs had to pay a yearly tribute known as "The Annual of Norway." And at an earlier period still, the Sudereys, or South Hebrides, and the Isle of Man, were included in this tributary kingdom. It is certainly worth considering whether the withdrawal of the legendary "marine people" from the Isle of Man, and their gradual disappearance (as "marine people") from the whole western and northern extremities of Scotland, which seems to coincide very closely, in time, with the decay of Scandinavian authority in these localities, ought not to be regarded as signifying that that authority was rooted in Mongoloid supremacy.

However, our present purpose is not to guess at the name or names by which these people must be known to history, but to emphasize their existence as a Mongoloid race. That the present British people show traces of such a line of ancestry is the opinion of many modern ethnologists. In his "Origins of English History" Mr. Elton recognizes a type "not unlike the modern Eskimo," as existent in certain parts of England. Mr. J. F. Campbell, in his "Popular

Tales of the West Highlands," contends strongly for the past existence in that locality of a race akin to modern Lapps. And the Iberian theorists discern a similar type in "the small, swarthy Welshman," "the small, dark Highlander," and the "Black Celts to the west of the Shannon." The question of complexion is, of course, but of minor importance, since it is anatomical structure that determines affinity. The modern Eskimo races themselves show this, for they include all shades, from dark or olive to actual red and white; although plainly of one general stock.

They exhibited an American-Eskimo chief, "as a Rarity," at some of the eastern seaports of Scotland, a few years ago. But it is probable that a considerable number of the spectators were looking at a man who almost exactly resembled one or more of their own ancestors, not many generations back; not only in the style of his dress and in his general appearance, as he shot his slender kayak across their waters, but also, to a very great extent, in his physical features. And it is much the same with many millions of Europeans (and their offshoots), who, chiefly through intermixture, and partly on account of altered conditions of life, are no longer recognizable, to a superficial observer, as in any degree connected with this "Eskimo" stock.

CHAPTER V.

WHEN the twelfth-century Norseman, Sigurd Slembe, with his twenty followers, spent a whole winter with the Lapps or Finns, as stated in the "Heimskringla"(Saga XIV), it is evident that the two sets of men were in intimate association. Their life at that time is thus described in Sigurd's song:

> " In the Lapland tent
> Brave days we spent,
> Under the grey birch tree ;
> In bed or on bank
> We knew no rank,
> And a merry crew were we.
>
> " Good ale went round
> As we sat on the ground,
> Under the grey birch tree ;
> And up with the smoke
> Flew laugh and joke,
> And a merry crew were we."

It was at that time, also, that the Lapps made for Sigurd those "sinew-fastened boats," in which he and his party voyaged southward in spring. In these accounts there is no mention made of the Lapp or Finn women, but their presence there must certainly be taken for granted. And there is no reason for supposing that they were less friendly to their guests than the Finn men were. There are evidences, indeed, that the Ugrians and the non-Ugrians of Scandinavia, of either sex, were on a friendly footing two centuries before Sigurd Slembe's day. When Eric, the son of Harald Haarfager, was in Lapland on one occasion, he there found his future wife, Gunhild, living in a hut with "two of the most knowing Laplanders in all Finmark." She had come there, she said, "to learn Lapland-art," in which these two Lapps were deeply versed. The way in which she entrapped her hosts, and went off with Eric, is described in the Saga (Harald Haarfager's, chap. xxxiv), and it argues something for Eric's magnanimity or indifference that he chose this lady to be his bride. However, the point is that in Gunhild we have a presumably non-Ugrian woman, living in the most friendly way with a couple of Lapp "magicians."

Again, we find Harald Haarfager himself actually marrying a Finn woman. We are told (chap. xxv of his *Saga*) how, one winter, when Harald was moving about Upland "in guest-quarters," he was induced by "the Fin Svase," who announced himself to the king's followers as "the Fin[1] whose hut the King had promised to visit," to not only fulfil the said promise, but then and there to marry Snaefrid, the daughter of the Finn. Whether he took this step by reason of the beauty of the Finn girl, or of the strength of the mead which she poured out to him, or of the "magic" which she and her father exercised upon him, is a matter of little moment. The fact remains that she became his queen, and in course of time bore to him four sons: Sigurd Hrise, Halfdan Haleg, Gudrod Liome, and Rognvald Rettilbeine: who, consequently, were half-bred Finns—that is, assuming that Harald himself was of pure non-Ugrian blood.

These four sons of Harald's Finn wife are subsequently to be met with in this Saga; which tells how "they grew up to be very clever men, very expert in all exercises." When Harald was fifty years of age, he gave to three of them, as to his other sons, "the kingly title and dignity," assigning to them, as their portion of his kingdom, the territories of "Ringerike, Hadeland, Thoten, and the lands thereto belonging." But one of the four, Halfdan, did not live to attain this dignity. Several years before, he, like Harald's many other sons, had resented his exclusion from place and dignity, and the advancement of mere "earls" instead; "for they [Harald's sons] thought earls were of inferior birth to them." Consequently, Halfdan and his brother Gudrod "set off one spring with a great force, and came suddenly upon Earl Rognvald, Earl of Môre, and surrounded

[1] In the edition of 1844, the word "Laplander" is used instead of "Fin" in these two instances, as also in the following chapter, where "the cunning of the Fin woman" is referred to. But the admirable edition of 1889 employs "Fin" in each case. Whatever may have been the original distinction between "Fin" or "Finn" and "Lapp," it is evident that these two terms have very often been used indiscriminately, from an early period.

the house in which he was, and burnt him and sixty men in it." Then, leaving his brother in temporary possession of that earldom, "Halfdan took three long-ships, and fitted them out, and sailed into the West Sea." The Earl of Orkney at that time was Einar ("Turf" Einar), and on Halfdan's unexpected appearance he fled. For six months the Finn woman's son ruled over Orkney. But in the autumn, Einar returned, and "after a short battle," totally defeated and put to flight Halfdan and his followers. "Einar and his men lay all night without tents, and when it was light in the morning they searched the whole island, and killed every man they could lay hold of. Then Einar said: 'What is that I see upon the Isle of Ronaldsha?' Is it a man or a bird? Sometimes it raises itself up, and sometimes lies down again.' They went to it, and found it was Halfdan Haaleg, and took him prisoner." Einar thereupon killed Halfdan, and he and his men raised a mound of stones and gravel over the corpse; which mound, if not yet opened, will no doubt disclose to some modern craniologist the exact ethnological status of this semi-Finn.[1]

With regard to another brother of Halfdan's, Rognvald Rettilbeine, it is stated that he ruled over Hadeland, and became famous for his skill in witchcraft, in which he was no doubt instructed by his Lapp relatives. This, indeed, was the cause of his death. For, at the instigation of their common father, his half-brother Eric (Bloody-axe) "burned his brother Rognvald in a house along with eighty other warlocks," on account of these same alleged malpractices.

These are only a few recorded instances, which reveal the Finns and the non-Finns as sometimes closely allied not only by association, but by blood. But from them it may be inferred that many other intermarriages between the two races took place, and that the Finns, although eventually con-

---

[1] It is stated of Einar that, although "he was ugly, and blind of an eye," he was "yet very sharp-sighted withal."

[2] Mr. John R. Tudor, in his very interesting book on "The Orkneys and Shetland" (London, 1883), indicates (p. 364) a certain district in the island of North Ronaldshay as the scene of Halfdan's death; and suggests that one of "three curious ridges, or mounds," is probably that raised over Halfdan's body. The saga certainly says that his death took place on that island. But, of course, there is plenty of room for conjecture in the whole story.

quered as a distinct people, were frequently men of rank and importance among the Scandinavians of eight or nine centuries ago. As an instance of a Finn occupying an official position (certainly much inferior to that of the semi-Finnish kings of Ringerike, Hadeland, and Thoten), we have the "Finn Sauda-Ulfsson," who appears as "engaged in drawing in King Inge's rents and duties" at Viken, Norway, in the twelfth century ("Heimskringla," Saga XIV, chap. vii). And a certain notable Ketill flat-nose,[1] or Ketill Finn, whose memory is doubtless embalmed in Ketill's-sæter (now Kettlester), in the island of Yell, Shetland, was clearly of Finn blood. When he, and such as he—the semi-Ugrian sons of Harald, for example—held sway in Shetland and Orkney, and when men and women of either race occasionally, perhaps frequently, lived together, a state of things existed that closely resembled that described in Mr. Karl Blind's Shetlandic traditions—when "Finns came ow'r fa Norraway" and practised magic and witchcraft, and domineered over the people of the northern islands.

Of course, it is impossible to say what proportion the Finn blood bore to the other. Yet it is quite evident that the Finns, while often at war with the race that overcame them, were also frequently their allies, and that the two peoples became to some extent blended in blood. Consequently, when one discovers among modern British people physical traces of a race "not unlike the modern Eskimo," in localities famed as the scene of many a Scandinavian raid, these traces may reasonably be attributed to those very inroads.

---

[1] Mentioned, for example, in Skene's "Celtic Scotland," i, 311-312. It is not out of place to refer here to a Mongoloid race of "Flat-noses" of whom Mr. Howorth speaks. These are the Nogais, who are known as "Mangats"; the word *Mangut*, or *Mangutai*, being "merely an appellative, meaning flat-nosed." "Dr. Clark says of them : 'They are a very different people from the Tartars of the Crimea, and may be instantly distinguished by their diminutive form, and the dark copper colour of their complexion, sometimes almost black. They have a remarkable resemblance to the Laplanders, although their dress and manner has a more savage character.' Pallas enlarges also upon their specially Mongolian features. Klaproth says: 'Of all the Tartar tribes that I have seen, the Nogais bear by far the strongest resemblance in features and figure to the Mongols'" (Howorth's "History of the Mongols," part ii, p. 2, and part iii, p. 71).

CHAPTER VI.

THE references made in the two preceding chapters bear specially upon those Finns who "came ow'r fa Norraway" to the islands of Shetland and Orkney. But if the assumption be correct that many of the Finns who landed in Shetland and fished in Shetlandic waters came thither direct from the Hebrides, it is to be presumed that Gaelic as well as English tradition has something to say regarding them. And as there are several words in use in Shetland which are also in use among West Highlanders,[1] it is not unlikely that these people may be known in the West Highlands by the same name as in Shetland.

It is quite clear that Highland tradition does bear testimony to the former existence of a special race or caste of people known by a name which resembles that of the Finns so closely that it may reasonably be regarded as only a variant of "Finn." In a certain charter of Alexander II. of Scotland (A.D. 1214-49), reference is made to a well which is known in Gaelic as *Tuber na Freine, Feinne*, or *Feyne;* and an old gloss (date unknown) explains that this term signifies "the Well of the grett or kempis men callit Fenis."[2] Or, in more modern English, "The Well of the great men or champions called *Fenus, Fenus, Fennies,* or *Fennies.*"[3] Here, then, we have record of a certain race of "kempies" or fighters, who were known in English as *Fenus*, etc., and in Gaelic as

---

[1] Such as *roo* and *wild* (each used to denote a bondland); *chevvy*, a reef; *rostle*, the "cuddy" or coal-fish, and *brock*; all of which are found in Gaelic as *ru* (*ruadh*), *maol*, *speir*, *cudain*, and *brag*.

[2] See p. lxxi of Dr. Skene's Introduction to "The Dean of Lismore's Book." Edinburgh, 1862.

[3] Perhaps the old Scotch termination "is" ought not to be modernised into a separate syllable, as, whatever the force once given to it, that termination represents the modern plural and possessive "s." But if the "Fenis" of the gloss was disyllabic, it has an equivalent in Shetland in the alternative "Finny," sometimes used instead of "Finn."

the *Feinne*. One does not require to know much of Gaelic tradition—one need not know anything of it—to be well aware of the fact that that legendary lore is fairly alive with stories of the "Feinne," whatever may have been the ethnological position of the caste thus named. And, just as in modern Shetland we have people proclaiming with pride their descent from the *Finns*, so have we West Highlanders and Hebrideans boasting that the *Feinne* were among their forefathers. Just as Mr. Karl Blind met with a modern Shetland woman who asserted that she was "fifth from da Finns," so did the late Mr. J. F. Campbell, in 1871, converse with a Skyeman, "Donald MacDonald, styled Na Feinne"—that is, "of the Feens." If the "Feinne" of Gaelic story are really the same people as the "Finns" of Shetlandic tradition, it will not be for lack of statements made regarding them if we do not learn a great deal more about these people through Gaelic channels.

Without either hastily accepting or condemning this hypothetical identification, let us look a little further into the circumstances of the Gaelic *Feinne*. And it may be as well first to decide upon an English equivalent of this Gaelic plural. Mr. J. F. Campbell states that the singular is *Fiann*; but, even when writing in English, he prefers to adhere to the Gaelic form of the plural—thus, "the Feinn" or "the Feinne." However, both Dr. Skene and another writer (the late Rev. J. G. Campbell, Tiree), have Englished this into "the Fians." This approaches so closely to the marginal "Fenis" of the old charter of Alexander II., that we may take "the Feens" as a good enough modern English equivalent for the Gaelic plural. (For the vowels in *Fians* and *Feinne* receive the old or Continental pronunciation, these words having the sound of "Feeans" and "Fane," or "Fayny," according to modern English spelling.) In order, therefore, to avoid the confusion that might arise from Englishing "the Feinne" into "the Finns" (although we are tacitly assuming, in the meantime, that the latter really expresses the ethnological position of the former), let us refer to "the Feinne" of Gaelic story as "the Feens."[2]

[1] See "Leabhar na Feinne," London, 1872, p. iv.
[2] It may be added, that while Dr. Skene frequently speaks of "the Fians,"

So lately as the latter part of the seventeenth century, certain districts of Scotland were recognized as specially "the land of the Feinne." Dr. Skene, on the page which tells us of the *Tobar na Feinne*, or Well of the Feens, states that Kirke (the Rev. Robert Kirke, minister of Balquhidder, in Perthshire), in his Psalter, which was published in 1684, refers to the territory stretching from Loch Linnhe northwest to, and inclusive of, the Outer Hebrides[1] as "the generous land of the Feinne."

"The land of the Feens," therefore, according to this Scotch writer of the seventeenth century, embraced the Outer Hebrides and a certain portion of the opposite mainland, known in the Highlands as "the rough bounds." It is thus evident at the outset that we do not obviously make a false start in assuming that the *Feens* of Gaelic tradition ought to be regarded as forming a section of the *Finns* who visited Shetland in the seventeenth century. In 1684 Kirke regarded the Hebrides as the land of the Feens; in 1688 Wallace records the occasional arrival of Finns or Finnmen on the coasts of Orkney and Shetland. And we have already seen that skin kayaks, such as those which bore the Finn visitors to the islands of the north-east were employed at about the same period by inhabitants of the Hebrides. Certain sections of the Hebrideans are recorded in history as making warlike descents upon the fisheries of Orkney and Shetland. And these Hebrideans dwelt in "the land of the Feens."

But the seventeenth century is much too recent a date for studying the Gaelic accounts of the Feens. These accounts go back to the period when Gaelic was peculiarly associated with what seems to have been its earliest home in the British Islands—Ireland. That they also relate to the more recent period of the Irish or Gaelic settlements in Scotland

and at other times of "the Feinne," he occasionally refers to "the Feniane." But, as this term has been recently usurped by a quasi-political faction, and as it is, moreover, less accurate than the other, we may at once reject it. The compound "Fingalian" has also little to recommend it.

[1] "The Rough-bounds (*Garbhcrioch*) and the Western Isles" is the expression used. The former term denoted that portion of the mainland between Loch Linnhe and Glenelg. Whether the Island of Skye ought to be included as one of the "Western Isles" is not quite clear.

is manifest. But they are substantially Gaelic (*i.e.*, Irish), and they deal with events which cannot be limited to the time of the Irish invasions of Scotland; and they relate to localities which are not merely British, but European.

"Who were the *Feens* of tradition, and to what country and period are they to be assigned?" is the question asked by one of the most learned of the authorities from whom these statements are obtained.[1] And his answer, after due consideration, is, that "we may fairly infer that they were of the population who immediately preceded the Scots [Gaels] in Erin [Ireland] and in Alban [Scotland, north of the Forth and Clyde], and that they belong to that period in the history of both countries before a political separation had taken place between them, when they were viewed as parts of one territory, though physically separated, and when a free and unrestrained intercourse took place between them; when race, and not territory, was the great bond of association, and the movements of their respective populations from one country to the other were not restrained by any feeling of national separation."[2]

Distinct and important as this announcement is, it requires still further consideration. Our guide in this question, has shown us that in such modern times as the seventeenth century, the Feens of Scotland were restricted to a small corner of the West Highlands and to the Hebrides; which territory was so far associated with them that an intelligent writer of that century spoke of it as the land of the Feens. But Dr. Skene points also to a much earlier period, when the Feens inhabited, if they did not possess and exclusively occupy, the whole of Ireland and Irish-Scotland. And he indicates further that they had dwelt in these districts before the advent of the Milesians (or Gaels). More than that, he shows us that the lands in which they lived included a portion of the continent of Europe.

In opposition to the theory manufactured by the Irish historians, that the Feens were "a standing body of Milesian

---

[1] Dr. Skene, p. lxiv of his Introduction to "The Dean of Lismore's Book." (Here, as elsewhere, I take the liberty of substituting *Feens* for the Gaelic plural *Fiann*.)

[2] *Op. cit.*, Introduction, p. lxxviii.

militia, having peculiar privileges and strange customs," Dr. Skene holds the conviction that, "when looked at a little more closely," they "assume the features of a distinct race."[1] As a proof of this, he quotes three verses from an old poem on the Battle of Gabhra (or Gawra, as the more softened pronunciation has it). This battle of Gawra is said to have been fought in Ireland, on the border of the counties of Meath and Dublin, and it is placed by some in the third century A.D. It appears to have been the outcome of the resolution made by the High King of Ireland, Cormac Mac Art, to renounce for ever the tributary position which he and other kings occupied towards their over-lords, the Feens. The Irish monarch is said to have aimed at the complete extermination of the race in one district at least; to have "Great Alvin [apparently the modern Allen, near Dublin] cleared of the Feens."[2] At any rate, whatever its position in time and place, this battle clearly marks a crisis in the history of that latter race. For to them the battle of Gawra was a complete and crushing defeat; and thereafter their suzerainty was ended. "The kings did all own our sway till the battle of Gawra was fought," sings the bard of the Feens, "but since that horrid slaughter no tribute nor tax we've raised." The chroniclers state that the leader and an immense number of his warriors were killed, and only two thousand of the Feens of Ireland were left alive when the battle was over. And their bard sings thus:

> "Fiercely and bravely we fought,
> That fight, the fight of Gawra;
> Then did fall our noble Palan,
> Sole to sole with Ireland's kings."[3]

But the Feenian army here engaged did not only consist of the Feens of Ireland; and this, indeed, is the reason why attention is now drawn to this battle. It is in regarding the battle of Gawra that we recognize the force of Dr. Skene's contention, that however the Feens may in later times have become restricted to this or that locality, they at one time

---
[1] *Op. cit.*, Intro., pp. lxxiii-lxxiv.
[2] *Op. cit.*, p. 56.
[3] For the above references, see pp. 36, 37, and 40 of "The Dean of Lismore's Book."

formed a very widely spread *race*, the various divisions of which were ready to hasten to the aid of any portion of this great confederacy in time of danger. Whether Dr. Skene is precisely correct in stating that "race, and not territory, was the great bond of association," is a mere question of words. Because the Gaelic traditions emphatically show that although Ireland and other neighbouring lands were occupied by people of non-Feenic race, who were governed by their own kings, yet, as these kings were *themselves* subject to the Feens, who drew tribute from them, the real owners of these various territories were the powerful though scattered over-lords, and not the races that were under their sway.[1] Mr. J. F. Campbell also states that the Feenic king was not distinguished by any *territorial* title: "always 'Righ na Finne or Féinne'" ("West Highland Tales," I, xiii). And in the pedigree which he gives on page 34 of his "Leabhar na Feinne," and which was compiled by a good archæologist, the title given to three successive generations of the "royal family" of the Irish Feens is "General of the Feens" of Ireland; not "King of Ireland" itself.

This battle of Gawra, then, which seems to mark the period when the great Feenic confederacy was on the point of breaking up, was brought about by the evident resolve of the non-Feenic population of Ireland to throw off for ever this intolerable yoke. And the three verses which Dr. Skene extracts from the poem descriptive of the battle disclose to us that other sections of the Feenic confederacy had come to the help of that division which was resident in Ireland. The poem is supposed to be sung by a Feen of Ireland; and he states that

> "The bands of the Feens of Alban,
> And the supreme King of Britain,
> Belonging to the order of the Feens of Alban,
> Joined us in that battle.
>
> "The Feens of Lochlin were powerful,
> From the chief to the leader of nine men,
> They mustered along with us
> To share in the struggle.
> . . . . . .

[1] Just as modern India is *British* India, although it is almost exclusively occupied by native races. (In this instance, of course, the position of master and alien is precisely the reverse from that which this "Feen" empire seems to denote.)

> "Boisne, the son of Brascal, exclaimed,
> With quickness, fierceness, and valour,—
> 'I and the Feans of Britain
> Will be with Oscar of Emhain.'"

"There was thus in this battle," says Dr. Skene, "besides Feens of Ireland, Feens of Alban, Britain, and Lochlan."[1] Alban, he explains, denoted the whole of Scotland lying to the north of the Forth and Clyde. Britain, he states in this place, was South-Western Scotland. But elsewhere[2] he tells us that "Britain" signified "either Wales, or England and Wales together"; and again,[3] that that term included "England, Scotland, and Wales." At the very least, then, it denoted a part of Great Britain, then inhabited—not necessarily to the exclusion of other races—by Feens.

These two names, "Alban" and "Britain," do not, however, take us outside of the British Isles. But the third term, "Lochlan," does. "Lochlan," says our guide, "was the north of Germany, extending from the Rhine to the Elbe." And the Feens of that territory, the poem tells us, "from the chief to the leader of nine men," "mustered along with us (the Feens of Ireland) to share in the struggle," on this fateful day of Gawra.

Why Dr. Skene should limit "Lochlan" to these dimensions is not made quite clear. For Norway, Sweden, and Denmark constituted the "Lochlan" chiefly known to Gaelic writers. However, he seems to be of opinion that the term was "transferred" to Scandinavia in the ninth century, and that previously (as, for example, when the battle of Gawra was fought) it peculiarly denoted the more southern territory. If he is right in this, we cannot assume the Lochlan contingent as including the Feens of Norway. On the other hand, there does not seem to be any strong reason for believing that, at the date of Gawra, "Lochlan" did not take in the whole of Scandinavia, as in the ninth century and afterwards. It is at least noteworthy, in this connection, that in the pedigree previously referred to,[4] the ruler of the Feens of Ireland, when the battle of Gawra was

---

[1] "Dean of Lismore's Book," p. lxxv. The spelling is here slightly modified.
[2] Op. cit., p. 8, note 1. [3] Op. cit., p. 49, note.
[4] "Leabhar na Feinne," p. 34.

fought, is stated to have been the grandson of a *Finland* woman. Quite apart from the assumed identity of *Feen* and *Finn*, this indicates a kinship that was not limited even by the river Elbe.[1]

But really the identity of *Feen* and *Finn* seems tolerably clear. Indeed, a contemporary writer,[2] who has studied ancient Ireland and its "Feinne" from his own point of view, appears to regard this identity as a thing perfectly manifest. And when, as tending to confirm this opinion, he embellishes his pages with several illustrations from scientific authorities in modern Finland, in which the ancient forms of art and dress are seen, it is plain that these designs are the same as those which are strongly associated with those portions of Scotland which were once known as The Land of the Feens.

Therefore, it appears probable that the "Feinne" of Lochlan, that is, of the country lying between the Rhine and the Elbe, who assisted their kindred in Ireland at the battle of Gawra, were simply the Finns of that territory. And that, consequently, that battle belongs to a period when the Mongoloid people, instead of being cut up, as now, into small detachments here and there, or amalgamated with other races, held a very distinct and important position throughout a considerable area of Europe.

However, this identity of "Feen" with "Finn" may not appear to some people as even a probability, without a fuller investigation into the circumstances of the people known to Gaelic tradition as the *Feinne*. It may therefore be desirable to continue to refer to the "Finns" of Gaelic folk-lore by the name of "Feens."

[1] The Gaelic traditions have a good deal to say regarding a race of sea-rovers, styled *Fomorians*; which word is by some believed to be a latinised form of a Gaelic term denoting a sea-faring people. As it is not improbable that this may be simply another name for the people now under consideration, the following is worth citing here: "That those adventurers whom our writers call Fomorians, have arrived hither in multitudes from that country whence the Danes, Swedes, and Norwegians came, is a circumstance that may be collected from this account, that the father-in-law of Tuathal is said, in the genealogy of the kings of Ireland, to have been king of the Fomorians of Finland." (O'Flaherty's "Ogygia," Hely's translation, Dublin, 1793, vol. i, p. 19.)

[2] Mr. Charles de Kay, in the course of several learned articles on early life in Ireland, contributed to *The Century Magazine* during the year 1889.

CHAPTER VII.

"THE Feens, then, belonged to the pre-Milesian races, and were connected, not only with Ireland, but likewise with Northern and Central Scotland, England and Wales, and the territory lying between the Rhine and the Elbe.[1] Now, there are just two people mentioned in the Irish records who had settlements in Ireland, and who yet were connected with Great Britian and the region between the Rhine and the Elbe. These were the people termed the Tuatha De Danann, and the Cruithné." So says the learned annotator of "The Dean of Lismore's Book."[2]

These two last-named races, we are told, are both traditionally brought from the Elbe and Rhine districts to Ireland and Scotland, and both are eventually subdued by the later-arriving Milesian Scots. The period given for the Milesian conquest of the Cruithné of Scotland, is the ninth century of the Christian era.

Leaving the "Tuatha De Danann" out of the question in the meantime, let us look at the contemporary and probably kindred "Cruithné." The Cruithné, Cruithneach, or Cruithnigh, are unquestionably deserving of study, for Dr. Skene has shown us[3] that this is merely another name for those people whom history chiefly knows as "the Picts." The traditional "Feens," therefore, are to be identified with the historical "Picts."

Now, although these people are, as we have just seen, believed to have come from the Continental country of "Lochlan" (Scandinavia, in the largest acceptation of that

---

[1] It is to be remembered that "Lochlan," the term used to denote the territory last named, was ultimately applied to the whole of Scandinavia, and may have been used in its widest sense at the period here referred to.

[2] Introduction, p. lxxvi. In the above, I have again taken the liberty of modifying the various designations.

[3] "Celtic Scotland," vol. i, p. 131; vol. iii, chap. iii, etc. See also his "Chronicles of the Picts and Scots."

term, or, in its most restricted sense, the region lying between the Rhine and the Elbe), and although there is every reason to believe that they spread themselves all over the British Isles, yet they seem—regarded as "Picts"—to be chiefly associated with North Britain. Their memory is still preserved, topographically, by the name of *Pentland* (formerly *Petland* or *Pehtland*, and *Pictland*), which is borne by the stormy firth separating the Orkneys from Caithness, and also by the range of hills lying to the south of Edinburgh. Both of these names are unquestionably derived from the time when there was a "land of the Picts" in either of these neighbourhoods. But the Picts, as such, are remembered all over Scotland, in history and in tradition. It is chiefly in connection with Ireland that they are spoken of as Cruithné.

If the "Feens" of tradition were *Cruithné*, or *Picts*, it is evident that whatever is known with regard to the history, customs, appearance, and language of the Picts will help us to decide as to whether the *Feens* were really one with the *Finns* of history, ethnology, and tradition. This, as already remarked, on general grounds, seems very probable. But, when a very able historian assures us that the historical Cruithné or Picts must certainly be at least classed with the Feens of tradition, if these three terms do not actually include one people, we are enabled, by proceeding upon this assumption, to obtain further proofs in corroboration of this belief.

Whether regarded as Feens or as Picts, these people, we are informed, had settlements throughout the British Isles during the earlier centuries of the Christian era, and the country of their origin was Northern Germany (or, more vaguely, Scandinavia); in which country large sections of their kindred continued to dwell, and to maintain a system of confederacy with the Western or British section long after the latter had settled in their new home. This, at any rate, when viewed as Feens.

On the other hand, such a writer as Mr. H. Howorth demonstrates that, during the same period, the Mongoloid races formed a most important, and in some places a preponderating, portion of the inhabitants of the countries of Northern Europe. But, during that period, these Mongolian races have—he points out—been subjected to an unceasing process of expulsion from their neighbours on the south and south-east. If any race, therefore, arrived in the British Islands from the neighbourhood of the Baltic in the centuries immediately preceding or following the birth of Christ, the probability is that that race belonged to one division or another of these dispossessed Ugrian people.

If this were so—if the Cruithné or Picts, who came to Britain from the Baltic lands, were one with, or closely akin to, the Finns and Lapps—their characteristics must have been those of such people. For example, their religious beliefs. Now, one cannot read Dr. Skene's references to the heathen religion of the Cruithné without seeing that it strongly resembles that of the Lapps and Finns.[1] Without quoting these references in detail, it may be pointed out that the power of bringing on a snowstorm and darkness, and unfavourable winds, was among the mysteries of the Pictish priests. And this gift of commanding the elements was peculiarly associated with the Finns and Lapps, as it still is with the Eskimo "sorcerers" of Greenland. "In the Middle Ages," says a writer on sorcery,[2] "the name of *Finn* was equivalent to sorcerer." And as the same writer observes that "the old authors often confounded the Finns with the Lapps, and when they speak of Finns, it is very difficult to know which of these two peoples they refer to" (a confusion of terms which we have already had occasion to remark), we may here use the term *Finn* to denote both divisions. Tentatively, at any rate. The actual Lapps appear to have been the most powerful magicians of all that caste. "It is proved by numerous documents," continues M. Tuchmann, "that the Finns called the Lapps sorcerers, although they themselves were reputed to be great magicians ; but they regarded themselves as inferior to their neighbours, for they habitually said, when speaking of their most famous sorcerers: 'He is a veritable Lapp.'"[3] However, since "Finn" has so fre-

[1] "Celtic Scotland," vol. ii. pp. 108-16.
[2] M. J. Tuchmann, in "Mélusine," t. iv, no. 16.
[3] Mr. Charles de Kay, in one of the valuable articles already referred to, remarks ("Women in Early Ireland," *Century Magazine*, July 1889, p. 439): "Although in the Kalewala the tribes of Pohjola, or the Lapps, are considered foul magicians, and even the foe of the heroes of Kaleva, or the Finns, yet it is

quently been used to denote the whole group, and since the most recent examples of these people in the British Isles, namely, the magic-working Finns of Shetland, have borne that title, we may adhere to the practice of referring to both divisions as "Finns."

The Picts or Cruithné, therefore, practised the magic of the Finns. That is, the *Feens* practised the magic of the *Finns*.[1]

Again, when we look at certain weapons used by the *Feens*, a similar resemblance is visible. According to a tradition, taken down from the recital of an old Hebridean, the spears or darts of the Feens, which were known in Gaelic as "*runnachan*," were of this description: "They were sticks with sharp ends made on them, and these ends burned and hardened in the fire. They [the Feens] used to throw them from them, and they could aim exceedingly with them, and they could drive them through a man. They used to have a bundle with them on their shoulders, and a bundle in their oxters [under their arm-pits]. I myself have seen one of them that was found in a moss, that was as though it had been hardened in the fire."[2] "This, then," justly remarks Mr. Campbell, "gives the popular notion of the heroes [the Feens], and throws them back beyond the iron period."

While the fashion of referring to "periods" of iron, bronze, etc., is very apt to mislead (since contiguous peoples have been, and are, in different "periods" of this nature, at the same moment of time), it is at least clear from the above tradition that the most primitive form of dart was associated with the Feens. But, although this species of weapon is of great antiquity, it does not follow that a tradition which relates to people who employed it, is necessarily of great

---

from Pohjola that Wainamoinen and his comrades always take their brides by force or by purchase." This quotation not only confirms the above account of M. Tuchassen, but it also illustrates the fact that even the most antagonistic races do not refrain from mixing their blood. Thus it may be seen how Lapps and Finns could eventually become almost identified. And the "Heimskringla" shows us how, in turn, this composite Finno-Lapp race could later on become blended with that of the Haralds and Sigurds of the Sagas.

[1] This has already been propounded by the late Mr. J. F. Campbell ("West Highland Tales," iv, 29-30).

[2] "West Highland Tales," iii, 394-5.

antiquity also. Or that those javelin-men were at all "prehistoric." We have already seen that a race of people employed darts in exactly the same way when fishing—or, perhaps, more correctly, when seal-hunting—within British waters, only two hundred years ago. And the people who in this respect resembled the *Feens* of Gaelic folk-lore are themselves remembered as *Finns*.

But perhaps the readiest and surest way of obtaining something like a true conception of these legendary Feens, is to regard them from the ethnological point of view, as well, that is, as our imperfect information will allow. We shall therefore look at them in this aspect, whether considered as *Picts* or *Cruithni*, or as *Feens*.

The great hero of the Feenic legends, and the "King" or "General" of the Feens of Ireland, was the famous "Finn" or "Fionn." If the battle of Gawra was really fought in the third century, as is alleged, and if this "Fionn" was a real man, and not the type or "eponymus" of his race, then he ought to be assigned to the third century. For he is said to have been present at that battle, where his grandson was slain and the supremacy of his race destroyed. At any rate, whether he lived at that date or not, and whether he was an individual or merely a personification of his race, Fionn figures throughout the tales of these people as a very Feen of the Feens.

Now, among the many stories told of him, there is one, entitled "How Fin¹ went to the Kingdom of the Big Men." It is unnecessary to give all the particulars of this tale. But Fin is pictured as starting from Dublin Bay in his little coracle (*curachan*) on his voyage to the country of the Big Men. Although he is described as "hoisting the spotted, towering sails," they cannot have been very large, or very many, for the coracle was so small that "Fin was guide in her prow, helm in her stern, and tackle in her middle," and when he landed on the coast of the Big Men's country, he drew his tiny vessel, unaided, up into the dry grass, above the tide-mark. It ought to be added, however, that this

¹ So spelt in the English translation given by the Rev. John G. Campbell, minister of Tiree, in *The Scottish Celtic Review*, Glasgow, 1885, pp. 184-90.

coracle was an open boat, capable of holding at least four persons; as is shown on the return voyage.

After landing, Fin encountered a "big wayfarer" (*taisdealach mòr*), who informed him that his king had long been in want of a dwarf (*troich*), and that Fin would suit him capitally. "He took with him Fin; but another big man (*fear mòr*) came, and was going to take Fin from him. The two fought; but when they had torn each other's clothes, they left it to Fin to judge. He chose the first one. He took Fin with him to the palace of the king, whose worthies and high nobles assembled to see the little man (*an duine bhig*"). And then and there Fin was installed as the royal dwarf.[1]

In this story, then, we have the tacit admission that, not far from Fin's home at the hill of Allen, Kildare, there was a country whose inhabitants were so much taller than the race of Fin, that the latter were mere dwarfs beside them. Now, this is precisely *the most striking* characteristic of the kayak-using Finns of Shetlandic tradition.

The *Finns* of Shetland folk-lore are, says Mr. Karl Blind, "reckoned among the *Trows*." The king of the *Finns* was hailed in the country of the big men as a *Troich*. And these are simply two forms of the same word. *Troich* or *droich*, among Gaelic-speaking people, is softened into *trow* or *drow* among the English-speaking Shetlanders.[2] In both cases it signifies "dwarf."

And, just as the Shetlanders have memories of a race of small men, who, in spite of their mean stature, were a terror to the taller people, whom they oppressed and took tribute from, so have the Gaelic-speaking people a mass of legends

---

[1] Referring to the component parts of Fin's army on a certain occasion, Mr. Charles de Kay remarks ("Early Heroes of Ireland," *Century Magazine*, June 1889, p. 204): "The battalion of 'middle-sized men' and that of 'small men' we may understand as recruited from the troe hunter and fisher tribes, who gave the name *Fenius* to the army itself, and Fion to the folk-hero."

[2] *Trow* is the favourite form among the Shetlanders; but other forms are given by Edmondston in his "Glossary," such as *drow*, *troll*, *trail*, *trailye*, and *traild*. The Shetland terms are, therefore, also variants of the Scandinavian *troll*, following a common Scotch tendency, which modifies *bull*, *knoll*, *pull*, *roll*, etc., into *boo*, *know*, *poo*, *roo*, etc. (the vowel sound being as in *now*). But whichever form may be the oldest, it is manifest that *trow* or *drow*, and *troich* or *droich*, are radically one.

which also tell of similar dwarfish but dreaded tyrants. The former designate their dwarfs "Finns": if the Gaelic traditions are not equally definite, they at least suggest that a caste of "Feens," who levied a tax upon the Gaelic-speaking people, were themselves dwarfs in stature. And the Highland tales abound in stories of fierce and tyrannical dwarfs.

CHAPTER VIII.

BUT, if the legendary "Feens" are identical with, or closely akin to, the Picts of history, then the historical Picts must also belong to this stunted Eskimo-like race. Let us look at the people called "Picts."

And, first of all, since the word "Pict" is admittedly the result of a pun or a misapprehension on the part of Latin-speaking people, it may be as well to discard that special spelling. The forms which the word appears to have most commonly taken in the mouths of the country-people of Scotland are *Pik*, *Pich*, *Pecht*, and *Peht* (the *ch* being of course pronounced as in German). Doubtless, other forms might be adduced; but perhaps the best compromise is *Pecht*. What, then, are the accounts given with regard to the stature of the Pechts?

The question is practically answered at once in considering the nature of the dwellings that the traditions of Scotland unanimously assign to these people.

"The only tradition which I heard current on the subject of the former inhabitants of the country," says a writer on Shetland,[1] "was, that the remains of old dwellings were Pechts' houses, and that those who lived in them were little men." And, in reporting to the Anthropological Society of London the result of an archæological tour in Shetland, Dr. James Hunt[2] remarks of such "old dwellings"—"These remains are called 'Pights' or Picts' houses.' Mr. Umfray [a local archæologist] surmises that they were originally 'pights' or dwarfs' houses.' Dwarfs, in this locality, are still called *pechts*."[3] And the present writer, when visiting a "Pict's

---

[1] Rev. J. Russell, "Three Years in Shetland." Paisley and London, 1887, pp. 135-6.
[2] See the Society's "Memoirs," 1865-6, vol. ii, pp. 294-338.
[3] The spelling *pight*, which Dr. Hunt uses above, must clearly represent the guttural and vowel sound of *licht*, *micht*, *dight*, etc., in "broad Scotch." Without this caution, the reader would naturally infer the sound of *pit*.

house" three or four miles north of the place just spoken of, and which had also been inspected by Dr. Hunt, obtained similar testimony. The place is known as Saffester, or Seffister, and its antiquarian features consist of the remains of a chambered tumulus and a separate subterranean gallery. The latter is referred to by one writer as a "Pict's house," although it is only a passage. As, however, local tradition alleges that it leads to the chambered mound, the name may be correct enough. Now, this tumulus was opened fifty or more years ago by the parish minister.[1] And an old man, who was then a boy, informed the writer that the entrance was effected by what he and his boy companions had always called "the *trow's* door." Another similar experience of the writer's yields a like result. Near Hamna Voe, at the south end of the island of Yell, there is a small loch and islet, with the remains of a "broch," the loch being known as "the loch of Kettlester." The "broch" that once stood there (for the ruins no longer retain their original shape) was built by "the Pechts," said the intelligent lad (a native of the district) who was the writer's guide, and these Pechts he described as very small people.[2]

The popular Shetland notions regarding the Pechts are again repeated by a lady writer, who has the advantage of being herself a Shetlander[3]: "The first folks that ever were in our isles were the Picts..... They had no ships, only small boats..... They were very small [people]." Indeed, so much has their small stature been impressed upon the popular memory, that, as we have seen, "dwarfs, in this locality, are still called *pechts*." Nor is it only in Shetland that this word has such a meaning. In Aberdeenshire *picht* denotes a

---

[1] Rev. J. Bryden: *see* "Anthrop. Soc. Mem.," *ut supra*.
[2] Close to Kettlester there is a noted haunt of the "trows," which bears the name of *Houlland*. With this may be compared *Troil-Houlland*, which adjoins Seffister, of "trow" memory. This very common Shetland termination "*ster*" or "*setter*" is the Icelandic *setr*, a dwelling; and these two names resolve themselves respectively into dwellings of *Kettil* and *Sift*. The former name at once recalls the ninth century *Ketill Flat-nose* of the Sagas, and this "*setr*," still associated with dwarfs (otherwise *trows* or *pechts*), may have been one of his dwellings.
[3] Mrs. Saxby, in "Folk-lore from Unst, Shetland" (part v), contributed to *The Leisure Hour*, 1880. (For another reference to the boats of the Picts, *see* pp. 178-9, *post*.)

dwarfish person, and Dr. Jamieson, in recording the fact,[1] suggests its connection with "the *pichts* or *pechts*, whom the vulgar view as a race of pigmies." In the south of Scotland also, this signification appears to prevail; for the Ettrick Shepherd, in the "Noctes Ambrosianæ," employs "pegh" as an everyday synonym for "dwarf." In point of fact, although it has just been stated that dwarfs "are still called *pechts*" in Shetland, because of the small size of the race so known to history, it is really a question whether the historical people did not so become historically remembered *because* a pre-existing word fitly described their dwarfish stature. But this etymological point is of little importance here.

Although Shetland has been chiefly considered in these recent remarks, it will be seen that the popular belief regarding the stature of the Pechts is apparently common to the whole of Scotland. Dr. Jamieson evidently thought so when he referred to "the Pichts, or Pechts, whom the vulgar view as a race of pigmies." And he does not stand alone. "Throughout Scotland," says another writer, "the vulgar account is 'that the *Pechs* were unco wee bodies, but terrible strang'; that is, that they were of very small stature, but of prodigious strength.'" "Long ago," quotes the late Robert Chambers,[3] and his quotation also applies to the whole of Scotland, "there were people in this country called the Pechs; short, wee men they were,"—and so on.

Enough has been said to show that the ideas held by the "vulgar" (whose traditions, once contemptuously rejected by scholars, are nowadays being rated at their true value), throughout Scotland, with respect to the Pechts, agree in describing those people as decidedly dwarfish in stature. And this belief is most convincingly borne out by the dwellings which the Pechts are believed to have inhabited;

---

[1] "Scottish Dictionary" (Supplement), *s. v.* "Picht."

[2] "The Topography of the Basin of the Tay," by James Knox, Edinburgh, 1831, p. 108. This writer adds that "they are said to have been about three or four feet in height"; and it may be mentioned that when I asked my young guide at Kettlester the exact height of the small Pechts he had just been speaking of, he said, "About that height," indicating at the same time a stature of three feet or so. Whatever their height really was, this young Shetlander's ideas were in agreement with those held "throughout Scotland."

[3] "Popular Rhymes of Scotland," 1870, p. 80.

the "Pechts' houses" which we glanced at a few paragraphs back, and which speedily led us to consider the Pechts themselves. No man of the average height of modern British people, who has personally inspected these "Pechts' houses," can arrive at any other conclusion than that they were built and inhabited by people of a stature very much less than his own. This is a point so manifest that it need not be emphasized to those who have stooped, squeezed, and crept among the chambers and passages of a "Pictish broch." A few particulars of measurement would quickly convince others; but such details need not be entered into here. However, something may be said with regard to the appearance of the dwelling which may best be regarded as the typical "Pecht's house."

In a "Notice of the Brochs and the so-called Picts' Houses of Orkney," submitted to the Anthropological Society of London,[1] Mr. George Petrie points out that "the name Pict's house is applied indiscriminately, in the northern counties of Scotland, to every sort of ancient structure." And as there is certainly a great difference, in degree, between the various structures referred to, we may here accept Mr. Petrie's guidance as to what constitutes the typical "Pict's house." "The class of buildings to which I have for many years restricted the appellation of *Picts' house* have been," says Mr. Petrie, "very different from the brochs,[2] both in external appearance and general structure and arrangements. The *Pict's house* is generally of a conical form, and externally closely resembles a large bowl-shaped barrow. It consists of a solid mass of masonry, covered with a layer of turf, a foot or more in thickness, and has a central chamber surrounded by several smaller cells. The entrance to the central

[1] *See* the Society's "Memoirs," 1865-6, vol. ii, pp. 216-223.
[2] The term "broch" has hitherto been used in a general sense in these pages. This its etymology permits; for it is the same word as *borough*, *burgh*, *bury*, *barrow*, etc. But the students of these ancient structures have recently restricted "broch" to the more elaborate and superior building of the round or "martello" tower order. This definition is very convenient, and saves much confusion. In spite, however, of the great difference that Mr. Petrie speaks of as between the so-called "Pictish" broch and the humbler dwelling that alone is recognised by him as a "Pict's house," it is yet evident that the "broch" is to a very great extent evolved from the more primitive and rudimentary "Pict's house."

chamber from the outside is by a long, low, narrow passage; while the cells are connected with the chamber by short passages of similar dimensions to the long one. The walls of the chambers and cells converge towards the top, where they approach so closely that the aperture can be spanned by a stone a couple of feet in length."

Another writer[1] describes a Pict's house—that on Wideford Hill, near Kirkwall—in these terms: "All that meets the eye at first is a green, conical mound, with an indescribable aspect of something *eerie* and weird about it, resting silently amid the moorland solitude. On closer inspection we discover an entrance passage, about eighteen inches high and two feet broad, leading from the lower side into the interior of the prehistoric dwelling."—and so on.

The resemblance between this kind of dwelling, or its more modern representative, the "bee-hive" hut of the Hebrides and Western Ireland, to the dwellings of modern Eskimos has long been recognised. But it may be permitted to quote here from the accounts given by two Arctic voyagers of the early part of this century, especially as these accounts, both relating to the most northern tribes of Greenland, appear to describe with peculiar exactness the "Pict's house" of Mr. Petrie.

Captain Scoresby, in the account of his explorations in the year 1822, thus describes the deserted dwellings of some of those northern Eskimos:

"The roofs of all the huts had either been removed or had fallen in; what remained, consisted of an excavation in the ground at the brow of the bank, about 4 feet in depth, 15 in length, and 6 to 9 in width. The sides of each hut were sustained by a wall of rough stones, and the bottom appeared to be gravel, clay, and moss. The access to these huts, after the manner of the Esquimaux, was a horizontal tunnel perforating the ground, about 15 feet in length, opening at one extremity on the side of the bank, into the external air, and, at the other, communicating with the interior of the hut. This tunnel was so low, that a person must creep on his hands and knees to get into the dwelling: it was roofed with slabs of stone and soda. This kind of hut being deeply sunk in the earth, and being accessible only by a subterranean passage, is generally considered as formed altogether under ground. As, indeed, it rises

[1] Mr. Daniel Gorrie, in "Summers and Winters in the Orkneys," London, 1869, p. 117.

very little above the surface, and as the roof, when entire, is generally covered with sods, and clothed with moss or grass, it partakes so much of the appearance of the rest of the ground, that it can scarcely be distinguished from it. I was much struck by its admirable adaptation to the nature of the climate and the circumstances of the inhabitants. The uncivilised Esquimaux, using no fire in these habitations, but only lamps, which serve both for light and for warming their victuals, require, in the severities of winter, to economise, with the greatest care, such artificial warmth as they are able to produce in their huts. For this purpose, an under-ground dwelling, defended from the penetration of the frost by a roof of moss and earth, with an additional coating of a bed of snow, and preserved from the entrance of the piercing wind by a long subterranean tunnel, without the possibility of being annoyed by any draught of air, but what is voluntarily admitted—forms one of the best contrivances which, considering the limited resources, and the unenlightened state of these people, could possibly have been adopted."[1]

Scoresby's description fully corroborates that given by Captain Ross a few years earlier, when relating his visit to the Eskimos living about the north-eastern corner of Baffin's Bay. These people he describes as "short in stature, seldom exceeding five feet," and he mentions that their sorcerers alleged that it was in their power to raise a storm or make a calm, and to drive off seals and birds."

With regard to their dwellings, he says:

"None of their houses were seen, but they described them as built entirely of stone, the walls being sunk about three feet into the earth, and raised about as much above it. They have no windows, and the entrance is by a long, narrow passage, nearly under ground. Several families live in one house, and each has a lamp made of hollowed stone, hung from the roof, in which they burn the blubber of the seal, etc., using dried moss for a wick, which is kindled by means of iron and stone. This lamp, which is never extinguished, serves at once for light, warmth, and cooking."[2]

It is not out of place to refer here also to an instructive article on "The Archæology of Lighting Appliances," read before the Society of Antiquaries of Scotland by Mr. J. Romilly Allen, F.S.A.Scot., in the course of which he describes the stone lamps found in the habitations known as "brochs"

---

[1] This extract is quoted from the review in the *Scots Magazine* of 1823 (pp. 457-8) of Captain Scoresby's "Journal" (published 1823).

[2] From an extract contained in the review (*Scots Magazine*, 1819, vol. iv. pp. 338-3) of Capt. Ross's account (published by John Murray, London, 1819).

(and popularly assigned to the Picts), with regard to which lamps he states that although not quite identical in shape with those used by modern Eskimos, they are substantially identical, and must have been used in precisely the same way. Comparing this with Baron Nordenskiöld's accounts, Mr. Romilly Allen observes: "The picture here given of the domestic life of the Eskimos at the present time enables us to form a tolerably correct idea of the way in which the inhabitants of the Scottish brochs lighted their dwellings during the long winter nights two thousand years ago." ("Proceedings of Soc. of Antiq. of Scot." 1887-88, p. 84.)

From all these remarks, then, it will be seen that the dwelling of the dwarfish Eskimo and the "house" assigned by Scottish tradition to the Pechts, or dwarfs, are substantially one. And a consideration of the statements also demonstrates clearly that, whatever the age of the word "pecht," none but a race of dwarfish stature would have built such places of abode. Indeed, the stature of the dwellers in the Pecht's house is doubly impressed upon the memory of the Northern Islanders. When Mr. Gorrie describes its outward appearance, he tells us (in similar terms to the Arctic voyagers), that "all that meets the eye at first is a green, conical mound ... resting silently amid the moorland solitude." But he really repeats himself, although he is not aware of it, when he refers on another page[1] to "the simple superstition (?) long prevalent among the inhabitants of Orkney and Zetland, that the strange green mounds rising by the sea-side and on solitary moors, were the abodes of supernatural beings known by the name of Trows." Of the "supernatural" attributes assigned to those people, or claimed by them—in early Scotland, in Lapland, and in Greenland—much remains to be said. But the people just referred to under two different, but synonymous, names, are undoubtedly one and the same.

The Pechts of history, then, were a race of dwarfs. Thus, when Dr. Skene identifies the Feens of Gaelic folk-lore with the historic Pechts, he reveals them to us as a race of dwarfs. Therefore, the traditional story of the Feen chief's visit to the "country of the big men," where he was regarded by that

[1] *Op. cit.*, p. 119.

latter race as a "droich," is entirely in accordance with Dr.
Skene's belief that the Feens were of the same race as the
historic Pechts. It is not at all unlikely that this identity
was taken for granted long before the nineteenth century,
and in Scotland. In Allan Ramsay's *Evergreen*, a collection
of Scottish poems written before the year 1600, there is a
certain "Interlude of the Droichs," also referred to as "The
Droichs' Part of a Play." Now, the spokesman of these
droichs (or trows, or dwarfs) announces himself as a grandson
of Fin, the great chief of the Feens of Ireland. And he
makes a statement which is identical with one contained in
a Feenic poem on the battle of Gawra. This statement need
not be particularized here, but it tells us unmistakably that
these "droichs" were regarded as the representatives of Fin
and his Feens.[1] Therefore, it would appear from this poem
that Fin and his Feens were regarded by the ruling class in
Scotland, prior to 1600, as dwarfs. That is, as *pechts*.

So far, then, all that has here been said tends to show that
the *Feinne* of Gaelic folk-lore, and the Finns of Northern
history and tradition, ought to be regarded as one and the
same people. And that one section, at any rate, of such
people ought to be identified with the Pechts, or Picts, of
history.

[1] The fact that the "Interlude" is allegorical does not at all affect the question.

CHAPTER IX.

WHILE the Picts, or Pechts, are remembered to a great extent as the builders of the subterranean and half-subterranean dwellings with which they are associated, these are far from being the only structures which popular tradition has stamped as the work of their hands. The architectural skill, of a kind, which they displayed in the construction of their own "Pechts' houses" may be seen from such a casual reference as this, gleaned from among certain specimens of Clydesdale folk-lore: "Our milkhouse," says a Clydesdale peasant, "whilk stude on the side of a dentie burn, and was ane o' thae auld vowts [vaults] whilk the Pechs biggit langsyne, had wa's sae doons strang that ane waud hae thocht it micht hae stude to the last day; but its found had been onnerminit by the last Lammas-spait."¹ If the "Pechts' houses" lacked, as they certainly did, evidences of high culture in the designers, or outward beauty of design in themselves, they were at least remarkable for their great strength and durability; so that, were it not for such accidents as a Lammas-flood, they might well have stood "to the last day." But the great bodily strength of this race, and their turn for masonry, were made use of in other ways than in the construction of the dwellings referred to; that is, if there is any truth in the popular ideas upon this subject.

The late Robert Chambers, in putting together the popular Scotch beliefs regarding these people,* not only states that they were "short, wee men," but he adds, still speaking as a Scottish peasant: "The Pechs were great builders; they built a' the auld castles in the kintry; and do ye ken the way they built them? I'll tell ye. They stood all in a row from the quarry to the place where they were building, and ilk ane handed forward the stanes to his

Scots Magazine, vol. III. 1818, p. 503.
¹ "Popular Rhymes of Scotland," 1870, pp. 80-82.

neebor, till the hale was biggit." A special example of one
of the buildings so reared is the Round Tower of Abernethy
in Perthshire, well known as one of the two towers of this
class still to be found in Scotland. "The story goes," says
the Rev. Andrew Small, in his "Antiquities of Fife,"[1] " that it
was built by the Pechts, ... and that, while the work was
going on, they stood in a row all the way from the Lomond
Hill to the building, handing the stones from one to another.... That it has been built of freestone from the
Lomond Hill is clear to a demonstration, as the grist or
nature of the stone points out the very spot where it has
been taken from, namely, a little west, and up from the
ancient wood of Drumdriell, about a mile straight south from
Meralsford." That Abernethy was long a seat of Pictish
power is what no historian would deny, and the tower referred to is always denominated "Pictish." Of the way in
which it was built we have just seen the local account.

Similar ideas are current in Northumberland. "The
erection of several of these old castles [e.g., Dunstanborough
Castle] is, by popular tradition, ascribed to the Picts ...
The building of the Roman wall, which is by country people
commonly called the Picts' wall, is also ascribed to them ;
and they are said to have formed the Catrail on the Scottish
border, which is frequently called the Picts-work ditch. The
Picts are described as men of low stature, but of superhuman
strength ; and on the moors of Northumberland the heaps
of stone, which are supposed by antiquaries to mark the spot
where 'bones of mighty chiefs lie hid,' are sometimes pointed
out to the inquiring stranger as places where a Pict's apron-
string had broken as he was carrying a load of stones to his
work."[2]

Although the tower at Abernethy, and the "Pechts' houses"
already spoken of, may be classed together as having been
built for the use of the builders themselves, it is quite evident
that if these people actually reared the many other structures
attributed to them, in Scotland and in Northumberland, they
did so in the character of serfs, working for people of other
races. If Dunstanborough Castle, the Wall of Hadrian, and

---

[1] Edinburgh, 1823, pp. 152-3.
[2] "Rambles in Northumberland," by S. Oliver. London, 1835, p. 104.

(perhaps also) the Catrail, not to speak of "a' the auld castles in the kintry," were built by the Pechts, the builders were evidently not working on their own behalf. This clearly must have been the case in the instance of the "Roman Wall," which was raised for the very purpose of checking the southward inroads of these fierce warriors. That it actually was a "Roman wall" is of course beyond question. But that fact does not interfere with the supposition that the drudgery was performed by captive Pechts, whose immense strength, and intimate acquaintance with the art of building such structures, would render them of the greatest use to their conquerors. That they, and not the Romans, were the actual *builders* of the wall, as Northumbrian tradition asserts, is therefore far from improbable. Indeed, there are one or two indications that the more northern "Wall of Antoninus" may also have been reared by kindred hands. And as with these early examples, so may the later buildings referred to have actually been unwillingly built by Pechts, at the command of other people.[1]

Not only walls and castles, or towers, but churches and cathedrals are also said to have been reared by the same dwarfish but powerful builders, as may be seen from the following instances.

One part of Scotland that continued to be a "reservation" of the Pechts, after that people had ceased to hold sway, is the hilly country lying to the south of Edinburgh, and known as "the Pentlands." Like the "Pentland Firth" on the north-east of Scotland, this district was so called because it was associated with the Pechts. We need not here concern ourselves as to the causes which made the name, in both instances, assume the modern form of "Pentland." But, in each case, the name was formerly "Pehtland," and it signified "the land of the Pehts, or Pechts." According to Dr. Skene, the Angles of Northumbria had, as early as the seventh century, established themselves pretty securely as the ruling

---

[1] The earliest instance which has come under my notice of such work performed in the British Islands by a subject people, who correspond in many ways with the Pechts, is that given by Lady Ferguson ("The Story of the Irish before the Conquest," London, 1868, p. 32), with reference to the rebuilding of the fort of Cruachan, in Connaught.

castethroughout the south-east of what is now Scotland, then a
part of "Northumbria." This territory seems to have reached
as far on the north-west as the modern county of Linlith-
gow, and one of the chief Northumbrian strongholds in that
neighbourhood has ever since been known by the name of
the Northumbrian king, Edwin. Edinburgh, therefore, in the
seventh century, appears as a seat of the Anglian race, which
ruled from the Forth to the Humber. Three or four centuries
later, the steadily growing power of "Scotia" annexed the
whole of Northumbria lying north of the Borders. But the
population, no doubt, remained little affected by this political
change, and its speech and traditions continued the same.[1]

But, although those Angles were the rulers of south-
eastern Scotland (in modern topography), there still remained
a remnant of the Pechts in at least one part of that northern
Northumbria.[2] And it was because of their residence there
that the Angles spoke of the hilly region lying to the south
and south-west of Edinburgh as "the Peht or Pecht land."
How long the Pechts maintained some kind of individuality
in that neighbourhood it is impossible to say. It is said
that, after Kenneth's great victory over the Pechts at Forteviot
or at Scone, in the middle of the ninth century, many of the
fugitives sought refuge in England. And, as the Pentland
Hills were then in "England," it is likely that they found
shelter among their kindred there. In other parts of Scotland
the Pechts are historically visible long after the seventh and
ninth centuries. At the battle of the Standard, in 1138, the
Galloway section formed one division of the Scottish army.[3]

---

[1] For Dr. Skene's accounts, on which these statements are based, see "Celtic Scotland," vol. i. pp. 136-241; and p. cvii of his Preface to the "Chronicles of the Picts and Scots."

[2] It is not meant to be implied that Angles and Pechts were exclusively the inhabitants of this territory at that time. But it seems clear that the former predominated, and gave to the district the impression of speech and custom which it yet retains.

[3] "Celtic Scotland," vol. i. pp. 203 and 467. "Reginald of Durham, writing in the last half of the twelfth century, mentions, in 1164, Kirkcudbright as being in 'terra Pictorum,' and calls their language 'sermo Pictorum.'" (Op. cit., p. 203, note.) Dr. Skene, quoting various authorities, gives us an interesting description of the Scottish army at the Battle of the Standard. It was composed, we learn, of Normans, Germans, English, Northumbrians, Cumbrians, men of Teviotdale and the Lothians, Picts (commonly called Gallo-

A popular tradition, to be presently referred to, also speaks of them as a distinct people in the Clyde valley, during the same century. It is therefore quite permissible to suppose that, once the people of the Midlothian "Pecht-lands" had realized that they were a conquered remnant, with no hope of ultimately recovering their lost power, they may have continued to live, if merely as serfs, not only to the twelfth century, but for several centuries longer.

That they did so is to be inferred from the following bit of "folk-lore," which relates to a locality that, though not strictly included in the district of the "Pecht-lands," is quite near enough to agree with this hypothesis.

The hill of Corstorphine, situated a little to the west of Edinburgh, is only about three miles north of the nearest point of the "Pecht-lands." Now, the village church of Corstorphine is one of the few churches in Scotland which are of interest to the antiquary. "Ancient it most unquestionably is," says a modern writer in the course of a description of the village and its church, and the foundation of the latter is placed in the year 1429. The fifteenth century is not very "ancient," as these things go, but perhaps the site has been occupied by a church from a much earlier period. At any rate, the writer just referred to, in visiting Corstorphine for the purpose of inspecting both church and village, obtained this piece of local tradition, believed to relate to the church of 1429. "Of this [church], in November 1881, an intelligent native assured the writer that it was 'wonderfully ancient, built by the Hottentots, who stood in a row and handed the stones on one to another from Ravelston quarry.'"—on the adjacent hill of Corstorphine.[1]

Now, if one compares this account with the traditional description of the *modus operandi* of the Pechts, already instanced in the case of Abernethy, and generally accepted

---

ways of Galloway-men), and Scots. This is the statement made by Richard of Hexham, a contemporary writer, and it seems to agree on the whole with the other accounts. His "Cumbrians" are identified with the "Welsh" of Strathclyde. No doubt his "Northumbrians" were those who, living on the north of the Border, belonged to that part of Northumbria which had then been Scottish for more than a century. The Galloway Picts, it may be added, were in the front of the battle, and "claimed to lead the van as their right."

[1] See the *Ordnance Gazetteer of Scotland*, Edinburgh, 1882, vol. i. p. 297.

throughout Scotland, one hardly requires the historical testimony of the "Pechit-lands" to recognize in these "Hottentots" the Pechts of tradition. It is not necessary to take the expression here used by the Corstorphine villager as absolutely correct. His statement, it may be remarked, succeeded a conversation in which our various wars in South Africa had been discussed,[1] and it is not unlikely that this had suggested to the speaker the term "Hottentot" as aptly enough describing a race that to his ancestors, whose ideas he inherited, had seemed savage and inferior. That he absolutely believed the labourers who reared the walls of the church to be of a different race from his own is unquestionably indicated by the whole tenor of his remarks.[2]

This Corstorphine tradition points to a body of Pechts still surviving as a distinct type, in the Midlothians of 1429; and then regarded by the general population as a caste of drudges. This, too, is the position accorded to that race in one phase of Highland tradition. "I am informed," says Dr. Jamieson,[3] "that in Inverness-shire, the foundations of various houses have been discovered, of a round form, ... and that when the Highlanders are asked to whom they belonged, they say that they were the houses of the *Driunich*

---

[1] This I am informed by the writer of the lines quoted.

[2] "The tradition that certain buildings were erected by men who stood in a row and handed the stones from one to the other is quite familiar to me with regard to buildings in Ireland," writes a correspondent (the Rev. J. Ffrench, of Clonegal, Fellow of the Royal Society of Antiquaries of Ireland); and he furnishes one example:—"Brash, in his 'Ecclesiastical Architecture of Ireland,' when describing the Round Tower of Ardmore, tells us: 'I have before stated that the materials of which this tower was built were brought from the Mountain of Slieve-Grian, some few or five miles distant. The local legend is that the stones were brought to the spot without "horse or wheel," and laid without the noise of a hammer, the meaning of which is that the stones were all dressed in the quarry, and a line of men being stationed along from the quarry to the tower, the stones were handed from one to the other.'" While this Irish tradition does not identify these builders with any special race of men, it is noteworthy that their method of building is that which Scottish tradition regards as peculiarly characteristic of the Picts, or "Pechts." Moreover, the building referred to by Brash is of precisely the same order as the Round Tower of Abernethy, said to have been built after the same fashion. And the builders of the Round Tower of Abernethy, as also the builders of the Round Tower of Brechin, are alleged by local tradition to have been "Pechts."

[3] In the "Dissertation on the Origin of the Scottish Language," prefixed to his Scottish Dictionary.

or *Trinnich*, i.e., of the *labourers*, a name which they give to the Picts." They may be seen in the Clyde valley, in the same position as those of Corstorphine, but three centuries earlier, on the testimony of tradition. "Throughout Scotland," says an antiquary previously quoted, "the vulgar account is, 'that the *Pechs* were unco wee bodies, but terrible strang'; that is, that they were of very small stature, but of prodigious strength. It is commonly added [he goes on] 'that the meal (oatmeal) was a penny the peck when they built the *His* Kirk [the Cathedral] of Glasgow;' for the building of all the cathedrals, and in general everything very ancient, is ascribed by the common people to the *Pechs*."[1] Now, the present Cathedral of Glasgow is said to have been built in the twelfth century, at which date the Pechts of Galloway formed a distinct and separate population in south-western Scotland. According to Reginald of Durham, as we have already seen, the town of Kirkcudbright was situated in the "Pecht-lands" (*terra Pictorum*), and the *serma Pictorum* was still spoken there. In the same century the Galloway Pechts formed the van of the Scottish army at the battle of the Standard; and the Pechts of this period are remembered in the popular memory, assisted by a homely enough detail, as having been employed in the building of the "High Church" of Glasgow. Of course, the Clyde valley is not situated in Galloway; but the presence of Pechts in twelfth-century Glasgow may easily be explained by assuming that they belonged to another detachment of the race, or that it was worth while sending to Galloway for such famous builders. Belonging to a period less easily defined are the Pecht masons of the famous Round Tower at Brechin. Regarding this tower a local writer states: "Tradition, in Brechin, as well as at Abernethy, ascribes the erection to the *Peghts*," and he adds, that "it has stated they were only allowed a trifle for this work, and were cheated out of part of this trifle."[2] In this instance, also, the Pechts are remembered as working for people of another race; which is somewhat remarkable, as the tower itself is one of

---

[1] Knox's "Topography of the Tay," Edinburgh, 1831, pp. 108-9.
[2] "History of Brechin," by David D. Black. Edinburgh and Brechin, 1867, 2nd edition, p. 247.

those which seem to have been built by the Pechts for *their own* purposes.

Without going much out of the way, it may be as well to point out that the popular idea of the Pechts being "men of low stature, *but of superhuman strength*," "unco wee bodies, *but terrible strang*," is not only supported by tradition on every side, but it is borne out by a consideration of the mementos they have left behind them. Much could be said on this subject; but it will perhaps be enough here to point to a hill-fortress in Forfarshire, which history and tradition agree in ascribing to these people. This is the stronghold known as the White Cater Thun, situated a few miles north-west of Brechin (which possesses the Pictish round-tower just referred to, and which was once a seat of Pictish monarchy). The fort crowns a hill which rises about 300 feet above the general level of the great valley of Strathmore, and is thus referred to:

"This is, perhaps, the strongest Pictish fortification extant. It is surrounded by a double rampart of an elliptical figure, being 436 feet long by about 200 broad, and containing about two imperial acres.... But the most wonderful thing that occurs in this Pictish fort is the extraordinary dimensions of the ramparts, composed entirely of large, loose stones, being 36 feet thick at the top, and upwards of 100 at the bottom, reckoning quite to the ditch, which, indeed, seems to be much filled up with the tumbling down of the walls. The vast labour that it must have cost to amass so enormous a quantity of large stones, and convey them to such a height, is astonishing.... In conveying the enormous quantity of large stones to the summit of White Cater Thun, the natives must doubtless have expended great labour, and much time. They seem, however, to have been familiar with a method of removing immense masses from considerable distances, and it is supposed they made use of hurdles on such occasions; it is not improbable they might have some kind of rude windlass for raising the larger stones from the bottom to the top of the hill."[1]

Whatever the method employed by the builders of this stronghold, the description just given will show the reader, what he cannot fail to be impressed with on a study of the Pechts, that these people and their buildings belonged to what is known as the "Cyclopean" type, and that they—the people—represented a race now quite extinct, in its purity,

[1] Knox's "Topography," pp. 92-94.

but which must undoubtedly have been remarkable for a prodigious strength of body, a strength that may well be spoken of as "superhuman," if it is to be compared with that of any existing race of men. It is this point that must always be borne in mind when one considers the traditions regarding the buildings of the Pechts, and this it is that justifies the very parts of those traditions which would otherwise appear utterly wild and incredible. Beyond question, there is much that demands criticism and inquiry in the traditional description of the way in which such edifices as Abernethy Tower and Corstorphine Church were reared. But two important points must not be overlooked. The one is that an immense number of people may have been simultaneously at work; the other is that the workers were of vast muscular strength.

CHAPTER X.

In the immediately preceding pages we have been considering the people known as "Pechts." But it is contended that the "Feens" of Gaelic story ought to be identified with the "Pechts." When the leader of the "Feens" landed in "the country of the big men," he was at once seized upon as eminently fitted to be the court dwarf, into which office he was duly installed; from which it was reasonably inferred that he was a "pegh," or dwarf. Now, in one of the many songs ascribed to the son of this "pegh," Oisin, who is ever bemoaning the departed glories of his race, he laments the fact that he finds himself in his old age "wearily dragging stones along to the church on the hill of the priest." "Here, where he is a drudge, he has seen the Feinne in their glory. . . . . Were they alive, shavelings would not hold this mound." Thus laments Oisin, the representative of the old heathen Feens, bitter in his denunciations of Patrick the priest, and the new order which he represents, and ever bewailing the vanished "glory of the Feinn."

We find Oisin, therefore, accepted universally as the type of his race, unwillingly occupied in "dragging stones for priests to build churches," in his old age and after the downfall of his people. Nor was it only as the serf of another race that he had so worked; because, he explains to Patrick that this old age of drudgery had been foretold to him by his leader, Fin, on a previous occasion, before the coming of Patrick, and on that occasion not only Oisin, but a great number of the Feens of Ireland, were engaged in a similar task. The great difference was that then they were not working as the drudges of another people, but for themselves, and at the command of their leader. And it was not a church, but a hill-fortress, that they were building, "on Cuailgne's bare and rounded hill." Oisin speaks of it as Fin's "famous fort," and the hill on which it was built is "said to be in the county of Armagh," or, as another writer states, in County Louth. According to Oisin, two-thirds of the materials for the fort were brought thither by the Feens of Connaught and the west of Ireland, and the remainder by the Feens of Leinster and the east of Ulster, to which section both Oisin and Fin belonged. Assuming these traditional accounts to be correct, we thus see the Feens, in the day of their independence, "dragging stones" to the top of a hill, in order to build a fortress; and later on we see them, personified by Oisin, occupied in a similar manner, but as the drudges of Christian priests and the builders of Christian churches. The one account applies to Scotland and the other to Ireland; but the Pechts of the White Cater Thun have their counterparts in the Feens who reared the "famous fort" "on Cuailgne's bare and rounded hill;" and the Pechts who built the churches of Glasgow and Corstorphine are also duplicated in the conquered Feens, "weary dragging stones for priests to build churches," in Ireland. Consequently, the traditional fame of the Pechts of Scotland, as a great race of builders, is not at all at variance with the belief that they and the Feens were of one nation.[1]

But, if Fin and his Feens were builders of the hill-forts of the "Pechts," and were themselves veritable Pechts, it is evident that the Feens built and inhabited the dwellings known as "Pechts' houses." This is quite borne out when we regard that class of building which, although an archæologist already quoted (Mr. Petrie) does not hold it to be strictly entitled to the designation of "Pecht's house," is nevertheless a variety of the same species, and often receives the same title. The variety referred to differs from what has been accepted as the true "Pecht's house," in that it has no superimposed covering of earth or turf. But the two varieties undoubtedly belong to the same general class. Now, with regard to this second order of "Pecht's house," we have such a statement as the following: "Glenlyon, in Perthshire, is remarkable for the great number of remains of

[1] For these references to Oisin and the Feens see Skene's "Book of the Dean of Lismore," pp. 12-14 (English version), and 10-11 (Gaelic). Also Mr. J. F. Campbell's "Leabhar na Feinne," pp. xiii, 47 and 49.

aboriginal works scattered through it, in the shape of circular castles built entirely of dry stones. The common people believe these structures to have belonged to their mythic hero, Fion, ... and have a verse to that effect:

> 'Bha da chaisteal dheug aig Fionn
> Ann an Crom-ghleann-nan-clach.'

That is, *Fion had twelve castles in the Crooked Glen of Stones* (such being an old name for Glenlyon)."[1] And a like belief prevails in other Perthshire glens, such as Glenshee and Glenalmond, beside the latter of which, as every reader of Wordsworth knows, Oisin himself is said to be buried.

The true "Pecht's house," however, is not this dry-stone circular "castle," open to air and sun. These "castles" are, indeed, popularly included among "Pechts' houses," but such an archæologist as the one recently referred to prefers to speak of them as "brochs." This word "broch" (akin to *burgh*, etc.) has been adopted by Dr. Joseph Anderson and other eminent students of such buildings, to distinguish this special structure; and although, etymologically regarded, the distinction is arbitrary, it is very convenient. But the "broch," standing visibly exposed like any other ruin, its stone walls uncovered to the sun, is by no means the same thing as the "Pecht's house" described by Mr. Petrie and others. This, it may be remembered, is almost or altogether identical with the dwellings of the North-Greenland Eskimos, as portrayed by the explorers of seventy years ago. It is approached through a long, dark tunnel, entered from the face of a bank or brae, so low that one has to crawl along it, its sides and roofs composed of large stone slabs, and the roof itself flush with, or even underneath, the surface of the ground. At the end of this long, dark, narrow passage one enters the central chamber of the dwelling of the North-Greenlander and the ancient Pecht. It, too, would be in darkness, were it not for the rude stone lamp, fed with the oil of seal or whale, soaking through moss or the pith of rushes, which hangs from the roof and is always burning. Here and there at the side of this central chamber are openings in the wall which lead into small cavities used as sleep-

[1] Chambers's "Popular Rhymes of Scotland," 1870, pp. 254-55.

ing-places. Briefly and imperfectly, that is the interior of the Pecht's house.[1]

Viewed from the outside, what does it resemble? The underground passage of approach is invisible. The "house" itself "is generally of a conical form, and externally closely resembles a large bowl-shaped barrow. It consists of a solid mass of masonry, covered with a layer of turf a foot or more in thickness, and has a central chamber surrounded by several smaller cells." Or, as another writer describes it, "all that meets the eye at first is a green, conical mound .... resting silently amid the moorland solitude." The entrance to this seeming hillock, situated sometimes at its base, more frequently, perhaps, at the extremity of a narrow, underground tunnel, was never very conspicuous, since it was only about a couple of feet high. In the days when the Pechts were actually inhabiting these "green hillocks," it is likely they took the precaution to conceal this outer orifice, small though it was, as well as possible. Thus, the adventurer or colonist of another race, arriving at a settlement of Pechts' houses, saw nothing but one or more grassy, conical hillocks rising out of the surrounding moor.

Since the Gaelic term *brugh* (for it is Gaelic, though not exclusively so) is used to denote the one variety of these "Pictish" dwellings, let us employ, if only temporarily, the Gaelic term which denotes the other. That kind of *brugh*, then, which is covered over with earth and turf so as to resemble a conical green mound, is known in Gaelic by the

[1] Although the Pechts made use of stone lamps similar to those of the northern Eskimos, it is perhaps too much to assume that the dwellings of the former admitted nothing of the light of day. Mr. Petrie states that the walls of the Pechts' houses "converge towards the top, where they approach so closely that the aperture can be spanned by a stone a couple of feet in length." If this aperture remained open during the day, which seems quite likely, then the above reference as to the ever-burning lamp is only applicable to the dwellings of the northern Greenlanders. For the sake of safety, while their lands were over-run by hostile forces, it is probable that the Pechts did cover the two-foot hole in the roof with a large stone, which itself would need to be hidden by earth and turf. But the fact that such an aperture was left in the building indicates that it was frequently uncovered; perhaps always at night, and also, during times of safety, in the day. In the latter case, the interior of this underground dwelling would then receive, through the hole overhead, enough light to fill the central chamber with a sort of twilight, although the smaller cells might have been quite in darkness.

name of *sith-bhrog*, or *sith-bhrugh*; that is to say, the broch of the *sith*. Still more commonly, it is styled a *sithean*, or *sith*-place. When rendered in our modern English spelling, according to its pronunciation, this distinctive *sith* becomes spelt *shee*; as in the case of *Gleann-sith*, which is written "Glenshee." And, similarly, *sithean* becomes *sheean*. It is the "sheean," then, and not the "broch" proper, that is regarded by such archæologists as Mr. Petrie as peculiarly the dwelling of the Pechts.

Now, if any Highlander were asked his opinion as to the former inhabitants of the "sheeans," he would have but one answer to give. And the nature of that answer is very clearly shown by those Highlanders who have compiled the leading Scottish-Gaelic dictionaries. *Brog* (i.e., "broch") is itself defined as an obsolete term for "a house"; but *bruth* and other variants connect, if they do not identify, the "broch" with the "sheean." The various definitions are these: *Bruth*, "a house half under the surface," "the dwelling of fairies in a hill"; *sith-bruth*, *sith-bhrugh*, "a fairy hill or mansion"; *sith-bhrog*, *sith-bhruach*, *sith-bhruth*, "a fairy hill," "a fairy residence," "fairyland"; *sithean*, "a little hill or knoll," "a fairy hill"; *sithein*, "a green knoll or hillock, tenanted, according to superstitious belief, by fairies."[1]

Thus, the houses of the Pechts or dwarfs were inhabited by the people known as "fairies." As the fairies were "little people," there is here no contradiction in terms. We have, moreover, seen that the same "conical, green mounds" are remembered in Orkney and Shetland as the homes of the "trows." "Trow," however, is itself equivalent to *droich*, or dwarf. Therefore, the belief that those outward-seeming "green hillocks" were the abodes of Pechts is quite in agreement with the traditions that refer to those mound-dwellers as *trows* and *fairies* (otherwise "the little people"). Because *pechs* (or *pechs*), *trow*, and *fairy* are all synonyms for "dwarf."

[1] See the dictionaries of Armstrong, McLeod and Dewar, and McAlpine. McAlpine also defines the word *dùn* as a "conical mound," "an abode of fairies"; and that more uncommon term is thus employed in an Islay story of Mr. J. F. Campbell's (*West Highland Tales*, ii. 484).

CHAPTER XI.

IN a reference to the popular traditions of Northumberland, the Picts are spoken of as "a race of people who are represented, in such legends, as endowed with supernatural power, and holding, in the scale of beings, an intermediate rank between men and fairies."[1] Sir Walter Scott also corroborates this belief as existent in Northumberland ("Rob Roy," ch. xxiii). And the writer previously quoted, in describing the local tradition with regard to the building of the tower at Abernethy by the Pechts, explains that "the people always, when they speak of these Peghs, associate that idea with a notion that they were a preternatural sort of beings, such as fairies and brownies." Therefore, without entering into any discussion as to what is or was meant by "supernatural power," we have ascertained from these extracts that the Pechts were regarded, in Northumberland and in Scotland, as a race of people possessing or claiming "supernatural" attributes. And that they were akin to "fairies and brownies," if they were not identical with them. This also is the position of the "Feens" of Gaelic folk-lore, as the following references will show.

When the celebrated Irish king, Brian Borumha, defeated the Danes of Dublin and their allies, in the year 1000 A.D., it is stated that he appropriated all the vast treasures that the Danes had gathered together:—"gold and silver, and bronze, and precious stones, and carbuncle-gems, and buffalo-horns, and beautiful goblets," as well as "various vestures of all colours."[2] And the chronicler explains that "never was

---

[1] "Rambles in Northumberland," by S. Oliver, London, 1835, p. 104.
[2] "The War of the Gaedhil with the Gaill," edited by J. H. Todd, D.D. London, 1867, p. 115. In the above quotation, the word translated "bronze" is *findruine*. This is referred to as "a metal, the constituents of which are not well known. O'Clery describes it as *prás go n-airgead buailte*, 'brass, with silver hammered on to it.'" It is also referred to as "white silver," "silver or

there a fortress, or a fastness, or a mound, or a church, or a
sacred place, or a sanctuary," which the Danes had not
plundered when it fell to their arms. The first three terms,
which in the Gaelic are *dún*, *daingean*, and *diongna*, are
closely allied, and each designates something akin to the
"hollow mounds" of which we have been speaking.[1] But
the succeeding sentence is quite explicit: " Neither was there
in concealment under ground in Erinn, *nor in the various
solitudes belonging to Fians or to fairies*, anything that was
not discovered by these foreign, wonderful Denmarkians,
through paganism and idol worship." With regard to which
last allusion, Dr. Todd says: "The meaning is, that notwithstanding the potent spells employed by the Fians and
fairies of old for the concealment of their hidden treasures,

---

white bronze," "brass," and "copper." It was employed to furnish such various articles as "leg armour," the rim of a shield, a royal chessboard, and, further, a bedstead—which surely ought to have been royal also. (*Op. cit.*, pp. cliii-cliv. *naw*, and 30 and 94; also Skene's "Celtic Scotland," ii. 507.) The passage relating to buffalo-horns is given in the Gaelic version ("War of the Gaedhill," p. 114), "*eras do chornaibh buabhill*." The word *corn*, of which *chornaibh* is an inflexion, is substantially the Latin *cornu*. The Scotch-Gaelic dictionaries give it chiefly the signification of "drinking-horn," and "sounding-horn or trumpet." Armstrong states that the drinking-cups of the northern nations were made from the horns of the "*urus* or European buffalo," referred to by Latin writers: *Fis adds*—"One of these immense horns, at least an ox-horn of prodigious size, is still preserved in the Castle of Dunvegan, Isle of Sky." *Buabhall* itself has the secondary meaning of "trumpet," or "cornet"; but its true meaning is "buffalo." Armstrong subjoins these comparisons—Armorican *boal*, French *buffle*, Latin *bubulus*, Greek *boubalos*. Also Cornish *buvuel*, with the meaning of "trumpet." And also *buabhall-chorn*, "a bugle-horn," with which he compares the Welsh *bual-gorn*. Halliwell has *bugyll*, "a bugle-horn," and *bugle*, "a buffalo"; and with reference to the latter spelling he says, "hence bugle-horn, a drinking-vessel made of horn; also a hunting-horn." Professor Skeat, who cites Halliwell also, defines "bugle" as "a wild ox." It is clear that these are all merely variants of one word, or rather of two words. The *u* in "bugle" has originally been broad. The hard *c* of "corn" has become a guttural in "chorn," and a mere aspirate in "horn," although it is still found as "corn" both in English and Gaelic dictionaries (with a very restricted meaning in the former instance).

[1] Dr. Todd (*op. cit.*, p. 45, *note*), in referring to another instance in which these terms occur, says:—"The words here used, *Dún, Daingen, Dingna*, all signify a fort or fortress. It is not easy to define the precise difference between them. *Dún* . . . seems to signify a fortified hill or mound. *Daingen* (dungeon) is a walled fort or strong tower; hence *daingnigim*, I fortify. *Dingna* (which he translates 'mound' in the above instance) is apparently only another form of the same word. Cf. 'Zeuss,' p. 30 a."

the Danes, by their pagan magic and the diabolical power of their idols, were enabled to find them out."[1] (The Gaelic from which Dr. Todd translates the above sentences is as follows:—"Ni raibh imorro *dún* no *daingean*, no *diamgna*, no ceall, no cadhas, no neimedh do gabhadh ris an ngláim nglifidhigh, ngloinnmair, ngnuismhir do bhí ag teaglaim, ocus ag teaccar na hédala sin, óir ni raibhe ifolach *fo thalmain* in Erinn ina fá dhiamhraibh dichealta ag *fianaibh* no ag *síthcuiraibh* ni na fuaratar na Danmargaigh allmardha ingantacha sin, tre geintlidhecht, ocus tre iodhaladhradh.")[2]

Like the Pechts in Northumbrian tradition, the Feens are here not absolutely *identified* with the fairies, although the two are so closely associated that it is difficult to distinguish between the one and the other. The traditions of the Feens themselves testify to a distinction between the two. Thus, in the "Dan an Fhir Shicair," or Ballad of the Fairy Man,[3] Fin and his six nobles, while walking out one evening, see a fairy-man coming towards them, who announces that he comes from the neighbouring Golden Doon (*Dún an oir*), and that his purpose is to cause those Feens to come, by enchantment, to dine that day with him and his people in their "hill." Here, then, we have the Feens associating, to some extent (though not, as it appears, on a very friendly footing) with fairies, and yet not themselves regarded as identical with that people.

From the foregoing reference to the plunder of the Danes at Dublin, in the year 1000, it is evident that "the Feens and Fairies" were understood, in the traditional history of the Gaels, to be then actually inhabiting those underground and half-underground dwellings known as "Pechts' houses." There is another reference, in the same history, that corroborates this belief. The date when Brian Borumha became

[1] *Op. cit.*, p. 115, note.
[2] Even the expression "*fo thalmain*" may be held to denote the "conical hill" of the fairies. *Talmhainn* is certainly the genitive of *talamh*, "the ground"; and so "*fo thalmain*" signifies "under the ground." But *talamh* particularly denotes "a mound." And it, or the variant *tulmon*, is used in a fairy tale of the island of Barra (Campbell's "West Highland Tales," ii. 39) with special reference to one of those abodes of the "little people." It may be added that the word translated the "solitudes" of the Feens, etc., might also be rendered the "secret places" or "concealed places."
[3] "Leabhar na Feinne," pp. 94-95.

possessor of those "fairy-hoards," which the Danes had previously obtained by their well-known process of "how-breaking,"[1] was the close of the tenth century. Now, a son of this same Brian, and also one of his father's chief warriors, are both described as asserting (on a certain occasion, in the reign of the same Brian)[2] that they had been tempted by the fairies to forsake their ancestral cause. "Often," says Murchadh, "was I offered, in hills and in fairy mansions [*i sithaib ocus i sithbrugaib*], this world and these gifts; but I never abandoned for one night my country nor my inheritance for them." As Murchadh's response was evoked by a similar statement on the part of Dunlang, it thus appears that, in rifling the abodes of the "how-folk," the Danes were robbing a race *then alive*, and were not merely appropriating unclaimed treasure. And, indeed, the Scandinavian accounts of "how-breaking" distinctly point out that this pastime involved a struggle of life and death with the armed inmate of the "how."

The evidence of Murchadh and Dunlang, then, shows that intercourse with "the fairies" was not a matter for wonder; and, moreover, that, for one reason or another, the latter desired to seduce the Gaelic-speaking people from their allegiance. That they were eventually successful with Dunlang seems pointed out by the statement, made elsewhere, that this Dunlang was himself a fairy (*siogaidhe*).[3] And it is well known that "Fairies," as well as "Feens," while possessing distinct innate attributes, were not averse to obtaining adherents from other races, who thus became "Feens" and "Fairies" by adoption.

In the instance of Murchadh and Dunlang, however, the *Feens* are not named; and it is a matter for conjecture whether they ought to be included among the Fairies there spoken of. But, at any rate, the incident shows that the

---

[1] The "fairy mound" was also known as a "how" or "hang," and its people as "how-folk." To "break," or break into a "how," in the hope of obtaining treasure (an early form of burglary), was a well-known custom of the Danes.

[2] "The War of the Gaedhil with the Gaill," pp. clxxviii-clxxix, note 5, and pp. 172-173.

[3] Dr. Todd, in mentioning this and the other relative circumstances, refers the reader to "Mr. O'Kearney's Introd. to the 'Feis Tighe Chonain' (Ossianic Soc.) p. 98 *sq.*"—and to O'Flaherty's "Ogygia," M. c. 22, p. 300.

Fairies (if not the Feens) formed an active, existent caste or race, subsequent to the date of Brian's famous victory over the Danes; and that the Danish inroads on their doons, brochs, hows, etc., in the neighbourhood of Dublin had not by any means annihilated them as a people.

Of this robbery of the "how-folk" by the Danes in the Dublin district, something further may be said in passing. The date of these raids is stated to have been 861 or 862 A.D., when the Danes overran the whole district of the Boyne and Blackwater (co. Meath), and broke into the "fairy hills" of that region; one of which, that of New Grange, is probably the most interesting example of its class that is at present known to archæologists.[1] Therefore, the booty which the Danes thus obtained in 862 must have formed a portion of that captured by King Brian, after his victory, in the year 1000. And it is clear enough that it was this special treasure that the chronicler referred to when he spoke of the hoards which the Danes sought out and discovered "in concealment under ground" and "in the various solitudes (or secret places) belonging to Feens or to Fairies."

Ought "Fairies," then, to be identified with the "Feens" and "Pechts" of history and tradition? We have already seen that, both in Scotland and in Northumberland, the Pechts are classed with the Fairies in the popular memory. And from the brief references just made, one would be disposed at the first glance to say that the two names applied to one people. But all the people who form the subject of consideration in these pages belong, even in their most modern and most modified phases, to the past; and in looking down that long vista one is often deceived by the "foreshortening" effects of distance, which seems to unite what is really distinct and separate. Still, it is evident that "Fairies" have so many points in common with "Feens" and "Pechts" that they must all, at least, be classed together."

The Ayrshire term *Fane*, which, according to Dr. Jamie-

---

[1] See Sir W. R. Wilde's "Beauties of the Boyne," Dublin, 1849, p. 202. The same work refers (p. 24) to "sidh Nectain, the fairy hill of Nechtain," where the river Boyne rises, but does not state whether early Dane or modern archæologist has ever investigated it. (It is now known as the Hill of Carbury.)

son,[1] signifies "a fairy," offers itself as very probably a variant of the Gaelic *Fian* (pl. *Feinne*). But Brittany affords even a better instance. There, we are told, the peasantry have memories of a race of *Fions*, who were dwarfs in stature, and are described as "living with the fairies."[2] And although we have endeavoured, as far as possible, to restrict these remarks to the British Islands, and even to a few special districts, yet the folk-lore of Brittany coincides so closely with that of the districts just referred to, and is so corroborative of the theories here stated, that it may be permissible to quote a few of the Breton beliefs bearing upon this subject.

Of those whom he states are called the *Christian* fairies of Brittany, M. Paul Sébillot gives several particulars.[3] These so-called "Christian" fairies were, he says, "neither wholly Christian nor wholly pagan," and in the traditions relating to them he dimly recognizes their possible identification with the heathen priestesses[4] of Brittany, at the time when they were gradually becoming converted to Christianity. They are celebrated, like the Pechts of Scotland, as the builders of churches. And just as local tradition states that the Pechts who built the Round Tower of Abernethy, in the manner already described, accomplished their work in the course of a single night, so a certain chapel in the Côtes-du-Nord is said to have been built in one night by the "fairies." Moreover, in two of the instances referred to by M. Sébillot, the top stone of the building is or was lacking, for the reason that the daylight had surprised the builders at their work.[5] Now, this is precisely what is stated of the Pictish builders of the Round

---

[1] "Scottish Dictionary," s. v. *Peer*.

[2] See the "Revue des Traditions populaires," Nov. 1889, p. 613. The reader is there referred to M. Paul Sébillot's "Contes populaires de la Haute-Bretagne" for those *Fions*; and also to Bézier's "Inventaire des monuments mégalithiques de l'Ille-et-Vilaine," (p. 36) for certain *Foins*, who seem very likely to be the same people.

[3] "Revue des Traditions populaires," Oct. 1889, pp. 515-519.

[4] These "Christian" fairies appear to be remembered as women; like the *banshee* or fairy woman of Ireland and Gaelic Scotland.

[5] Another illustration of these special features is afforded by the church at Eckwadt, in Denmark, which is said to have been built by a "hill-man," or dwarf. In this case, also, the last stone was not put on. Of this builder, too, it

Tower at Abernethy, who are said to have been much irritated because an early riser in the village discovered them at work, and thus deprived the building and its builders of their claim to a "supernatural" origin.[1] Further, these Breton "fairies" are spoken of as carrying the stones in their aprons, like the Picts of Northumberland, the castle-building "genii" of Yorkshire, and the "witch" who helped to build the Forfarshire fort of Cater Thun.[2] And, as in the two latter instances, as well as in several of the others referred to, the stones were carried from "a great distance" by the Breton fairies, on at least one occasion.

To this Breton comparison one is tempted to add that of the Netherlands. In referring to the dwarfs who once inhabited the neighbourhood of Tienen, M. Pol de Mont states that "they were uncommonly small of stature, but of extraordinarily great strength"[3]; a statement which is paralleled by "the vulgar account" in Scotland, "that the Pechs were unco wee bodies, but terrible strang." And, in the Journal of Folk-lore just quoted from, the same kind of people are again suggested by the *Gypuissen*; "queer little women," who lived in a "castle" which had been reared in a single night, and who, like the Scotch "brownies" (with whom the Pechts are classed by the Scotch), were content to perform such everyday drudgery as washing the clothes of the taller race living near them, for no higher remuneration than their daily food.[4] The "castle" in which they dwelt is not spoken of as visible at the present day, but the probability is that it was of the same nature as the *Aschberg*, near Casterlé,

---

is stated that "he worked only during the night."—(Thorpe's *Northern Mythology*, III. 32-39).

[1] In this mysterious method of working,—first preparing the stones in a quarry at some distance off, and then conveying them to the chosen site, and erecting them according to a pre-arranged method, and all in the course of a single night (as the nature and dimensions of the buildings rendered quite possible)—one seems to discern one of the methods by which these dwarf tribes asserted and maintained the "supernatural" qualities ascribed to them.

[2] For these latter references, see pp. 99-100 *post*. Of course, the "aprons" of the traditional dwarfs, it need hardly be added, were *leather* aprons.

[3] *Volkskunde*: "Tijdschrift voor Nederlandsche Folklore," 2ᵉ Jaargang, 9ᵉ Aflevering, p. 182.

[4] *Op. cit.*, 2ᵉ Jaar. 9ᵉ Afl., p. 89.

which M. Pol de Mont states[1] is declared by tradition to be a chambered mound, capable of housing as many as fifty *bergmannetjes*, or mound-dwarfs (the Dutch term being equivalent to the Scotch "how-folk" or the English "hill-men").

Nor can one omit the following testimony from the island of Sylt, off the Schleswig coast, supplied by Mr. William George Black. Referring to a story of "Finn, the king of the dwarfs," Mr. Black explains as follows:—"These were an odd, small, tricky, people whom the Frisians found in Sylt when they took possession. They lived underground, wore red caps, and lived on berries and mussels, fish and birds, and wild eggs. They had stone axes and knives, and made pots of clay. They sang and danced by moonlight on the mounds of the plain which were their homes, worked little, were deceitful, and loved to steal children and pretty women: the children they exchanged for their own, the women they kept. Those who lived in the bushes, and later in the Frieslanders' own houses, like our own brownies, were called 'Pucks,' and a sandy dell near Braderup is still known as the Pukthal. .... They had a language of their own, which lingers yet in proverbs and children's games. The story of King Finn's subjects is evidently one of those valuable legends which illuminate dark pages of history. It clearly bears testimony to the same small race having inhabited Friesland in times which we trace in the caves of the Neolithic age, and of which the Esquimaux are the only survivors." Mr. Black has himself visited one of those "green mounds" which are said to have been inhabited by this Sylt "Finn," and he states that when it was first scientifically examined, in 1868, it was found to contain "remains of a fireplace, bones of a small man, some clay urns, and stone weapons."[2]

These Continental instances may be regarded as relating rather to the "Feens of Lochlin" than to those of Ireland and Great Britain. But one thing quite evident from the foregoing references is that the "Fians and Fairies" of

[1] *Op. cit.*, 2ᵉ Jaar, 5ᵉ Afl., p. 89.
[2] *Heligoland*; by William George Black, Blackwood & Sons, 1888, Chapter IV.

Ireland, the "Flons, or Feins, and Fairies" of Brittany, and the similar people in the Netherlands and in Friesland, were all nearly identical, if they were not quite identical, with the "preternatural sort of beings" known to Scotch folk-lore as Pechs, or Pechts, or Piks, and to history in general as Picts.

CHAPTER XII.

THE Gaelic accounts do not, of course, refer to the "Fairies" under that name. It is therefore unnecessary to add anything here to the many attempted solutions of the etymology of "Fairy." But the Gaelic records speak of these people as the *Fir Sithe*, or *Daoine Sithe*—the *Sithe*-folk. As already pointed out, this word is pronounced as if spelt *Shee* or *Sheey*. It is also written *Sidhe*, and this brings us to the older spelling before the dental had been aspirated out of existence. The older form of the word is *Side*, presumably pronounced as *Sheede*. What are the conclusions arrived at with regard to these *Fir Sidhe*?

"We know now," says a recent writer, already quoted, "that the Sidhe were early peoples and their gods, incorporated into the following races. . . . We find under the Arctic Circle and among the Finns and other 'Altaic' or Turanian tribes of Russia, the same belief in 'Tshuds' or vanished supernatural inhabitants of the land, pointing to the same mixture of ideas we find in Ireland concerning dispossessed peoples of a different tongue but high civilisation, whose record remains only in legend. The 'Shee' of Ireland is the same word we find in Asia, but softened down in pronunciation. Among the early Russians and Irish we can safely infer the Turanian underfolk with its myths and manners of life, its subterranean dwellings and repute as magicians; in both we perceive remarkably clever members of the Finno-Ugrian women-folk gaining a power over chiefs of the conquering hordes, and going down into legend as supernatural Sidhes or Tshuds."[1] According to this writer, then, the "Fairies," whose treasures were seized by the Danes of Dublin in the ninth century, belonged to the Turanian or Finno-Ugrian race of the Tshuds. And the traditions

[1] Mr. Charles de Kay, in *The Century* of July 1889, p. 437.

current in Ireland and Scotland regarding the *Fir Sidhe*, are counterparts of those current in the north of Europe with regard to the *Tshuds*. It does not certainly tend to the simplification of a very complex question to discover that the North Europeans, who remember so much about those *Tshuds*, are the very people who, of all modern Europeans, seem to have most resemblance to the *Fir Sidhe*. In reviewing a recent collection of Lapp folk-tales, Mr. Ralston states that "the traditions relating to the constant struggle maintained between the Lapp aborigines and their foreign enemies" forms an important portion of the collection. "The first nine stories all refer to the foes known as *Tsjuderne*, the *Tsjuder*—the Chudic Finns of the Baltic and other coasts. When these dreaded enemies appeared, the Lapps would take refuge in their underground retreats."[1] Thus, in accepting Tshud as identical with *Side* or *Sidhe*, we have to recognize that the people so named were the bitter foes of the very race that most resembles them—the "underground" folk of Lapland. Perhaps the explanation of this apparent contradiction is, that the fact of antagonism existing between two nations is no proof of any great racial difference between them.

Whether the word "Tshud" is, or is not, a variant of *Sidhe*, there seems good reason for believing that such a variant ought to be recognized in the *seid* of the Sagas. We are told by Thorpe that witchcraft was *seidhr*, which word some derive from *siodha* (modern *sothe*), to boil. "Boiling 'seid,' or the witches' broth, was the chief art in witchcraft," says Mr. Du Chaillu; who adds that "the witchcraft songs which were used for the seid" were called *Vard-lokur*,—"weird or fate songs." The "seid" platform and the rites performed on and around it are described at the same place (*Viking Age*, ii., 394-398):—"Seid was to be performed. A *Seidhjall*, or platform consisting of a flat stone, was laid upon three or four posts, and women were to be found who knew how to recite or sing the so-called Vardlokun. When all this was ready, and the *Volva* [sibyl] on the platform, the women formed in a circle round it, and the effective song was chanted

[1] See Mr. Ralston's review in *The Academy* of May 11, 1889.

while the seeress, with the strangest gesticulations, made her conjurations and received her revelations." "Once at a feast, according to ancient custom, Ingjald prepared incantation (*seid*), that men might know their fates. There was a Finn woman skilled in witchcraft. .... The Finn woman was placed high, and splendid preparations made for her; each of the men went from his seat to inquire of her about their fates."

Similar accounts are given by Thorpe, who states that it, *seid*, "was regarded as unseemly for men, and was usually practised by women only: we nevertheless meet with seid-men." And again:—"On account of its wickedness, it was held unworthy of a man to practise seid, and the seid-man was prosecuted and burned as an atrocious trollman.[1] The seid-women received money to make men hard, so that iron could not wound them." "The most remarkable class of seid-women were the so-called Valas, or Völvas. We find them present at the birth of children, when they seem to represent the Norns." "That the Norns, who appeared at the birth of children, were of the race of the dwarfs," is elsewhere suggested by Mr. Thorpe.[2]

Scott, also (*The Pirate*, Note R), quotes from Kaspar Bartholin a long account of one of those "Valas," as given in the *Saga of Erie Rauda*. From which it is seen that, according to the custom described by Thorpe and Du Chaillu, she stood "on a sort of elevated stage," when delivering her prophecy.[3] Scott adds that Bartholin "mentions similar instances" to that of "the little Vala" (as this one was called), "particularly of one Heida, celebrated for her predictions," who attended festivals for the purpose of telling

[1] These trials and executions for "witchcraft" were the precursors of those which were carried down almost into our own times; and the above allusions to the "wickedness" of those rites only serve to strengthen the growing belief that the relentless persecution of "witches" was based upon most reasonable grounds, and that the motives actuating the "persecutors" were far higher and more sensible than a mere fanatical and narrow-minded hatred of paganism.

[2] For these extracts, see Thorpe's *Northern Mythology*, I., 14, 212, 213, 214, and 238.

[3] The flat stone, supported on three or four posts, or pillars (as Thorpe calls them), upon which the seid-woman stood, is very suggestive of the *cromlechs* or *dolmens*. (Cf. the *grottes aux fées* of Brittany.)

fortunes, accompanied by "thirty male and fifteen female attendants."

In all these accounts we see the fairies of tradition, notably the "fairy godmother" who came to the birth or christening of children. The man who practised *seid* rendered himself liable to be prosecuted and burned as a *trow*, "an atrocious trollman;" or, in the Gaelic, a *fear-side*. If the words "seid" and "side" are not practically one, it is at least evident that they relate to the very same people. And the *bean-side* (banshee) of Gaelic tradition is simply the seid-woman, remembered chiefly in her less pleasing aspect, as the foreboder of death or misfortune.

Thus, whether *side* ought to be held as primarily denoting the incantations, or the enchanters themselves, it is this worship that is indicated in the metrical life of St. Patrick, which says of him (Skene's "Celt. Scot.," II. 108):—

> "He preached threescore years
> The Cross of Christ to the *Tuaths* [people] of Feni.
> On the *Tuaths* of Erin there was darkness.
> The *Tuaths* adored the *Side*."

Nor is there anything inconsistent with these deductions in the appearance of a *Finn* woman as a celebrated seid-woman. For, in Shetland, the Finns are even yet "reckoned among the Trows."[1]

To return, however, to the *Sidhe* people of the British Islands. The Blackwater valley of Leinster, whose "fairy" strongholds and abodes were entered and plundered by the ninth-century Danes, reminds one by its name that the Blackwater valley of Munster is also famous for its fairy associations. In one of Mr. William Black's novels ("Shandon Bells") there are frequent references to a chief of the Fir Sidhe named *Fierna*,[2] who is remembered as the

---

[1] The magical power of the Finns is still recognised by the Swedish peasantry of to-day. An illustration of this appears in an anecdote related in the London *Standard* of 26 January, 1877, with regard to a Swedish lady "who had been so ill-advised as to insult a Finn, whose magical powers exceed those of the gipsies."

[2] It is no doubt owing to the infusion of Spanish blood in Southern Ireland, still visible in the complexion, as well as in the surnames (such as Costello and Jago, *i.e.*, Diego) of people in that neighbourhood, that this Fierna receives the most un-British title of "Don" prefixed to his name.

leader of the "little people" of the south-west. His chief residence appears to have been a certain *Knockfierin*, or Fierna's Hillock, which has perhaps been investigated by local archæologists. Several of the Limerick traditions relating to Fierna have been contributed by Mr. David Fitzgerald to the "Revue des Traditions populaires" (April 1889), and one of these tells how a mysterious stranger one night aroused a poor cripple and gave him a letter to take to Fierna. The messenger entered the fairy "hill," where he saw the chief—an old, white-bearded man. On reading the letter, Fierna declared it to be a challenge of battle on the part of the "King of the Sidhfir of the North"; a challenge which Fierna was loath to accept, because, as he explains, "my people of Munster are the weaker party."

This legend, then, shows the Fir Sidbe (or Sidhfir) as a people not always friendly to each other, although of kindred race. Moreover, it suggests that those of Ireland were divided into at least two sections—the Sidhfir of Munster and those of "the North." When we remember that in the ninth century "Feens and Fairies" were equally regarded as owners of the "underground" dwellings which were then plundered (and which still remain), it is noteworthy that in this very detail we have another parallel between the two castes—if they were two. For the Feens of Ireland were also divided into sections, and it may be remembered that two of these—"the Feens of Leinster and the east of Ulster," and those of "Connaught and the west of Ireland," were referred to on a previous page as engaged in building a famous hill-fort for their great leader, Fin. If the "Sidhfir of the North" were not the same as the Feens of Leinster and the east of Ulster, they occupied much of the same ground, and had so many points in common, that it is difficult to say wherein they differed.

Nor is this deduction at variance with the belief that the people just named were one with the Pechts of history. For the *Cruithni* of Ulster formed a distinct division of the Pechts; and, indeed, to be still more specific, were latterly associated with the *eastern* part of that province. And, as for internecine warfare, that forms no obstacle to the identification of the historical Pechts, in their later stages, with the *Sidhfr* of popular legend.[1]

Like the rivers of the same name in Leinster and Munster, there is a Blackwater in Perthshire which has fairy traditions, and, in consequence, the valley through which it flows is known as Glenshee (*Gleann-sith*). It is also remembered as a favourite hunting-ground of the Feens. Here they used to come, says an ancient poem,[2] to chase the deer and elk. The stories of Fin and his Feens are full of references to their hunting exploits. And an old poem[3] recites how, even while Ireland was chiefly peopled and ruled by another race, the ancient rights of the Feens, in this as in other respects, were still duly acknowledged. Fin, we are told,

> "possessed the old rights
> Which previously were his.
> From Hallowmass on to Beltin,
> His Fives had all the rights.
> The hunting without molestation,
> Was theirs in all the forests."

The "rights" possessed by these people between All Hallow-tide and Beltin, or from the first of November to the first of May, were, according to Keating,[4] that they were quartered upon the country-people, who had to support them during all that period. But from the first of May on to the first of November, the Feens were obliged to support themselves, which they did by hunting and fishing. It was during this latter period, therefore, that "the hunting without molestation was theirs in all the forests." Perhaps the expression "*all* the forests" is too comprehensive. Mr. J. F. Campbell, in referring to the Feens,[5] speaks of their "maintaining themselves by hunting deer, extensive tracts of land being allotted to them for that purpose." Perhaps, also, the

---

[1] Compare this tradition, recorded by Thorpe (*Northern Mythology*, III., 39):—"In very old times the dwarfs had long wars with men, and also with one another."

[2] "The Death of Diarmaid," by Allan MacRuaridh. *See* the "Dean of Lismore's Book," p. 30 (Eng. version), and p. 21 (Gaelic).

[3] "Dean of Lismore's Book," pp. 141-43 (Eng.) and 108-11 (Gaelic version).

[4] "History of Ireland"; Reign of Cormac Ulfada.

[5] "West Highland Tales," I. xlii.

word "forest" ought to be understood much in the way that "deer forest" now is.

"It was said at that time," says a West Highland tale,[1] "that Ireland was a better hunting-ground than the Scotch Highlands; that there were many great beamed deer in it, rather than in the Highlands. It was this which used to cause the Feens to be so often in Ireland." Nevertheless, the poem by Allan MacRuaridh, already referred to, states that the Perthshire Glenshee (or rather, the more important of the two Perthshire glens so named) was famous as a hunting-ground of the Feens, for the reason that it abounded in "deer and elk." Whether the "elk" of the one writer, and the "great antlered deer" of the other represent the same animal, or two separate species now extinct in these islands, is uncertain. In the account contributed to the (Old) Statistical Account of Scotland, the minister of the parish of Clunie, Perthshire, which is not very far from Glenshee, remarks (ix. 256-7, note): "The head of the urus has been dug up in this neighbourhood, as also the palmated horns of the elk, together with the horns and skeletons of large deer, supposed to be the moose-deer."[2] One of the tales of the Feens, which is common from County Mayo to Sutherlandshire, says Mr. J. F. Campbell, has reference to the hunting of an animal called the *lon-dubh*, which word Mr. Campbell, on the suggestion of his collector (Mr. MacLean), believes ought to be translated "black elk." This "black elk," then, which the Feens used to hunt, was an animal of much greater size than the deer, on the testimony of these tales, told in the degenerate days when the "black elk" and its hunters had become only a memory. "These [tales] may date from the days when men hunted elks in Erin, as they now do in Scandinavia," says Mr. Campbell.[3] It is to be remembered, however, that at the battle of Gawra, and, indeed, long after that date, the Feens of Scandinavia were in association with those of Ireland and of Scotland; and traditions relating to animals long extinct in Britain might really refer to incidents

---

[1] The Lay of Osgar : "West Highland Tales," III. 304-5.
[2] He adds :—" Some of these horns, which are of an amazing size, are in the custody of the Duke of Atholl, and of Mr. Farquharson of Invercauld."
[3] "Tales," II. 107. The story referred to is on pp. 102-6.

in Scandinavia, within comparatively modern times. But, on the other hand, there is the visible testimony of the " palmated horns of the elk, together with the horns and skeletons of large deer, supposed to be the moose-deer," dug up in the very neighbourhood which is famous as a favourite hunting-ground of the Feens, where they came " to chase the deer and elk." The inference is, then, that either the tales which relate to that time are very old, or else that the animals referred to did not become extinct in these localities at a very remote date.

And the latter inference is, in point of fact, the right one; if we do not restrict *lon-dubh* to the precise meaning of "black elk." Mr. J. F. Campbell not only tells us that certain "great antlered deer" were formerly hunted by the Feens, but he also points out Sutherlandshire traditions which tell how witches and fairies used to *milk* the female deer. And this statement forms one of the reasons which lead him to believe that Fairies, Picts, and Lapps were practically one people; for his deduction therefrom is this:—" Fairies, then, milked deer, as Lapps do." Now, the point of this is that the deer milked by the Lapps is the *reindeer*, and not any variety of deer now existing in the British Islands. Mr. Campbell's further reference to "a story published by Grant Stewart, in which a ghost uses a herd of deer to carry her furniture," quite bears out his belief that the reindeer was domesticated, as well as hunted, by the little people. And it is an actual historical fact that the reindeer was hunted in Caithness so recently as the twelfth century. In a very full and exhaustive "Notice of Remains of the Rein-Deer, *Cervus tarandus*, found in Ross-shire, Sutherland, and Caithness,"[1] the late Dr. John A. Smith, Sec. S. A., Scot, has pointed out that the seventeenth-century historian, Torfæus, mentions that it was the custom of two earls of Orkney, during the twelfth century, to cross over to Caithness from the Orkneys, for the purpose of hunting the roe-deer *and the reindeer*. Dr. Smith adds that the correctness of Torfæus' statement having been at one time called in question, the matter was placed beyond all doubt by a reference to the

[1] *See* " Proc. of Soc. of Antiq. of Scot." : First Series, VIII. p. 186, *et seq.* (with a special reference to pp. 203-6).

work of a learned annotator and editor of Torfæus (of the year 1780), who shows that the original manuscript whence Torfæus derived his information uses the words " rauddýri edr *hreina* " to denote those roes and reindeer of Caithness. Indeed, Dr. Smith's paper affords plenty of confirmation of this historical statement, since it is chiefly devoted to a consideration of the reindeer's horns found in various parts of the north of Scotland; some of them in those very "brochs" which are so associated with "the little people." And as, even at the present day, the higher mountains of Scotland abound in reindeer-lichen, there is nothing in the natural condition of the place to contradict the assertion of the historian. Therefore, Mr. Campbell's hypothesis that the fairy "herds of Glen Odhar" were herds of reindeer, receives every confirmation from history, tradition, and fact. And, thus, the figure of the reindeer incised on the monumental stone near Grantown, in the same quarter of Scotland (of which a representation is given on page 132 of Dr. Anderson's "Scotland in Early Christian Times"), may have been "drawn from life" at that very place, and need not be any older than the twelfth century.[1]

"Hunting appears all along to have been a favourite amusement of the *Seelie Court*," says a writer on the fairies of Clydesdale,[2] "and innumerable are the stories which are told concerning the magnificence and splendour of the royal retinue." There is also a Highland tale[3] which describes how the dwarfs used to be seen "hunting on the sides of Ben Muich Dhui, dressed in green, and with silver-mounted bridles to their horses which jingled as they rode." And a writer of the seventeenth century[4] tells "how there was a King and Queen of Pharie, of such a Court, and train, as they had, and how they had the teind [tithe] and dutie, as it were, of all corn, flesh, and meale, how they rode and went alongs the sides of hills, all in Green apparel." That green was the special colour of the fairies, everybody knows. And that it

---

[1] For Mr. Campbell's references, see "West Highland Tales," I., cl.-clx., and II., 96. This parallel has also been drawn by Miss Gordon Cumming ("From the Hebrides to the Himalayas," Vol. I., p. 283).
[2] *Scots Magazine*, Vol. III., 1818, p. 154.
[3] One of Mrs. Ewing's "Old-Fashioned Fairy Tales": The Laird and the Man of Peace. [4] George Sinclair, in "Satan's Invisible World Discovered."

was also the colour of the Feens is what certain sections of the people of modern Ireland do not allow one to forget.

Thus, in regarding these people as hunters, any distinction between "Feens and Fairies" seems to vanish altogether. Although it does not appear to be stated in so many words that the Feens "had the tithe and dutie, as it were, of all corns, flesh, and meale," yet the same fact is practically stated when we are told that, during the six months of autumn and winter, the Feens were kept in idleness by the people of the country ("billeted upon the country," as Keating has it), and this as a matter of right. The very dates upon which this period began and ended—Hallow-E'en and Walpurgis-night—are pregnant with "fairy" associations. And when the green-clad Feens, typified by their dwarf chief, had the exclusive right of hunting, during the spring and summer months, up till the end of October, over "extensive tracts of land allotted to them for that purpose," they could not have greatly differed from those little people who are even yet remembered as "hunting on the sides of Ben Muich Dhui, dressed in green." And it was distinctly understood that this right was theirs "without molestation." There is a real matter-of-fact meaning in the ballad, placed in the mouths of people of a taller race, and relating to that period and those privileged hunters—

> "Up the airy mountain,
> Down the rocky glen,
> We daren't go a-hunting,
> For fear of little men."

Of which the historical interpretation, as applied to Scotland, apparently is, that these popular traditions relate to the time when the Pechts, conquered by the Scots, who subsequently were reinforced by various later immigrant races, still retained a certain amount of independence, with special rights in certain districts, reserved to them as "Pecht lands." Their dwarfish stature is seen from the very word by which they are known, as well as from the dwellings they inhabited. Their small horses are spoken of in the earliest accounts of them,[1] and indeed still survive, though no doubt in blended

---

[1] *See* Ritson's "Annals," Vol. I. p. 12 (quoted from Dion Cassius, L. 76, c. 12).

forms, as the small breeds of Galloway, Shetland, and various parts of England. Their favourite colour gave them, in their earliest days, the title of Green Men or *Viridi*; although then the colouring was applied in a more primitive fashion.

Apart from all the resemblances specially referred to, there is a general association in the popular mind between Pechts and Fairies. Both are regarded as extinct races, and the date of their disappearance, though vague, points to the one period; and localities known as the abodes of Pechts are also known as the abodes of Fairies. For example, an antiquary of that neighbourhood (Sir Herbert Maxwell) states that "the fortified promontory of the Mull [of Galloway] is locally believed to have been the last stronghold to which the Picts of Galloway retired before an overwhelming force of Scotic (?) invaders." In the same paper,[1] and referring to the same promontory, the writer specifies "a small fortification called the 'Dunnan,' credited with having been a favourite haunt of the fairies." Again, the famous Pictish hill-fort in Forfarshire, known as the "White Cater Thun," is equally famous as a fairy stronghold. This celebrated fortress has been described on a previous page. It crowns a hill in the neighbourhood of the ancient city of Brechin, the centre of a district which was indisputably a territory of the Pechts. Even yet one may discern in the ruins of this fort the traces of the dwellings which so closely characterize the architecture of the Pechts, the chambers made within the thickness of the wall. Within the long elliptical enclosure of the White Cater Thun there are, indeed, faint traces of other buildings; but the great majority of its garrison must have been housed, after the fashion of the race, in the chambers that are traceable all along the actual rampart itself. And of this chambered fortress local tradition states that it was "the abode of fairies, and that a brawny witch carried the whole [of the stones] one morning from the channel of the West Water [a neighbouring river] to the summit of the hill, and would have increased the quantity .... but for the ominous circumstance of her apron-string breaking, while carrying one of the largest! This stone was allowed to lie

[1] Which appears in the "Proceedings of the Society of Antiquaries of Scotland," 1885-86, pp. 76-90.

where it fell, and is pointed out to this day on the north-east slope of the mountain! This tradition, it may be remarked," continues our authority,[1] "however *outré*, is curious from its analogy to that concerning the castles of Mulgrave and Pickering in Yorkshire, the extensive causeways of which are said to have been paved by genii named Wada and his wife Bell, the latter, like the Amazonian builder of Caterthun, having carried the stones from a great distance in her apron!" Among all the exaggeration and confusion of these statements two things are quite discernible—the identity of Pechts with fairies or other "supernaturals" in general—and (in particular) the identity of the descriptions given of people so denominated, in the region of Caterthun and of Yorkshire, and the descriptions of the Northumbrian Pechts as quoted on a previous page.[2] Indeed, the accounts given of the Pechts in the locality last-named, as well as some features of the traditional builders of Abernethy Round Tower, render it impossible to distinguish, in these two cases, between "Pechts" and "Fairies," or "Witches." And this, indeed, as we have seen, was the popular belief.

The conclusion, therefore, to be drawn from what has been said upon this subject is that, although the term *Pict* or *Pecht* has been chosen by History as that by which a certain race of people, once found in Scotland, ought to be remembered, yet that term indicates nothing more[3] than *Trow* or *Dwarf*, either of which names might as reasonably have been chosen as their synonym *Pecht*. And that when one speaks of *Pechts, Trows,* or *Dwarfs,* one is speaking of the same kind of people—the mound-dwellers, or "underground" races of the past. Further, that the people traditionally remembered in Shetland as *Finns* belonged to that group; as also those whom Gaelic folk-lore styles the *Feinne.* And that, along with many other popular terms not here enumerated, one of the names by which such people have been widely known is that of "the Fairies."

[1] Mr. A. Jervise, "The Land of the Lindsays," Edinburgh, 1853, p. 265.
[2] Page 67.
[3] The Latin term *Picti*, though pointing to another characteristic of the dwarfs, is not here taken into account, as it misinterprets the original word.

CHAPTER XIII.

THERE is one variety of the underground dwellings which, in the northern counties of Scotland if not elsewhere, is more specially indicated by the term "Earth House," or "Eirde House." With regard to this class of structure, an experienced archæologist[1] makes the following remarks:—

"The whole of these have been formed after one idea, viz. to secure an unobserved entrance, and to preserve a curved shape. From the entrance the first part of these structures is generally a low and narrow passage, growing in width and height from the point where the direction is changed, and terminating in a rounded extremity.

"The part of them last referred to is generally from five to nine feet in width, with a height barely sufficient to permit a man to stand erect. In some cases, however, they have been found to be of much more contracted dimensions throughout. The Eirde House at Migvie, in Cromar, only admits a single person to pass along; while that at Torrich, in Strathdonan, Sutherlandshire, is barely three feet in width.

"Dr. Mitchell has described another at Erribol, in that county, which is more like a large drain than anything else.

* * * * *

"These underground houses have occasionally smaller chambers, as offshoots from the main one, which are entered by openings of small size.

"They occur at times singly, and at others in groups. On a moor near Kildrummy, in Aberdeenshire, a group of nearly fifty were discovered.

* * * * *

"It has been doubted if these houses were ever really used as places of abode, a purpose for which they seem in no degree to be suited.

"But as to this there can be no real doubt. The substances found in many of them have been the accumulated *débris* of food used by man, and indicate his presence as surely as the kindred kitchen-middens which have recently attracted so much attention, while their occurrence in groups marks the gregarious habits of the early people. The bones of the ox, deer, and other like creatures have been found, as well as the shells of fish, mixed with fatty earth and charred wood. Ornaments of

---

[1] John Stuart, LL.D., "Proc. of the Soc. of Antiq. of Scot.," 1st Series, viii. 83 *et seq.*

bronze have been found in a few of them, and beads of streaked glass. In some cases the articles found would indicate that the occupation of these houses had come down to comparatively recent times, as in the case of the Irish crannogs, where objects of the rudest times are found alongside of those of the seventeenth century."

These underground passages or galleries are also known as Pechts' or Picts' houses; and they unquestionably belong to the same family as the other structures so denominated. But they are the rudest and most primitive of all. Between them and a chambered mound such as Maes-how, in Orkney, the difference is great; and still greater is the difference between them and a non-subterranean "broch," such as that of Mousa, in Shetland. Yet all these are so united by intermediate forms that it is difficult to say exactly where the one passes into the other. The nature of the difference may be expressed etymologically by saying that they are *burrows*, *barrows*, and *brochs*, or *burgs*; the "drain"-like Eirde House belonging to the first class, the chambered mound to the second, and the above-ground structure, such as that of Mousa, to the third. The three terms just used are radically one, as the buildings themselves are. But they represent different phases of one idea; and the last phase is very much in advance of the first. Whether the superiority of the one class of building over the other has been caused by the gradual advancement of one homogeneous race, during a long stretch of time, or by the blending of a higher race with a lower, within a limited period, must be regarded as an open question.[1]

But, although that crude form of earth-house which we have described as a burrow, is included among the Pechts' houses of Scotland, it differs in several respects from that variety which has been regarded as the typical "Pecht's house," namely, the chambered mound, or "hollow billock." One of the salient features of the burrow, the "unobserved entrance," is equally a feature of the hollow mound; and the latter has also the same narrow, low, subterranean passage of

[1] Examples of those "burrows," or underground galleries, in Ulster are given by Mr. S. F. Milligan, M.R.I.A. (*Jour. of Roy. Hist. and Arch. Assn. of Ireland*, No. 80, Vol. IX., Fourth Series, pp. 245-246), who remarks:—"These souterrains are good examples of the dwelling-places of a very early race of settlers in this country."

approach, formed of huge stone slabs. In each, too, as in the more advanced and elaborate "broch," it is seen that the builders knew of no other kind of arch than that formed by the gradual convergence of the walls, by means of each course overlapping the course immediately below it, until only a single slab was required to crown the whole by way of "keystone." The better kind of "burrow," with its "smaller chambers, as offshoots from the main one," is also closely akin, in that respect, to the so-called "hollow hill." But, while having all these points of resemblance, the latter differs from the former in that its passage dispenses altogether with the curve which distinguishes the "burrow;" and, greater difference still, in that it is not merely an underground dwelling, but that the earth over it is heaped so high above the level of the adjoining ground that it presents exactly the appearance of a conical or rounded green hillock, when looked at from the outside. Moreover, it is only rendered an "underground" dwelling by the earth-heap imposed upon the original structure, which itself was built upon what was then the surface of the ground. Whereas the long, curved gallery, which has more specially been styled an "earth-house," is below the surface of the surrounding land, and is generally discovered by some ploughman whose plough happens to break or disarrange the stone slabs forming its roof.

There is no special reason for limiting the term "earth-house" to the underground gallery just spoken of, because the chambered mound is also as much an "earth-house." In either case, the structure itself is of stone. Therefore, we need not here restrict the term "earth-house" to one of these two varieties, but apply it equally to both. Each variety is popularly known as a "Pecht's house," and the one is as much an "earth-house" as the other.

The "hollow hill," however, will be the variety of earth-dwelling chiefly considered in this place. But, before leaving the ruder structure, reference may be made to a Shetland specimen, examined in 1865. It is described as "of a semi-circular form, two feet or so beneath the arable land, about thirty feet in length, three feet in breadth and height, widening out at the western extremity to the form of a chamber of five feet square; ponderous slabs of mica-slate form the lintels. These stones have been transported from Norwick, which is the nearest depôt for such, and distant two miles." Like other similar structures this was locally known as a "Fairy Ha'."[1]

Thus, the two varieties of earth-house, each known popularly as a "Pecht's house," are also both remembered as the dwelling-place of fairies. For the chambered mound is equally a "Fairy Knowe"; in Gaelic, a "sheean" (*sitheun*), or abode of fairies.

And as the "little people" of Scotland have been chiefly chronicled as "Pechts," or "Picts," we may further consider them in that twofold character; continuing also to regard them in the territories which have already been most frequently named. Of these, none are more worthy of examination than the districts—insulated or otherwise—in the neighbourhood of the Pecht-land Firth.

"By an authentic record of Thomas, Bishop of the Orkneys, dated 1443, and published in Wallace's "Orkneys," edit. 1700; when the Norwegians conquered these islands they found them possessed 'by two nations, the Pets [Pehts, or Pechts] and Papas'"[2] (*i.e.*, popes or priests). The "popes" referred to are understood to have been the Irish missionaries from Iona, and of them there seems to be no distinct tradition surviving. But the other "nation" is well remembered in both of the Northern groups. "The first folks that ever were in our isles were the Picts," says Shetlandic folk-lore; "they were very small [people]."[3]

What appears to be a popular tradition relating to the time when the territory of the mound-dwelling Pechts was beginning to be invaded and settled by colonists of another race, is furnished us by Sir Walter Scott. The ballad of "Alice Brand," in "The Lady of the Lake," speaks of a

---

[1] "Memoirs of Anthropological Society of London," vol. ii. 1865-6, p. 343.
[2] Kam's "Topography," etc., Edin., 1831, p. 211, note.
[3] Regarding the original home of the Picts, there is considerable difference of opinion among ancient writers; but the above traditional belief receives support from the statement that "by Beda, by the 'Historia Britonum,' and by the Welsh traditions, they appear as a people coming from Scythia, and acquiring first Orkney, and afterwards Caithness, and then spreading over Scotland from the north."—(Skene's *Chronicles of the Picts and Scots*, p. xcvi.)

"moody Elfin King, who won'd[1] within the hill." And we are told in the *Appendix* that this legend "is founded upon a very curious Danish Ballad, which occurs in the 'Kæmpe Viser,' a collection of heroic songs first published in 1591." It begins "*Der ligger en vold i Vester Haf*," which is rendered in English, "There lies a wold in Wester Haf." Scott says:—"As *Wester Haf* . . . means the *West Sea*, in opposition to the Baltic or *East Sea*, Mr. Jamieson inclines to be of opinion that the scene . . . is laid in one of the Orkney, or Hebride Islands." Both in this old ballad, and in Scott's adaptation, there is an element of the magical, or impossible, or, at least, unexplainable kind; but some of the leading facts are these:—A "husband," or yeoman, goes to this "wold in Wester Haf," taking his wife and all his belongings with him, and there he proceeds to settle down as a colonist. Like many other "backwoodsmen," he begins by felling the trees of the forest[2] for his new home, much to the indignation of the dwarfs who inhabit a certain "knock" (Gael. *cnoc*), or chambered mound, in that district, and who, indeed, are the owners of the soil.

> "He hew'd him hipples,[3] he hew'd him bawks,[4]
> Wi' mickle moil and haste,
> Syne spear'd the Elf i' the knock that bade,
> 'Wha's hacking here sae fast?'"[5]

The dwarfs are discomfited in their attempt to enter the "husband's" house, but finally one of them succeeds:—

> "The huswife she was a canny wife,
> She set the Elf at the board;
> She set before him baith ale and meat,
> Wi' mony a weel-waled[6] word.

> "'Hear thou, Gudeman o' Villenshaw,'[7]
> What now I say to thee;
> Wha bade thee bigg[8] within our bounds,
> Without the leave o' me?'

---

[1] Dwelt (cf. Dutch *wonen*, Germ. *wohnen*).
[2] This feature does not accord with the appearance of modern Orkney or the Hebrides, but both groups were once thickly wooded. Buchanan refers to various Hebridean islands as being "*darkened* with wood" in the sixteenth century.
[3] Couples.   [4] Balks (cross-beams).
[5] From Jamieson's Scotch version, as given by Scott.   [6] Well-chosen.
[7] The dwarf is here addressing the settler by the name of his new possession.   [8] Build.

> "'But, an' thou in our bounds will bigg,
> And bide, as well as may be,
> Then thou thy dearest huswife maun
> To me for a lemman gie.'"

However, the husband is not even temporarily bereft of his wife; and, indeed, after all the threatenings of the "howfolk," the settlers are allowed to remain quietly in possession of their homestead, and their daughter is afterwards married to the dwarf visitor.[1]

Though this song is from a Danish collection, there is another of very similar nature in Unst, Shetland. It begins "Der lived a king into da aste," and it recounts how a certain "wedded wife" was carried off by "the King o' Ferrie." Her husband afterwards goes in search of her; and "one day, in his wandering quest, he sees a company passing along a hillside, and he recognizes among them his lost lady." They go into "a great 'ha'-house,' or castle," which is said to be *on* the hillside; but as nothing is visible but "a grey stane," after they have entered, it would seem that *the hill itself* was the castle, and the grey stone the entrance door, as in the case of the Orcadian Maes-how, or many another residence of the "how-folk." This assumption is quite borne out by the song itself. The same writer[2] indicates that such abductions were quite common in Shetland, when she states that a "witch" who married a dwarf returned once to her mother's house, and, while imparting to her various other counsels and warnings, "gave many instructions how to provide against the enchantments used by Trows for the purpose of decoying unsuspecting girls into their unhallowed domain." And her parting injunction was to be sure and have the maidens "weel cóst about" (? protected by charms) "when the grey women-stealers are wandering." But instances of such intercourse between the dwarf races and others, the abduction being by no means confined to one side, could be quoted almost interminably.

The celebrated "how" known as Maes-how, in Orkney,

---

[1] It ought to be added that he is only an "elf" by adoption; but this does not affect the general situation. He bears all the outward characteristics of the dwarf.

[2] Mrs. Jessie E. Saxby, "Folklore from Unst, Shetland" (*Leisure Hour*, 1880).

has just been referred to. It is so admirable a specimen of the "Pecht's house" proper that no better selection can be made for a more particular description of such a dwelling. "It stands about a mile to the north-east of the great stone ring of Stennis. Its external appearance is that of a truncated conical mound of earth, about 300 feet in circumference at the base and thirty-six feet high, surrounded by a trench forty feet wide. Nothing was known of its internal structure till the year 1861, when it was opened by Mr. Farrer, M.P., but the common tradition of the country represented it as the abode of a goblin, who was named 'the Hogboy,' though no one knew why."[1] In Lincolnshire, this term "hog-boy" is pronounced as "shag-boy."[2] The word pronounced *shag* in one place and *hog* in another, is understood to be the same as *haug* or *how*; and the term is therefore a variant of the plural "how-folk." It was one of those "shag-boys" or "hog-boys," then, that local tradition remembered as the inhabitant of Maes-how. And nowhere is the tenacity of the popular memory more strongly illustrated than in this instance. For, during many centuries prior to 1861, this had been nothing more, to the passing stranger, than a grassy hillock, utterly void of any indication that its interior was "hollow," and that the whole structure—stone-built dwelling, and super-imposed earth—was entirely artificial,—the work of a vanished race. And yet, so full of vitality is tradition, that the descendants of those who had seen its inmate or inmates, knew, in spite of the lapse of a thousand

---

[1] Dr. Joseph Anderson, in his Introduction to the "Orkneyinga Saga," p. ci.
[2] In an article ("From the Heart of the Wolds") contributed to the *Cornhill Magazine* of August 1882, the following is stated with regard to the traditions of this part of Lincolnshire:—"Ghosts, bogies, and the supernatural generally have utterly vanished from this commonplace district before schools and newspapers. Even an old lady more than ninety years old said to us, 'Fairies and shag-boys! lasses are often skeart at them, but I never saw none, though I have passed many a time after dark a most terrible spot for them on the road at Thorpe.'" The identity of "shag-boy" with "hog-boy" (as used in Orkney) is asserted by the writer of the *Cornhill* article; who also states:—"In an adjoining field [near Bechby] lingers one of the few legends of this prosaic district. A treasure is supposed to be hidden in it, and at times two little men, wearing red caps, something like the Irish *leprechauns*, may be seen intently digging for it." These little "red-caps" are not identified with the "shag-boys," but popular tradition generally would pronounce them to be the same people.

years, that this was no ordinary grassy mound, but that once upon a time it had been the habitation of people of a certain race, whose characteristics are even yet remembered, if only in a confused and imperfect manner.

However important and necessary a written description may be, it is very incomplete without a personal inspection of the place described, or in lieu of that, the "counterfeit presentment," which is almost as serviceable. From the view here given of Maes-how, as it appears from the outside, and also from the following diagrams, one obtains an

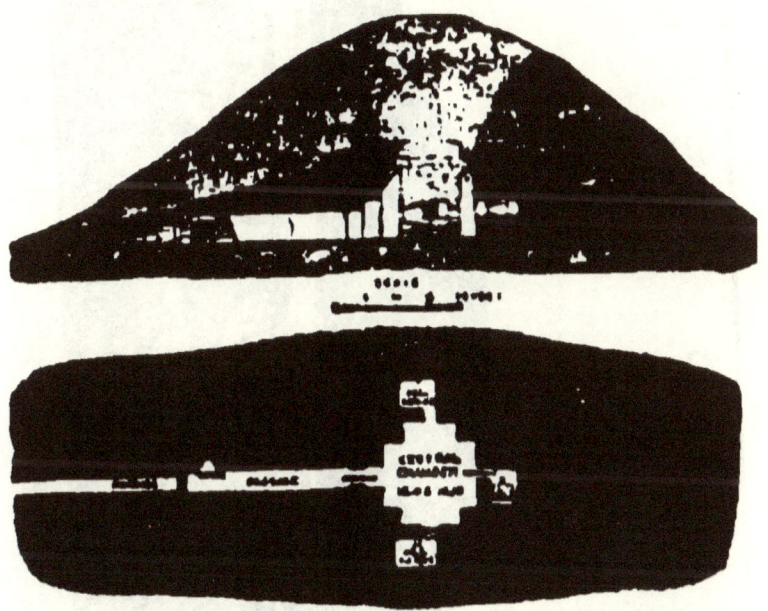

SECTIONAL VIEW AND GROUND-PLAN OF MAES-HOW.

admirable idea of the exterior and interior of a *sheean*, Fairy Hillock, or Fairy Ha'.

After examining these pictures of this famous "how," one is able to fully understand the traditional accounts of the "hollow hillocks" of the dwarfs. One can fit any of the many stories that tell of visits paid to such "hills" into this particular scene. There is the small, concealed entrance at the base of the hill (at which, or beside which, the visitor used to knock until "the hill opened"—revealing a low,

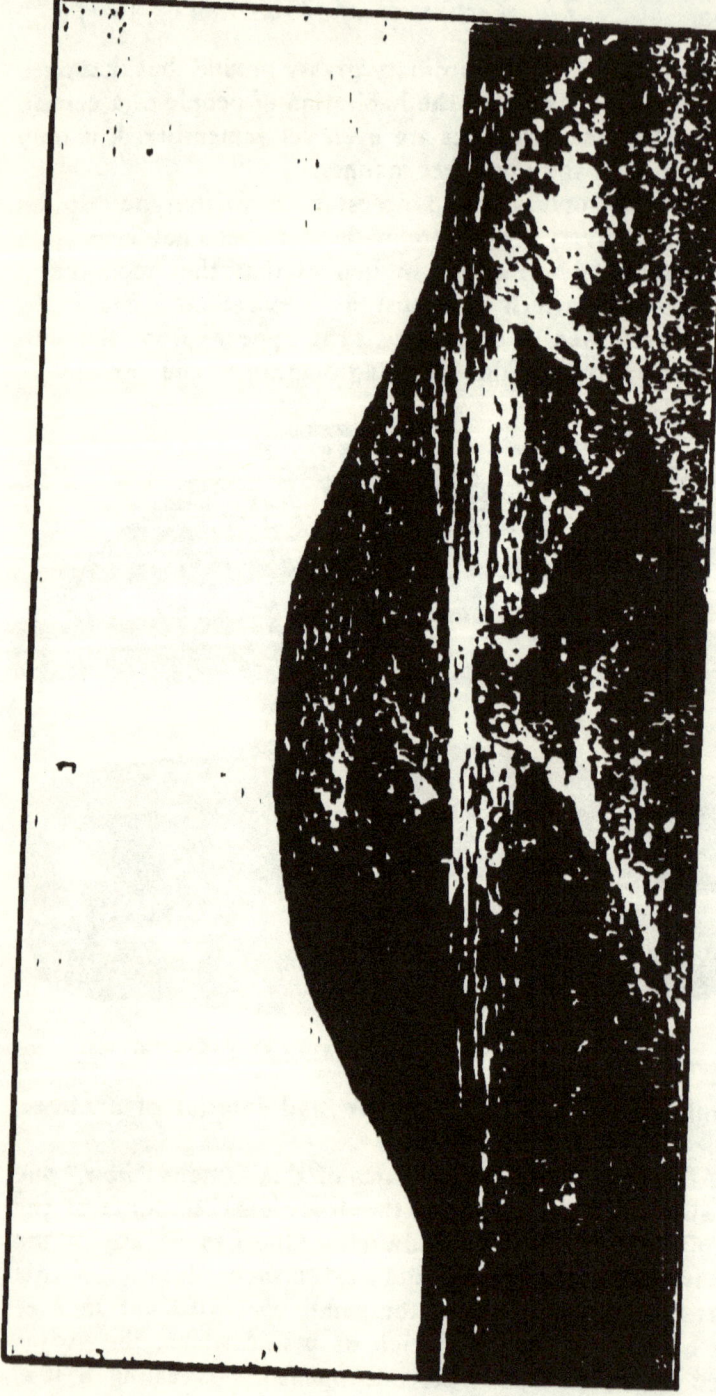

narrow, dark passages. In this instance the aperture is two feet four inches in height, and of exactly the same breadth; and its dimensions continue the same for the first twenty-two and a half feet into the hill; for it will be seen that the mound of stone and earth that surrounded and covered the actual building gave the habitation a fictitious base, which had to be penetrated by this passage until the walls of the

main building were reached—in the centre of the "hill."[1]

[1] One is apt to think of this introductory passage as though it had actually penetrated a pre-existing earthy mound. But the construction of all these chambered mounds shows plainly that the original stone structure, not only the central building but the long passage of approach, was originally reared upon the surface of the level ground; in the open air. Now that the "fairy hillock" had no existence at all over the top or at the sides of the stone structure, but became above it all—chambers and gallery—the masses of earth and stones that afterwards transformed the whole exterior into a "green hillock," and so completely disguised its real nature from all but the initiated.

In Maes-how the passage of approach is fully fifty-three feet long. Its height, as already stated, is only two feet four inches, during the first twenty-two feet of length; so that no one, unless an actual dwarf, could walk erect along this portion. After this the roof of the passage rises to four feet four inches; and it retains this height during the next twenty-eight feet of length. The remaining distance—scarcely three feet—is four inches higher; and then the passage "enters the middle of one of the four sides of a chamber which is fifteen feet square, and has, when complete, been about twenty feet high in the centre. The walls of this chamber are perpendicular for about six feet, after which the slabs, which generally extend the whole length of a side, project beyond the courses on which they rest, until in this way the roof has been completed in the shape of an inverted pyramid formed of successive steps."[1] In the three sides of this central hall (excluding the side at which the long passage emerges) there are respective entrances into three small chambers. The largest of these is less than seven feet long, less than five feet broad, and its roof is only three and a half feet from the floor.

In assuming that the roof of this building, now open to the sky, was "completed in the shape of an inverted pyramid formed of successive steps," Colonel Leslie is at variance with the description given by an eighteenth-century writer (in connection with similar buildings), and at variance also with tradition. The difference is a slight one, but it ought to be referred to. The roof was not precisely *completed* in such buildings, according to the writer referred to; it "was carried on round about with long stones [each successive course projecting, and thus gradually narrowing the orifice], till it ended in an opening at the top, which served both for light and a vent to carry off the smoke of their fire." Without this opening the dwelling had very little light or air; for little of either could have straggled in from the mouth of the narrow, underground passage, which reached the open air at a distance of fifty-three feet from

---

[1] For these details see Colonel Forbes Leslie's "Early Races of Scotland," vol. ii. pp. 338-40.

the dwelling, and whose entrance (besides) was nearly always closed during the day.[1]

While tradition seems clearly to indicate that the roof of the dwelling communicated with the open air above, there is necessarily some uncertainty on this point. The writer who speaks of the roof of such a building being "carried on round about with long stones, till it ended in an opening at the top," may have had in view a structure more resembling the open air "broch" than the *sith-bhrug*; although he mentions that the kind of building he describes often "looks outwardly like a heap without any design."[2] It is undoubted that many such mounds, for example, those of New Grange and Dowth, in the Boyne district, have their rude, "Pelasgian arch," crowned with one large stone as keystone; and that, therefore, any upward exit from the chamber must have led off in a slant from some portion of the wall. On the other hand, there are several indications that when one ascended the outside of a *sheann*, in the days when it was inhabited, one found oneself at the edge of a hollow or crater, at the foot of which was the narrow orifice that gave light and air to the chamber below. More than one fairy-hill of the present day, not yet explored, has a small hole on its summit, and when a stone is dropped therein, it is heard to rumble and fall into some unknown cavern below. And the existence of such "craters" was well known (we are

---

[1] Even with this roof-light the interior of the dwelling can only have received a limited supply of daylight. And this explains the statement made by a Scotch peasant who was taken by a "fairy" woman into her abode. "Being asked by the judge [before whom he was tried for 'witchcraft'] whether the place within the hill, which he called a hall, were light or dark, he said '*Indifferent, as it is with us in the twilight*.'"

At night, when the abode of the "hillman" was lit up with the glow of the fire, the cavity above the building, and the atmosphere overhead, must have also received some share of the firelight. This would account for the statement made by Wallace (who wrote at the period when "Evil Spirits also called Fairies" were "frequently seen in several of the [Orkney] isles dancing and making merry,") to the effect that, "in the Parish of Evie, near the Sea, are some small *Hillocks*, which frequently, in the Night time, appear all on a fire." And when Mrs. Ewing, in her "Old-Fashioned Fairy Tales," says that *sithean* is "a Gaelic name for fairy towers, which *by day* are not to be told from mountain crags," she evidently alludes to the same feature.

[2] See the description in an Appendix to Pennant's Tour, written by the then minister of the parish of Reay, Sutherlandshire.

told by Scott, in his Introduction to the *Tale of Tamlane*) to the people of Scotland. "Wells, or pits, on the top of hills were supposed to lead to the subterranean habitations of the Fairies." Legendary stories in connection with these there are many—of men descending such "pits," sometimes well knowing what to expect, and of having hand-to-hand fights with the natives of these abodes. At other times the attack was made by those "hillmen" themselves; who seem to have emerged by this entrance as often as by the other. "A savage issuing from a mount" was once a well-known bearing in Scottish heraldry. Mr. J. F. Campbell records a Ross-shire tradition of a dwarf who inhabited *Tombuidhe Ghearrloch*, "The Tawny Hillock of Gairloch," and who was the terror of the neighbourhood (whose chief inhabitants, in his day, belonged to another race). Before he was himself slain, this formidable dwarf had killed many of the latter race; none of whom (with one exception) dared to venture near his "hillock" after dusk. He was at length killed by a local champion, still remembered as "Big Hugh" (Uistean Mor, MacGhille Phadrig;) who was celebrated as a slayer of dwarfs; and who appears to have devoted himself to their extermination in that particular district. And in the story of the killing of this noted dwarf, it is stated that Uistean climbed to the top of the hillock (*Tom-buidhe*) and attacked its inhabitant, who emerged from the foot of its "crater" or "pit"; in other words, from the roof of his dwelling.[1]

Such a "*sheen*" is the Denghoog in the Danish island of Sylt, one of the mounds believed to have been the residence of Finn, the dwarf king. Mr. W. G. Black, who has visited this "how," describes it thus:[2]—

"Externally merely a swelling green mound, like so many others in Sylt, entrance is gained by a trap-door in the roof, and descending a steep ladder, one finds himself in a subterranean chamber some seventeen by ten feet in size, the

[1] "Popular Tales of the West Highlands," vol. ii. pp. 97-101. In the *Book of Clanranald*, a portion of which is translated by Dr. Skene, a certain "Haladhan," whose paternal grandfather was Donald of the Isles, is stated to have been also the grandson (through his mother) of "Giolla Phadraig." This "Huisdean" appears to have lived in the fifteenth century. (See *Celtic Scotland*, III., 408-409.)

[2] "Heligoland," 1888, pp. 84-85.

walls of which are twelve huge blocks of Swedish granite; the height of the roof varies from five feet to six feet. The original entrance appears to have been a long narrow passage seventeen feet long and about two feet wide and high. This mound was examined by a Hamburg professor in 1868, who found remains of a fire-place, bones of a small man, some clay urns, and stone weapons."

This example, then, of the abode of one of the "Feens of Lochlan," corresponds exactly with Maes-how and all similar "*shiens*." And, like them, it is locally remembered as the residence of a dwarf.

This, of course, is tradition. But the northern sagas (though "tradition" also) are accepted as "history," in some degree. And the sagas bear a like record. Their heroes break into those dwellings, make their entrance by the hole at the bottom of the "crater," and attack the inhabitants, who, seizing their weapons, defend their lives and (in many cases) their treasures. And before leaving the "hollow hill" of Maes-how, it may be stated that this particular *broch*, or *shiens*, is believed to have been invaded about a thousand years ago. It was entered in the twelfth century by some of those North-men who were on their way to the Holy Land; and these have incised various inscriptions on its inner walls. But at that date it was empty—and had been rifled many centuries before. One legendary tale places the date of its original despoliation as far back as the year 920; and states that "Olaf the Norseman" was its invader; and that he encountered its possessor, whom he overcame—after a deadly struggle. And, since "the common tradition of the country [up to the year 1861, when it was reopened] represented it as the abode of a goblin, who was named 'the Hog-boy'," it would seem that the prevailing blood of the country-people in that district is akin to that of this "Olaf the Norseman;" and that, therefore, in this instance, the popular memory reaches back for nearly a thousand years, with the most perfect precision.[1]

[1] For fuller information as to Maes-how, and references to more detailed accounts, see Dr. Anderson's "Orkneyinga Saga," Introduction, pp. cl-cviii.

It may be added that one feature in the first of the Maes-how diagrams conveys a wrong impression of the probable appearance of the mound, when inhabited; because the "well or pit" ("or crater") is represented as being as solid

The Ross-shire *Tombuidhe*, the Sylt *Denghoog*, and this Orcadian *breck* are all specimens of the one class; and, both as regards the character of the dwellers and the dwellings, they have many counterparts. How many we do not yet know. It is probable that, in the British Islands alone, they may be numbered by thousands (and we need not here speculate as to the continent of Europe, and other parts of the globe). Colonel Forbes Leslie, referring only to Scotland, says that "even in the present day many a green mound ... is shunned by sturdy peasants who would not fear the hostility of any mortal"—and this because that mound once contained one or more people of a race of whom that peasant's ancestors stood greatly in awe. That the valleys of the Forth and Teith alone contain a great number of those "green hillocks," as yet unexamined, has been stated by an eminent investigator of the Scotch *brochs*, Dr. Joseph Anderson. How many other districts can tell a similar story is a problem that will some day be solved.

The collector (who is, to a great extent, the exponent also) of the "Popular Tales of the West Highlands," appends several very interesting remarks to one of these stories: that of "The Smith and the Fairies" (vol. ii. pp. 46-55). Among other things he says: "The belief that the 'hill' opened on a certain night, and that a light shone from the inside, where little people might be seen dancing, was too deeply grounded some years ago to be lightly spoken of; .... 'In the glebe of Kilbrandon in Lorn is a hill called Crocan Corr ... where the fairies ... were often seen dancing around their fire.'" And reference is also made to "a certain hill in Muckairn, known to be the residence of the fairies." The incident connected with it is capped with a similar one "told of a hill called Ben-cnock in Islay;" and "another hill, called Cnock-doun" (presumably in Islay), has a like history. But such "hills" are too numerous to mention in detail.

as the rest of the outer covering. That it gradually became filled up with drift and rubbish, after the dwelling ceased to be occupied, is evident. But when the edifice was newly reared, and as long as people continued to inhabit it, the upper part of the mound was probably a hollow shaft; admitting light and air into the dwelling below; "carrying off the smoke of their fire;" and occasionally serving as a way of ingress and egress.

Owing to the great mass of earth which was heaped over the dwelling—the actual "kernel" of the mound—it will be seen that new-comers of another race from the mound-dwellers might build houses, or bury their dead, above the homes of the "little people," without being aware that the hill they were so utilizing was entirely of artifical origin. Nor are there wanting illustrations of this in fact and in tradition. Legendary lore, indeed, is full of incidents arising from the contact, often unexpected on the one side, of the two races; and many such tales reveal the mound-dwellers in a very homely light. The following story from the Hebridean island of Barra, for example:

"There was a woman in Baile Thangasdail, and she was out seeking a couple of calves; and the night and lateness caught her, and there came rain and tempest, and she was seeking shelter. She went to a knoll with the couple of calves, and she was striking the tether-peg into it. The knoll opened. She heard a gleegashing as if a pot-hook were clashing beside a pot. She took wonder, and she stopped striking the tether-peg. A woman put out her head and all above her middle, and she said, 'What business hast thou to be troubling this takman in which I make my dwelling?' 'I am taking care of this couple of calves, and I am but weak. Where shall I go with them?' 'Thou shalt go with them to that breast down yonder. Thou wilt see a tuft of grass. If thy couple of calves eat that tuft of grass, thou wilt not be a day without a milk cow as long as thou art alive, because thou hast taken my counsel.'"[1]

This story exemplifies the well-known prophetic or "supernatural" powers of the dwarf races, while at the same time it presents the "fairy abode" to us in a very matter-of-fact light. Equally homely and matter-of-fact is this story from Wigtownshire:—

"A shepherd's family had just taken possession of a newly-erected onstead, in a very secluded spot among 'the hills o' Gallowa,' when the goodwife was, one day, surprised by the entrance of a little woman, who hurriedly asked for the loan of a 'pickle saut.' This, of course, was readily granted; but the goodwife was so flurried by the appearance of 'a naibor' in such a lonely place, and at such a very great distance from all known habitations, that she did not observe when the little woman withdrew or which way she went. Next day, however, the same little woman re-entered the cottage, and duly paid the borrowed 'saut.' This time the goodwife was more alert, and as she turned to replace

[1] "West Highland Tales," II. 59.

'the saut in the sautkit' she observed 'wi' the tail o' her e'e' that the little woman moved off towards the door, and then made a sudden 'bolt out.' Following quickly, the goodwife saw her unceremonious visitor run down a small declivity towards a tree, which stood at 'the house en'.' (She passed behind the tree, but did not emerge on the other side, and the "goodwife," seeing no place of concealment, assumed she was a fairy.] In a few days her little 'nesbor' again returned, and continued from time to time to make similar visits—borrowing and lending small articles, evidently with a view to produce an intimacy; and it was uniformly remarked that, on retiring, she proceeded straight to the tree, and then suddenly 'ga'ed out o' sight.' One day, while the goodwife was at the door, emptying some dirty water into the *jaw-hole* [sink, or cess-pool], her now familiar acquaintance came to her and said: 'Goodwife, ye're really a very obliging bodie! Wad ye be sae good as turn the lade o' your jaw-hole anither way, as a' your foul water rins directly in at my door? It stands in the howe there, on the aff side o' that tree, at the corner o' your house en'.' The mystery was now fully cleared up—the little woman was indeed a fairy; and the door of her invisible habitation, being situated 'on the aff side o' the tree at the house en',' it could easily be conceived how she must there necessarily 'gae out o' sight' as she entered her sight-eluding portal."

This story[1] relates to a district that is noted as being one of the very latest to retain a population that was distinctively Pictish, and it unquestionably offers a parallel to that of the "Gudeman o' Villenshaw," and the "elves i' the knock that bade." In either case, we have the arrival of a new-comer of another race, all unconscious that the place is already inhabited by an earlier, mound-dwelling[2] people.

Of houses built upon the summit or the slope of a fairy hill a modern instance is furnished by Hugh Miller, in his reminiscences of Sutherlandshire ("My Schools and Schoolmasters," 1881 ed., p. 108), wherein he mentions that a cousin of his had built his house "half-way up the slope of a beautiful tomhan,"[3] which was regarded as a fairy residence.

---

[1] Which will be found at pp. 30-32 of "Legends of Scottish Superstition," Edinburgh, 1848.

[2] The Wigtownshire tale perhaps relates rather to an example of the rude underground Fairy Ha', or Pecht's house, described in the beginning of this chapter. While the word "how" signifies in Orkney a *heap*, or *mound*; the "howe" of other parts of Scotland means a "hollow." In fact, the story says that the foul water ran down to the entrance of the dwarf's house, which was therefore either an underground gallery of the kind referred to, or else a chambered mound placed on a lower level than the shepherd's cottage.

[3] Cf. *Salmon* in the Barra anecdote quoted above. See also p. 82 *ante*, note 2.

This "tomhan" appears to have been near Lairg, and in "the Barony of Gruids." The neighbouring countryfolk had expected that "the little people" inside the hill would resent this intrusion on their privacy, but, of course, nothing of this kind happened—as this occurred in the present century, when the mound-dwelling Pechts lived only in the memory of those by whose forefathers they had once been greatly dreaded. But there are various traditional accounts which point to a time when members of the intruding race, unaware that the hillock on which they began to build was itself a building, were obliged to desist by reason of the opposition of the dwarfs. Thus, a former Grant of Ballindalloch, in Strathspey, who attempted to build his castle upon a mound, found every morning that the previous day's work had been undone, and the stones removed from the site. One night, while he watched for these disturbers, he heard a voice bid him to "build on the Cow Haugh," or meadow, which he accordingly did, without further interruption.¹ A similar account is given in connection with a hill in Aberdeenshire. "When the workmen were engaged in erecting the ancient church of Old Deer, in Aberdeenshire, upon a small hill called Bissau, they were surprised to find that the work was impeded by supernatural obstacles. At length the Spirit of the River (says Sir Walter Scott, who tells the story²) was heard to say,—

> "It is not here, it is not here,
> That ye shall build the church of Deer;
> But on Taptillery,
> Where many a corpse shall lie."

The site of the edifice was accordingly transferred to Taptillery, an eminence at some distance from the place where the building had been commenced." In this case the interruption merely took the shape of a warning, but the midnight work in the former instance is entirely in keeping with all that tradition says of the Pechts.³

¹ From "Grantown-on-Spey," by the Rev. A. Gordon (in a "Budget of Holiday Letters," Edinburgh, 1889).
² "Lay of the Last Minstrel," Note M.
³ Chambers, in his "Popular Rhymes" (241-2), has a story corresponding in one feature to that of "Taptillery." This is of a certain Laird of Craufurdland,

Hugh Miller again points out a fairy locality, when referring to a boating excursion on Loch Maree, in 1823, on which occasion he learned from the boatman that one of the islands, *Eilean Suthainn*, was the annual rendezvous of the fairies, where they paid to their queen the yearly "kain" or tribute, due to "the Evil One." This reference is quoted by the author of "Gairloch,"[1] who also states:

"In Gairloch we have Cathair Mhor and Cathair Bheag, names applied to several places; and the Sitheanan Dubha on Isle Ewe and on the North Point. There is Cathair Mhor at the head of Loch Diaree, and Cathair Bheag (the Gaelic name of the place) at Kerrysdale. These names mean respectively the big and little seats of the fairies....

"The name Sitheanan Dubha signifies the black knowes or hillocks of the fairies. It is applied to two places in Gairloch, viz., to the highest hill-tops at the north end of Isle Ewe, and to a low hill and small round loch a full mile due north of Carn Dearg house."

Further south than Loch Maree, and situated in the deer-forest of Mamore, in the Nether Lochaber district, there is an alleged "hollow hill" which is also exceptionally famous. It is thus described by a local gillie:—

"Coming up the Ulnach, sir, you saw a corrie away to the left? Well, that's Corrie Vinnean; and the round hillock in the centre, which you must also have noticed, is a Shian or fairy-knowe; and in all the *garbh-chriochan* (rough-bounds) around us, from Kinloch Leven to Ardverikie, there is no other shiàn so famous as this shiàn, and it is the chief palace of the fairies of all these upland wilds, and it is always occupied by a company of them. It is never altogether deserted even for a day, though many other shiàns are sometimes unoccupied for weeks together."[2]

who had dammed up a stream in order to get at a treasure believed to be hidden in its bed, "when a brownie called out of a bush:

"Pow, pow !
Crunkiefand's tower's a' in a low !" (i.e., on fire)

which sent the laird home to save his tower; and when he returned from his fool's errand the dam had been destroyed, and the stream was flowing as before.

[1] Mr. J. H. Dixon, F.S.A.Scot. See "Gairloch," Edin.' 1886, pp. 159-61.
[2] See the modern *Scots Magazine*, Vol. L., No. 1, Dec., 1887 ("Damh Dhu Bhainn Chralain," a sporting story).

CHAPTER XIV.

So numerous are the mounds that, owing to the traditions attaching to them, invite their own destruction at the hands of the archæologist, that only a limited number of them can be specified in these pages. Among these were, until recent years, two "fairy knowes," long known by that term in the adjoining countryside. They lie between the rivers Forth and Teith, about four miles to the south of Doune. One of them was broken into a good many years ago, and it is now known to antiquaries as the "Broch of Coldoch" (from the estate on which it is situated).[1] It appears to be one of those structures which form a connecting link between the open-air broch, such as that of Mousa, and the more visible "hill," such as Maes-how. It is circular in form, has the central chamber and three small chambers in the thickness of the wall; and the lower portion of a winding-stair, also in the wall, which shows it to be the remains of an inferior "Mousa." Its dimensions are like those of other "brochs," and these are such that, in this case, they evoked the remark from the writer's guide (a native of the district) that "it had never been built for men like him." This, indeed, is the remark that naturally falls from any visitor to such buildings; as the writer has noticed on several such occasions (nor can he forget that one, at any rate, of his companions, in a recent visit to "the hidden places of the Finns and fairies" in the valley of the Boyne, was debarred from inspecting these interesting works for the simple reason that the underground passage of entrance was so strait, in every way, that for him to worm himself along it, as all visitors must do, was a physical impossibility). The

[1] This "fairy knowe" is described in the "Archæologia Scotica," vol. v. and the "Proc. of the Soc. of Antiq. of Scot.," 1st Series, ii. 37-38.

popular belief that such mounds were tenanted by dwarfs has no stronger testimony than the obvious fact that none but dwarfs would have thought of raising such structures; or could have properly utilized them when erected. And although the most famous of the Boyne mounds just referred to has been styled "the firm mansion of the 'Dagda'" in ancient records, and, by a modern singer,

> "The Royal Brugh,
> By the dark-rolling waters of the Boyne,
> Where Angus Og magnificently dwells,"

yet such a "mansion" would be a most impracticable kind of abode for men of the ordinary height of modern Europeans, if any such felt disposed to imitate the "magnificence" of Angus Og.

Of this "Royal Brugh" the outward appearance is well delineated in the engraving which constitutes the *Frontispiece*. All that has been said as to the adaptability of Maes-how to any of the well-known fairy stories is equally applicable to this Irish "how." The Boyne mound, however, as will be seen from its measurements, is much larger than the Orkney one; though the stone structure in its interior is of much the same dimensions as the other. The interior of the "Broch of the Boyne," however, represents a much ruder and more primitive stage in such architecture, and compared with it, the Orkney "how" is a most finished and elaborate work.

This, then, is what a fairy hill, of the larger class, looks like to the outsider. And it is clear that, when its entrance is concealed, as it once was, no stranger, ignorant of such a thing as a mound-dwelling, would ever think that this innocent-looking hill was artificially made, and that the chambers within it were the residence of a family or families. One might well begin to build, and even to fell trees, upon the outer "walls" of such a "house," without knowing that such a proceeding might be resented by "the moody elfin king that won'd within the hill."

The entrance to this underground hall, which has been rediscovered for about two centuries, may be discerned almost at the base of the hill, slightly to the left of the figures of the man and boy in the foreground. This entrance or door-

SECTIONAL VIEW OF THE BRUGH OF THE BOYNE.
(From the West.)

way is represented below, and, like the others of this series, it is the work of an artist who is also an eminent Irish archæologist, than whom no one possesses a more intimate acquaintance with the interior and exterior of the Boyne mounds. This, then, is an Irish illustration of what the Shetland boys used to call a " trow's door ! "[1]

The (not too portly) explorer who enters this doorway and creeps, sometimes laterally, along the passage, at one point very low and narrow, works his way at length into the com-

DOORWAY OF THE BRUGH.

paratively large chamber that forms the main part of the structure. The relation which this passage and chamber bear to the mound which was heaped over them will be seen from the transverse sectional view of the "hill," which is

[1] Judging from memory, and also from the reputed smallness of the hole into which one was expected to plunge, it seems to the present writer that the human figure seated at the doorway has been drawn too small. If one compares him with the standing figures in the general view, and with the aperture there seen, this criticism will be borne out.

represented in the accompanying plate. The dimensions and general appearance of this underground gallery and "hall" will also be fully understood by an examination of this and the other designs. And one point will be noticed, namely, that no access to the top of the mound, as in such a case as Finn's dwelling in Sylt, or the Orkney Maes-how, is here visible. But it must be borne in mind that, over those portions of the mound which are represented as solid, the word "Unexplored" might fitly be written. If this is like some of the "fairy hills" of tradition, it ought to have a channel, or passage, leading upward to the summit, and, indeed, the lower end of such a passage, though at present choked up, is suggested at one side of the inner chamber (on the right hand of the explorer), as may be seen in the plan of the year 1889.

It is necessary, however, to discriminate between one kind of "fairy hill" and another. Maeshow and the Sylt Denghoog appear to closely resemble the modern Lapp *gamme*, as regards the upper portion of the structure, for access to both of these may be gained from the roof. The "trap-door" to which Mr. Black refers in the Sylt instance appears to have always existed in one shape or another; and its original use may be guessed from the following notice of the same portion of a Lapp *gamme*. The gamme "is generally circular, or oblong, having the appearance of a large, rounded hillock, which indeed it may be termed," says a Lapland traveller of sixty years ago.[1] And he further states that "an opening in the roof, nearly over the fire-place, served to let out the smoke; and might be covered at times with a kind of trap-door, to retain the internal warmth, when the fire is burnt out. This is always let down at night." That this was the usage in the dwelling of Finn, or whatever may have been the name of the Sylt dwarf whose bones were found in the Denghoog, seems very probable. But to such chambered mounds as the Broch of the Boyne, another traditionary egress, whether for the dwellers or for the smoke, seems more applicable. It has already been noticed that "pits on the top of hills were supposed to lead to the subterranean habitations of the Fairies." But another

[1] A. de Capell Brooke; *A Winter in Lapland*, London, 1827, p. 320.

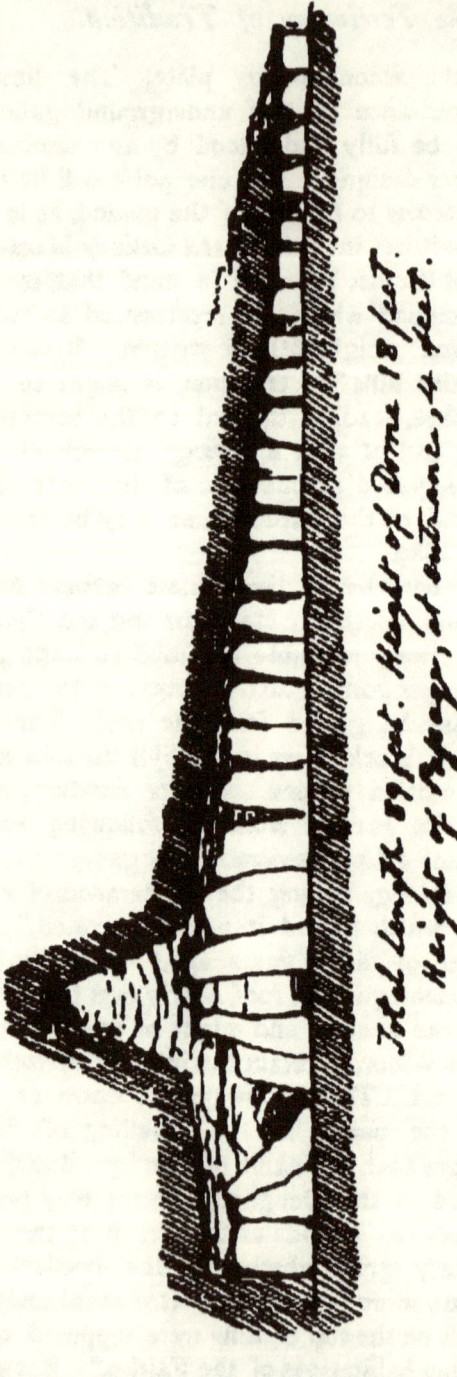

ENLARGED SECTIONAL VIEW OF PASSAGE AND CHAMBER, BRUGH OF THE BOYNE.
(From the West.)

Total Length 89 feet. Height of Dome 18 feet.
Height of Passage, at entrance, 4 feet.

version says that "pits on the tops of mountains are regarded in the border [i.e., the Anglo-Scottish Borders] with a degree of superstitious horror, as the porches or entrances of the subterraneous habitations of the fairies; from which confused murmurs, the cries of children, moaning voices, the ringing of bells, and the sounds of musical instruments are often supposed to be heard. Round these hills the green fairy circles are believed to wind in a spiral direction, till they reach the descent to the central cavern."[1] Assuming that "mountains" ought to read "hillocks," and that the spiral passages are akin to those which wind down the interior of the walls of such a "broch" as that of Mousa, this tradition would lead one to believe that the Broch of the Boyne has a winding passage to the upper air. A recent visitor has observed that "on the exterior top of the mound there appears to be a small crater-like depression,"[2] which he attributes to a subsidence of the structure, but which, on the other hand, may have always been there. The suggestion of an upward passage in the interior has just been referred to. This latter is not indicated at all in the plan of the year 1724; but as a matter of fact, this detail was not known until quite recently, when the displacement of a slab revealed this cavity (as well as some additional spiral incisions on the slab).

It will be observed that the plans of 1724 and 1889 differ considerably as to the dimensions and outline of the central chamber. Although the earlier one was "delineated with care and accuracy, upon the place," by "Mr. Samuel Molyneux, a young gentleman of the college of Dublin," one must rather accept the testimony of so experienced and careful an archæologist as Mr. Wakeman. But the plan of 1724 has this great merit, that it was executed only twenty-nine years after the re-opening of the "brugh"; and, consequently, it shows (marked with the letter H) "a pyramid stone now fallen, but formerly set up erect in the middle of the cave." Moreover, Mr. Molyneux was able to give a sketch of the carvings above the right hand, or eastern recess,

[1] Jeffrey's "Roxburghshire"; 1899, I., 54-5. (Quoted from Leyden.)
[2] "Journal of Roy. Hist. and Archl. Assocn. of Ireland," No. 81, Vol. IX., Fourth Series, p. 327.

when these were much fresher than at any period during this century. A fac-simile of this picture is here given; and if the artistic style of the draughtsman is not very admirable it will at least be admitted that his work possesses a high archæological value. But before quitting the subject of the drawing of 1724, it must be pointed out that although Mr. Molyneux shows, in the northern recess of his ground-plan, a rude basin similar to those still occupying the eastern and western recesses, yet the account of Mr. Edward Llhwyd, stated to have been written in 1699,[1] distinctly says that that recess was *then* vacant. If Mr. Llhwyd's statement is correct the plan of 1724 is obviously misleading in this respect.

The statements of those early writers are deserving of full consideration, for they wrote before the effects of the outside air and the unscientific tourist could have appreciably altered the appearance of the chamber, since it was entered in 1695. Their accounts, therefore, are quoted afterwards at greater length.[2] But, from what has been said, and from an inspection of these illustrations, a good idea may be gained of the exterior and interior appearance of the habitation in which tradition states that Angus Og "magnificently dwelt."

Something may here be said regarding this personage, and the race to which he belonged. He is said to have been the King of the Tuatha De Danann, a race traditionally believed to have been the immediate precursors of the Gaels in Ireland. They are sometimes spoken of as "the Danann" or "Danaans"; sometimes also as "the Tuatha De, or Dea." *Tuatha* merely signifies "people"; but the two other names do not seem to have received any definite interpretation. It is said that they migrated from "Lochlin" (Scandinavia, or perhaps also Northern Germany) to the north-eastern Lowlands of Scotland; and Dr. Skene notes that the topography of that district supports the theory in several details.[3] After living there for several generations, they are understood to have crossed to Ireland, then inhabited by the race of the "Fir-

---

[1] See the "Jour. of Roy. Hist. and Archl. Assocn. of Ireland," No. 81, Vol. IX., Fourth Series, p. 266.
[2] See Appendix A.
[3] *Celtic Scotland*, I., 222.

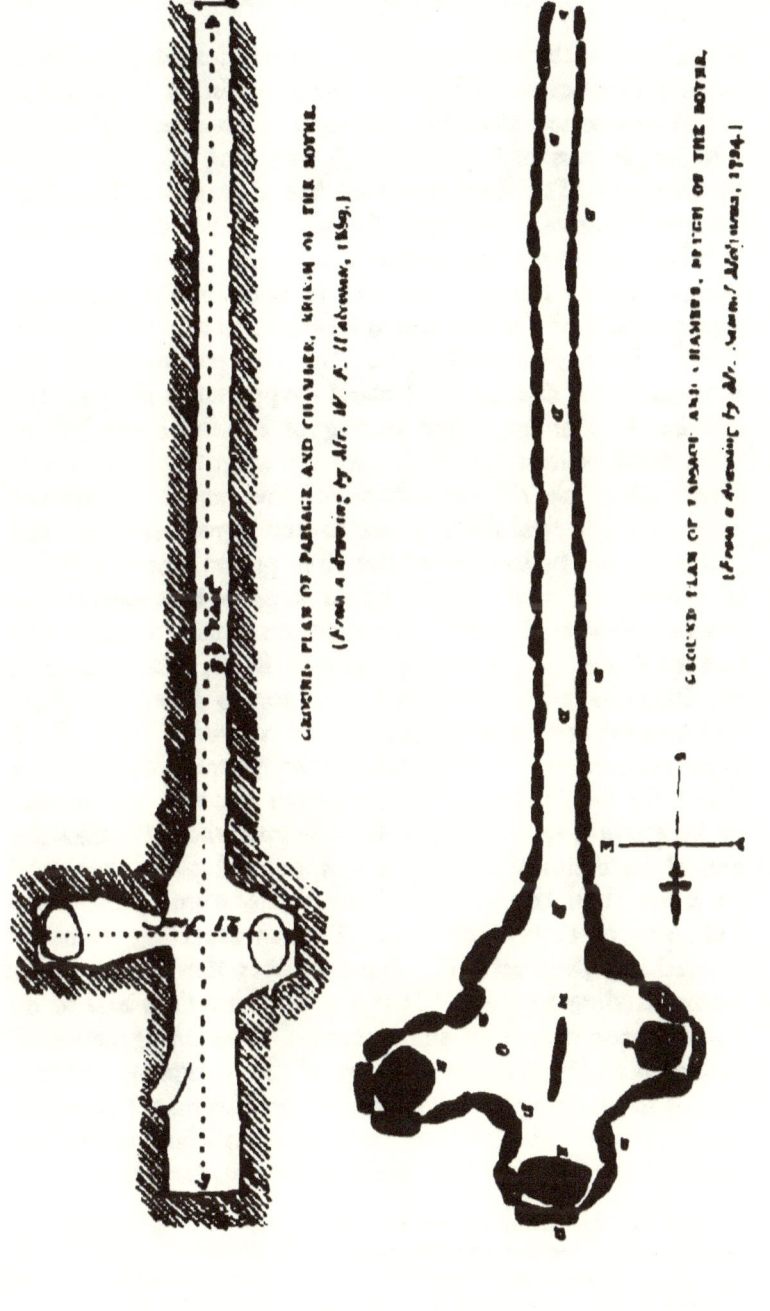

GROUND PLAN OF PASSAGE AND CHAMBER, KNOWTH OR THE BOYNE.
(From a drawing by Mr. W. F. Wakeman, 1869.)

GROUND PLAN OF PASSAGE AND CHAMBER, DOWTH OR THE BOYNE.
(From a drawing by Mr. James McInerney, 1834.)

Bolgs," whom they subdued.[1] Two centuries later the Gaels (or Milesians) came to Ireland—from Spain, it is said. It was at this period that "Aonghus Mac an Daogha," otherwise Angus, son of "the Dagda," was king of the Tuatha De Danann. The story goes that the Dananns, recognizing that the Gaels came as powerful and warlike invaders, and as colonizers, told them on their first arrival that if they could effect a landing in open day, and in spite of the Dananns, then one-half of Ireland would be ceded to the new-comers. The Gaels were successful; but the two parties could not agree as to the division of Ireland,—apparently because the Tuatha De Danann, while willing to surrender one-half of the island, wished to retain the sovereignty of the whole. Then, after the simple fashion of the heroes of ancient chronicles, the rival forces came to the agreement that the matter should be laid before the first person whom a party of deputies from either side should happen to encounter at the outskirts of a certain town, on an appointed day, and this man's decision should be held as final. Now, although the Dananns are remembered as "adepts in all Druidical and magical arts," the Gaels also had a *druidh* (*i.e.*, wizard or *magus*) among their number; who proved more than a match for the Dananns. For, between him and the leaders of his party it was arranged that the man whom the deputies should accidentally meet at the appointed place should be no other than this *druidh* of the Gaels, whose person was unknown to their opponents. The unsuspecting Dananns walked into the trap. The first man that the delegates met was a strolling harper. "It is a great thing thou hast to do to-day, good master of the sciences!" was the greeting of Angus Mac Dagda, who was one of the company. "What have I to be doing to-day?" quoth the wise man, "except to go about with my harp, and learn who shall best reward me for my music."[2] "Thy task is far greater than that,"

[1] The Fir-Bolgs themselves, well known to all readers of Irish tradition, have many points in common with the people under discussion. Compare, for example, Lady Ferguson's reference to "a fierce tribe of Firbolgic origin, the *Gamanraw*, who were compelled to labour unremittingly at the earthworks [the Rath of Cruachan], and are said to have completed the dykes *in our day*." "The Story of the Irish before the Conquest," London, 1868, p. 32.

[2] The Dananns themselves were notably "professors of musical and entertain-

answered Angus, "thou hast to divide Ireland into two equal portions." Thereupon the *druidh*, having obtained the promise of either side that they would abide by his decision, pronounced as follows:—"This, then, is my decision. As ye, O magical Dananns, have for a long period possessed that half of Ireland which is above ground, henceforth the half which is underneath the surface shall be yours, and the half above ground shall belong to the Sons of Miledh (the Milesians, or Gaels). To thee, O Angus, son of the Dagda, as thou art the king of the Tuatha De Danann, I assign the best earth-house in Ireland, the white-topped *brugh* of the Boyne.[1] As for the rest, each one can select an earth-house for himself." Against this grotesque decision there was, obviously, no appeal, and the Dananns surrendered the surface of Ireland to the Gaels; "and retaining only the green mounds, known by the name of Sidh, and then being made invisible by their enchantments, became the Fir Sidhe, or Fairies, of Ireland."[2]

In this legend of the "halving" of Ireland, Dr. Skene recognizes the memory of a historical fact,—the conquest of Ireland by the Gaels, and the terms meted out by them to the natives. The tradition has of course its defects, like most traditions. The "earth-houses" referred to[3] must have already been in existence before they could be spoken of, and particularized, by the magician of the Gaels. The inference to be drawn from the story is that the Tuatha De Danann were themselves mound-dwellers, and that the terms

---

ing performances"; and indeed the term *druidh*, applied to them also, seems to have indicated the possessor of many accomplishments, in art and in a pseudo-science.

[1] *Brugh barraghdal as Boinne* is the phrase given in "The Glenbard Collection of Gaelic Poetry" (Hazzard, Charlottetown, Prince Edward Island, 1888, p. 78) where the above story is told. The term "white-topped" is somewhat vague. Had the word been *barrachaol*, "pyramidal," the meaning would have been quite clear.

[2] *Skene's Celt. Scot.*, III, 106-107. See also p. 93 of the same volume, and pp. 178 and 220 of Vol. I.

[3] The words translated "earth-house," as used by the *druidh*, are "brugh" and "bruighin." These, as already mentioned, signify "fairy hill" or "underground dwelling of the fairies." But the alternative rendering of "earth-house" has been preferred, as being rather less of an anachronism than the assumption that such dwellings were styled *fairy hills* before ever they had been assigned to the "fairies."

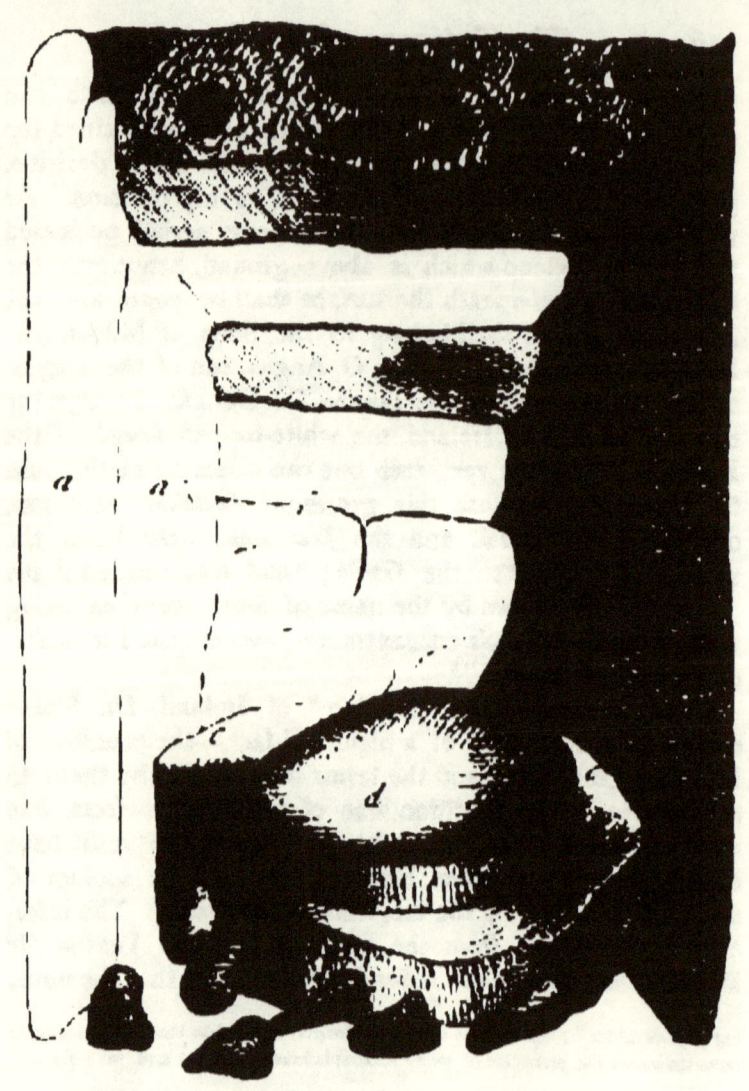

EASTERN RECESS OF CENTRAL CHAMBER, AS DRAWN BY MR. HOLYNESS IN 1774.

imposed upon them by the Gaels restricted the conquered people to their own habitations, presumably with the reservation of a small portion of the adjoining territory. That, in short, the Gaelic conquest denoted a state of things analogous to the European conquest and settlement of North America, where the native races, having once submitted, were allowed to live on "reservations," scattered here and there throughout the country. Thus, as in America, the two races would live side by side, though perhaps, as in America, presenting the most opposite characteristics.

The above story states that the Fir Sidhe, or Danann, were confined to those "hollow hills" by the Gaels, through the instrumentality of their *druids*. The version which Mr. William Black indicates as current in Southern Ireland, ascribes this act to *the saints*. In his novel of *Shandon Bells*, he introduces the hero and heroine as standing in "the very headquarters of the elves and the pixies"; and the girl asks "'Is this where you said the saints shut up Don Fierna and the pixies?' 'No,' he said, 'that was away over there in the mountains. But they say the little people can get out into this valley; and you won't catch many of the Inisheen natives about here after dark!'" Here, then, it is a Gaelic *saint* and not a Gaelic *druid* who was instrumental in confining "the little people" to their homes; but, after all, there is perhaps not much difference between *saint* and *druid*. The Fierna here referred to, it may be remarked, is that King of the Sidhfir of Munster, who has been spoken of on a previous page,[1] and whose dwelling, according to tradition, was the hill of *Knockfierna*, in the neighbourhood of Limerick.

The Tuatha De Danann, therefore, are the Sidhfir, or Fairies, of Irish tradition. But the Tuatha De Danann have been already referred to in these pages.[2] "Who were the Feinne of tradition, and to what country and period are they to be assigned?" This is the question put by Dr. Skene. And after considering the various Irish traditions relating to "the Feinne," his conclusion is this: "The Feinne, then, belonged to the pre-Milesian races, and were connected, not only with Ireland, but likewise with Northern and Central

---

[1] Page 93, *ante*.   [2] Page 51, *ante*.

Scotland, England and Wales, and the territory lying between the Rhine and the Elbe. [This last-named territory, being "Lochlin," ought perhaps to be held as including the whole of Scandinavia.] Now, there are just two people mentioned in the Irish records who had settlements in Ireland, and who yet were connected with Great Britain and 'Lochlin.' These were the people termed the Tuatha De Danann, and the Cruithne. .... These two tribes were thus the prior race in each country [Ireland and North and Central Scotland]. Both must have been prior to the Low German population of Lochlan. The Cruithne were the race prior to the Scots [Gaels] in North and Central Scotland, and the Tuatha De Danann the prior colony to the Milesian Scots in Ireland. The Feinne are brought by all the old historic tales into close contact with the Tuatha De Danann; a portion of them were avowedly Cruithne; and if they were, as we have seen, in Ireland, not of the Milesian race, but of the prior population, and likewise connected with Great Britain and the region lying between the Rhine and the Elbe, the inference is obvious, that, whether a denomination for an entire people or for a body of warriors, they belonged to the previous population which preceded the Germans in Lochlan and the Gaels in Ireland and North and Central Scotland. This view is corroborated by the fact, that in the old poems and tales the Feinne appear, as we have said, in close connection with the Tuatha De Danann. They are likewise connected with the Cruithne. .... In answering, then, the preliminary questions of who were the Feinne? and to what period do they belong? we may fairly infer that they were of the population who immediately preceded the Gaels in Ireland and in North and Central Scotland."[1]

The Feinne, then, belonged to the population which comprised the Cruithne and the Tuatha De Danann, or Sidhfir, or Fairies. But the Cruithne, as we have seen,[2] were the Picts of history, and the "Pechts" of Scottish folk-lore.

---

[1] *Dean of Lismore's Book*: Introduction, pp. lxiv, lxxvi-lxxviii. (As in former quotations, I have slightly modernised such terms as "Erin," according to Dr. Skene's own rendering of these terms.)

[2] Page 51, *ante*.

Thus, the Feinne were of the population of "Pechts and Fairies." It has already been shown that to draw a hard and fast line between these two divisions is impossible. Nevertheless, there seems to have been once some kind of distinction between the two. And if the Feinne must necessarily have been "Pechts *or* Fairies" (as the above conclusions of Dr. Skene's seem to warrant), then they appear to have belonged to the former division. Or, in other words, they were *Cruithne* rather than *Tuatha De Danann*. It may be remembered that in such a Fenian ballad as the *Dan an Fhir Shioair*, or Song of the Fairy Man,[1] the Feinne are represented as associating with the Sidhfir (say Tuatha De Danann), but yet not as *identical* with them. Again, the same dubiety was seen in the references to the hoards of treasure obtained by the ninth-century Danes from "the hidden places belonging to Fians *or* to Fairies,"[2] in the valley of the Boyne.

The Brugh of the Boyne is several times spoken of by Professor Eugene O'Curry in his "Lectures on the Manu-

---

[1] Page 82, *ante*.

[2] The custom of the "earth-man" to bury his treasures is known all over Europe. A special instance has been cited in these pages (p. 107, *ante*, note 7), when two little men, wearing red caps" are remembered as "intently digging" for their lost treasure, in a certain field in Lincolnshire. Mr. J. F. Campbell, in drawing his Fairy-Lapp parallel, says (*Tales*, Introd. cviii.): "Fairies had hoards of treasure—so have Lapps. A man died shortly before one of my Texa trips, and the whole country side had been out searching for his buried wealth in vain. Some years ago the old silver shops of Bergen and Trondhjem overflowed with queer cups and spoons, and rings, silver plates for waist belts, old plate that had been hidden amongst the mountains, black old silver coins that had not seen the light for years. I saw the plate and bought some, and was told that, in consequence of a religious movement, the Lapps had dug up and sold their hoards." Another writer (A. de C. Brooke : *A Winter in Lapland*, London, 1827, pp. 109-111), in referring to this practice, says that sometimes the Lapp "forgets himself where he has hidden it, and his hoard of silver remains so effectually concealed, after he has been absent some time, that he is unable to discover the place, and it is consequently lost to him for ever." And this writer refers to a Lapp of his acquaintance who had concealed his treasure "so securely that, notwithstanding the regular searches he had made for it," he could not recover it. This feature offers an explanation of the traditions of dwarfs seeking for treasures which they themselves had hidden. It may be added that the custom of burying money was still so prevalent in Shetland, in the beginning of last century, that it was held to be illegal, and the offenders were duly fined.

script Materials of Ancient Irish History."[1] For example, as an illustration of the use of the word *sidh* to denote "a hall or residence" of the *sidh*-folk, Mr. O'Curry cites a stanza "taken from an ancient poem by Mac Nia, son of Oenna (in the Book of Ballymote, fol. 190, b.) on the wonders of *Brugh* (or *Brog*) *na Boinne* (the Palace of the Boyne), the celebrated Hall of the Daghda Mór, who was the great king and oracle of the *Tuata Dé Danann*. This poem," continues Mr. O'Curry, "begins: '*A Chaemu Bregh Brig uad Breg*' ('Ye Poets of Bregia, of truth, not false,') and this is the second stanza of that poem:

> '*Fegaid in sid ar far shil
> Is follers dib is trcb rig,
> Ro gnid Iath in Dagda achlur,
> Ba dum, ba dun, amra brig.*'

> 'Behold the *Sidh* before your eyes,
> It is manifest to you that it is a king's mansion,
> Which was built by the firm *Daghda*;
> It was a wonder, a court, an admirable hill.'"[2]

In the same work we read of an incident, placed in the time of St. Patrick and subsequent to the Battle of Gawra, when the conquered "Fianna" were only represented by a few straggling survivors, one of whom was the well-known *Caeilté* (as the name is here spelt). "Saint Patrick, with his travelling missionary retinue, including Caeilté we are told, was one day sitting on the hill which is now well known as Ard-Patrick, in the county of Limerick." Questioning Caeilté as to the former name of this hill, St. Patrick learned that it had been called *Tulach-na-Feinê*, and obtained also an anecdote suggested by it. "One day that we were on this hill," says Caeilté, speaking of himself and his brother "Fianna," "Finn observed a favourite warrior of his company, named Cael O'Neamhain, coming towards him, and when he had come to Finn's presence, he asked him where he had come from. Cael answered that he had come from *Brugh* in the north (that is the fairy mansion of *Brugh*, on the Boyne).[3] 'What was your business there?' said Finn. 'To speak to

[1] Dublin, 1861. [2] *Op. cit.*, p. 505.
[3] This parenthesis appears to be Mr. O'Curry's.

my nurse, Muirn, the daughter of Derg,' said Cael. 'About what?' said Finn. 'Concerning Credé, the daughter of Cairbré, King of Kerry (*Ciarraighe Luachra*),' said Cael?" And so on. At another place¹ the dialogue goes thus:—
"'Where hast thou come from, Cael?' said Finn. 'From the teeming *Brugh*, from the North,' said Cael. ('*As in Brug Bramach atuaid,' ar Cael*)." And so on, to the same purpose as in the other version. In this story, then, we see the "Fians and Fairies" associated with each other, as in *The Ballad of the Fairy Man*; and the nurse of one of the Fians is described as living in the "brugh" which was built by the celebrated chief of the Tuatha De Danann, and was afterwards tenanted by his son, Angus Og.

Among Mr. O'Curry's notes there is this reference to Angus Og:² "In the *Dinnseanchus* it is stated that '*Edin Baili*' were Four Kisses of Aengus of *Brugh na Boiand* (son of the *Daghda Mor*, the great necromancer and king of the *Tuatha Dé Danann*), which were converted by him into 'birds which haunted the youths of Erian.' This allusion," remarks Mr. O'Curry, "requires more investigation than I have yet been able to bestow on the passage." Whatever the "*Edin Baili*" may have been, or have been assumed to be, this passage brings into prominence the fact that the people known as Tuatha De Danann, or Fir-Sidhe, were regarded by other races as possessed of supernatural power, and were indeed actually revered as gods at one era. As the biographer of St. Patrick says of him:—

> "He preached threescore years
> The Cross of Christ to the *Tuatha* (people) of Feni.
> On the *Tuatha* of Erin there was darkness.
> The *Tuatha* adored the *Sidhs*."³

(Here, of course, the *Fir* Sidhe, or people of the "sidhs" are denoted; the word being sometimes used to indicate the dwellers, sometimes the dwellings.) And the exalted character of the inmates of the Brugh of the Boyne is indicated also in a verse of a Gaelic poem entitled *Baile Suthain Sith*

---

¹ Pp. 996-7; the first version being at pp. 308-9.
² *Op. cit.*, p. 478.   ³ *Celt. Soc.*, II., 108.

Eamhna, which dates back to the year 1457 at least. The subject of the verse referred to is thus apostrophized:—

> "Thou, the son of noble Sabia,
> Thou the most beauteous apple rod;
> What god from Brugh of the Boyne
> Created thee with her in secret?"[1]

This exalted position "the little people" seem to have retained in some measure long after their subjugation, and even the household drudge or "brownie" was feared for his alleged "supernatural" power. The fact that the common people of Ireland at the present day speak of the inhabitants of the "brughs" or "sheeans" as "the gentry," may also be regarded as a witness to the superior rank once held by that caste whose mound-dwellings are exemplified by this "Brugh of the Boyne" and others in its neighbourhood.

Of the undoubtedly historic spoliation of those Boyne "hillocks" in the ninth century, something more may be said here. "We have on record," says Lady Ferguson,[2] "both in the Irish chronicles and the Norse *Sagas*, that in the year 861 the three earls, Olaf, Sitric, and Ivar, opened, for purposes of plunder, the sepulchral mounds of New Grange, Dowth, and Knowth on the Boyne, and the mound of the wife of the Gobaun Saer,[3] the mythic builder, or Wayland Smith of the Irish Celts, still a conspicuous object at Drogheda."

One of the Irish chronicles referred to by Lady Ferguson is that known as the "Annals of Ulster" ("compiled in the year 1498," says Dr. Skene), and the passage is as follows: "Aois

---

[1] *Celt. Scot.*, III., 413. The above translation is by Mr. W. M. Hennessy, from the following:—

> Tusa (tusea) mac Sadbhba moire,
> As (la) tu an slat (rutahlos) abhla as (ar) aille,
> Ca dia do bhra na boinne
> Do roine rin tha a tathbe.

[2] "The Irish before the Conquest," p. 237.

[3] More correctly, *Gobhan Saer* ("Free or Noble Smith"). From the description given by Mr. Elton (*Origins*, p. 131) of "Wayland's Smithy" at Ashbury, Berkshire, it is evident that it also belongs to the same class as the Boyne mounds.

Cr. ocht coed seascca a haon, ... Amlaoibh, Iomhair, 7¹ h Uailsi, tri toisigh Gall 7 Lorcain mc Cathail tigerna Midhe, do ionnradh ferainn Floinn mc Conaing. Uaimh Ach Alda hi Mugdhornaibh Maighen, Uaimh Cnoghbhai, Uaimh Feirt Bodan os Dubath, 7 Uaimh mna an Gobhand ag Drochat atha do croth 7 d orggain las na Gall cedna."²

This is rendered into Latin by Dr. O'Conor thus: "Ætas Christi DCCCLXI. . . . . Amlafus, Imarus et Magnates trium Ducum Alienigenarum, et Lorcanus filius Cathaldi Princeps Midiæ, vastant terras Flanni filii Conangi. Crypta subterranea campi Alda in regione Mugdornorum planitiei, Crypta Cnovæ, Cryptæ miraculorum Bodani supra Dubath, et Crypta fœminæ fabri apud Droghedam, vastatæ et destructæ ab Alienigenis iisdem."

Neither Dr. Todd nor Dr. Skene, however, have a high opinion of O'Conor's translation.³ And his rendering of "Uailsi" by "Magnates" is palpably a blunder based upon the acceptance of that word as *uaisle* or *uaisis*, a nobleman; whereas, Uailsi, Oisli, Oisill, &c., was the name of a comrade (some accounts say a brother) of the Olaf and Ivor referred to.⁴ Thus, the Annals state that in 861, Olaf (or Anlaf, or Aulay), Ivor and Uailsi (or Oisli), three chiefs of the Foreigners, and Lorcan, son of Cathal, lord of Meath,⁵ devastated the lands of Flann, son of Conang; in other words, the territory of "Bregia,—a district including the counties of Meath, Westmeath, Dublin (north of the Liffey), and part of Louth."⁶ And these same "foreigners" pillaged and destroyed certain underground chambers, which O'Conor refers to as "crypts." The term is correct enough, signifying, as it does, an underground place of concealment. But the Gaelic term is more suitable, if the quickened pronunciation which in many parts of Scotland has occasioned the spelling "weem" (*i.e.*, *uaim*) be adopted. For by "weem" is

---

¹ The symbol for the Gaelic *agus*—"and."
² Dr. O'Conor's *Rerum Hibernicarum Scriptores veteres*, 1824, III., 363–364.
³ "Bad translation and wretchedly erroneous topography," says the former; "by no means accurate," says the latter.
⁴ *Wars of the Gaedhill with the Gaill*, lxxii, 83.
⁵ Properly, of one-half only of Meath. (*Wars of the Gaedhill*, lxx, n°.)
⁶ *Op. cit.*, lxxviii, xci, *notes*.

understood the subterranean gallery previously described, if it is not at any time applied to the actual "hollow hill."[1] Of the "weems" in the territory of Flann, which the *Annals* state were plundered, three are easily recognized;—viz., that of "Cnoghbha," the modern "Knowth" (which is portrayed in the accompanying plate), the still more celebrated "Uaimh Feirt Bodan," described as "above Dubath,"[2] now known as Dowth, which is also here represented, and thirdly, the "weem" of the wife of the *Gobban Saor*, or "noble smith," at Drogheda. The first-named of all is said to be that of the "Brugh of the Boyne," at New Grange; and no doubt there is evidence for this identification, although the term "Mugdhornaibh Maighen" would otherwise lead one to place this "weem" at "Mugornn or Mugdhorn, now Cremorne,"[3] in the county of Monaghan.

Two of these "weems" are mentioned in the Gaelic poem of *Sith Eamhna*, wherein, as has been seen,[4] the son of noble Sabia" was assumed to be equally the son of some god "from Bru of the Boyne." In this poem, whose meaning is somewhat obscure, there are several references to the Boyne and to various "broghs," of which one is "the cave of Ferna, the fair cave of Knowth (*uaim fhearna, uaim chaomh cnodhbha*, or *cnaghdha*)." This *Sith Eamhna* itself appears to have been of the same order, and not improbably was that Eamhain which was "the ancient palace of the kings of Ulster." "The ruins of Eamhain, or, as it is now corruptly called, the Navan Fort, are to be seen about two miles to the west of Armagh," says Mr. O'Donovan, in a note to his "Book of Rights."[4] This is certainly farther north than the territory of Flann Mc Conang, ravaged by the "foreigners" in 861, as defined on a previous page; but one writer states that that territory of "Bregia" (or *Breagh*) extended into Ulster, in the eighth century;[5] and if the plundered "weem" first-named in the *Annals* was really in county Monaghan, that would show that a portion of "Breagh" was situated in Ulster in 861.

---

[1] For references to Scotch "weems" (specially so called), see Col. Forbes Leslie's "Early Races of Scotland," 1866, Vol. II, pp. 351-354. Also *ante*, p. 102.
[2] ? The "black foal." [3] *Wars of the Gaedhill*, xel. n°.
[4] Dublin, 1847, p. 22. [5] "Book of Rights," pp. 11-12, note.

Eamhain, or Emania (in the Latinized form), appears to have given its name to all Ulster, but in its proper application the term refers to the stronghold itself. Dr. Skene speaks of "the fall of the great seat of the Cruithnian kingdom called Emania, before an expedition, led by a scion of the Scottish (i.e., Gaelic) royal race, who established the kingdom of Orgialla on its ruins."[1] It is this place that is associated with Oscar, the hero of the "Fians," at the time of the Battle of Gawra; and it may be remembered that, in a poem describing that battle, a chief of one section of the "Fian" confederacy is made to exclaim:—

> "I and the Fians of Breatan
> Will be with Oscar of Eamhain."

And as Oscar is stated to have been slain at the Battle of Gawra, and the power of the "Fians" destroyed, one is tempted to believe that the legendary battle of Gawra coincides with the historical capture of Oscar's stronghold of Emhain, and the downfall of the historical Cruithné of Ulster. However, Sith Eamhna has been mentioned here not for its own sake, but for the casual references in that poem to the "Brugh of the Boyne" and "the cave of Ferna, the fair cave of Knowth."

The Gaelic records as well as the Scandinavian have many tales of "how-breaking" exploits. For, although the accounts of the Feenic "heroes" have been preserved to us in the Gaelic language, as those of the Longobards have been preserved in Latin, it does not follow in the one case more than in the other, that the language of the chronicle was the language of the chronicled. Whatever may have been wrought eventually, by time and intercourse, the Gaelic-speaking people appear originally as the plunderers of "the hidden places of the Fians and Fairies." Professor O'Curry states that among the Historic Tales in the *Book of Leinster*, there are many which deal specially with adventures in "caves" or, otherwise, "weems." Tales of this class are called *Uatha*.[2] "These are tales

---

[1] *Dean of Lismore's Book*, Introd., p. xlii.
[2] "*Uatha*, plural of *Uath*, a word not easily translated. *Uath* is evidently formed from *Uaimh*, a cave, or cellar; and signifies some deed connected with, as the attack or plunder of, a cave." (O'Curry, *op. cit.*, p. 586, note.)

respecting various occurrences in caves; sometimes the
taking of a cave, when the place has been used as a place of
refuge or habitation,—and such a taking would be, in fact, a
sort of *Toghail* [the *Toghail* having been previously defined
as a history 'which details the taking of a fort or fortified
palace or habitation by force. . . . . the term always implies
the destruction of the buildings taken.']; sometimes the
narrative of some adventure in a cave; sometimes of a
plunder of a cave." Mr. O'Curry gives a list of the *uatha*
in the "Book of Leinster"; and of these the most noteworthy
is the *Uath Uama Cruachan*, or the Plundering of the Weem
of Cruachan. This is referred to as "a very curious story,"
and the ravagers are said to have been "the men of Connacht,
in the time of Ailill and Meadhbh, as told in the old tale of
Thin Bo Aingen." This Meadhbh, or Maev, of Cruachan,
"the Semiramis of Irish history," as Lady Ferguson calls
her, has herself been identified with the "Queen Mab" of
fairy tradition. She appears to have occupied this "Uama
Cruachan" after it had been plundered; for it is stated that
her husband "re-edified the Rath of Cruachan, employing
for the purpose a fierce tribe of Firbolgic origin, the *Gowanree*,
who were compelled to labour unremittingly at the earthworks, and are said to have completed the dyke in one day."[1]
Mr. O'Curry has another reference to this place. "I have in
my possession," he says, "a poem in the Ossianic style,
which gives an account of a foot race between Cailté, the
celebrated champion of Finn Mac Cumhaill, and an unknown
knight who had challenged him. The race terminated by
the stranger running into the Cave of Cruachain, followed
by Cailté, where he found a party of smiths at work, etc.
No copy of the full Tale has come down to us." This incident is remarkable for its association of one of the "Fians"
with the underground smiths of tradition. Another *uath*
mentioned by Mr. O'Curry is the *Uath Dercc Ferna*, regarding which he says:—"There is an allusion to the trampling
to death of some sort of monster, in the mouth of this cave,
by a Leinsterwoman, in a poem on the Graves of Heroes
who were killed by Leinstermen, preserved in the Book of
Leinster (H. 2. 18, fol. 27, Trin. Coll. Dubl.)." The same

[1] "The Irish before the Conquest," p. 32.

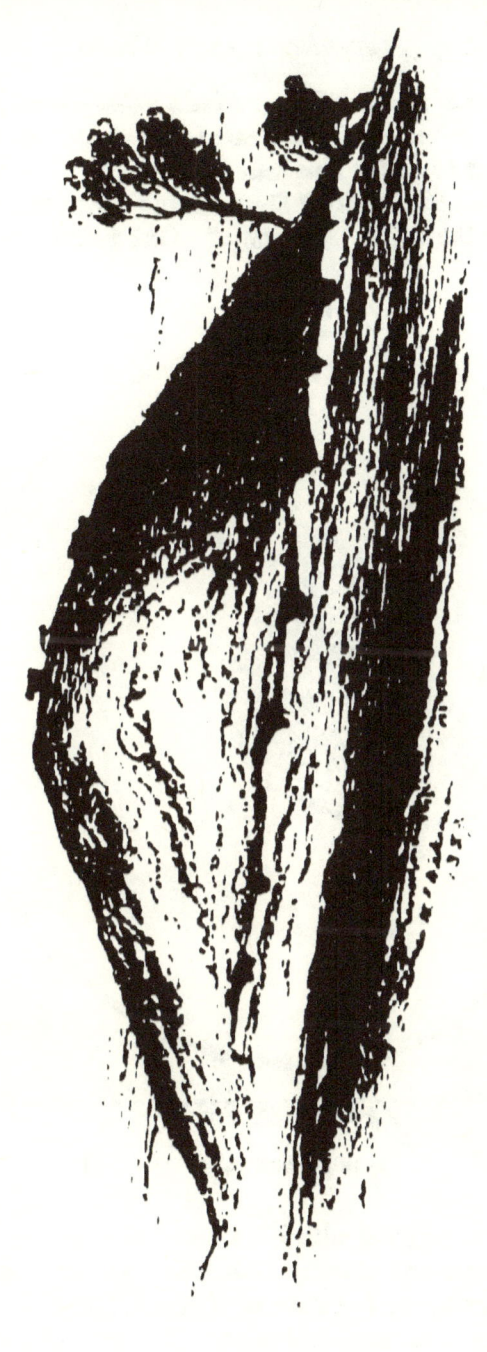

TOWER ((and Fort Sinian at Lisbeth), COUNTY MEATH.

(From the West)

place is the scene of the tale *Echtra Find a nDeircfearna*, "The Adventures of Finn in Derc Fearna"; but unfortunately Mr. O'Curry has to add "This tale is now lost." It is not clear why he should identify "Derc Fearna" with the "Cave of Dunmore in the county Kilkenny." One would naturally,

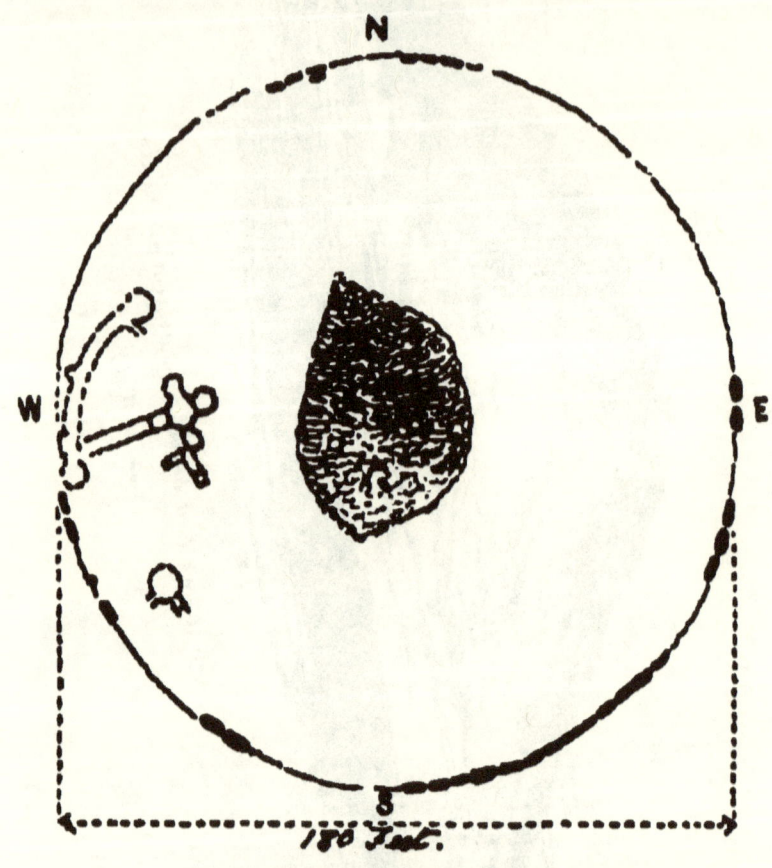

PLAN OF LOWTH.

considering its association with Finn and "Heroes who were killed by Leinstermen," assume that this was the same as "the cave of Ferna, the fair cave of Knowth."[1]

Of the plans and sectional views of these chambered

[1] For Mr. O'Curry's various statements, see his *Letters*, pp. 257-8, 283, 586-7 and 589.

mounds of the Boyne valley which are here given, it is not necessary to say much in these pages. "Dowth" has been explored and described by others, although the accompanying pictures, being new, and the work of the experienced archæologist referred to, add very considerably to the knowledge of the subject. The main gallery and chamber of Dowth resembles generally that of the "Brugh of the Boyne" at New Grange; but the central chamber is not nearly so spacious. The "bee-hive" chamber which the Dowth mound also contains has no duplicate at New Grange, but it is quite possible that each of these mounds has yet something to disclose.

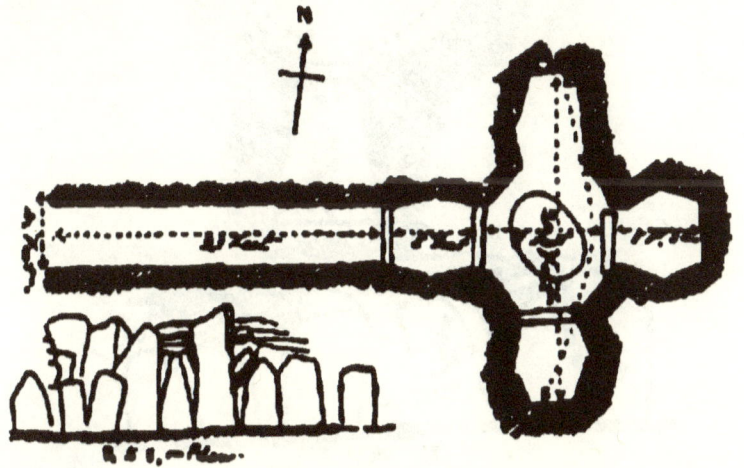

PLAN OF PASSAGE AND CHAMBER AT DOWTH, AND TRANSVERSE SECTION OF CHAMBER (SAME SCALE).

Dowth also reminds the explorer and excavator, by the deep hollow made in the upper portion, in the course of a fruitless and abandoned search, some years ago, that to attack these mounds at random is to run the risk of much useless and disappointing labour. It moreover shows that any upward exit from the central chamber did not in this instance ascend perpendicularly as in the Denghoog at Sylt, or the Orcadian Maes-how. In trying to find the entrances to such "hollow hills," we moderns have no light to guide us as the Danes had in the ninth century. It will be remembered that there never was, "in concealment under ground in Erian, nor in the various secret places belonging to Fians or to fairies, anything that was not discovered by these foreign, wonderful Denmarkians, through paganism and idol worship." This is otherwise explained by Dr. Todd, " that, notwithstanding the

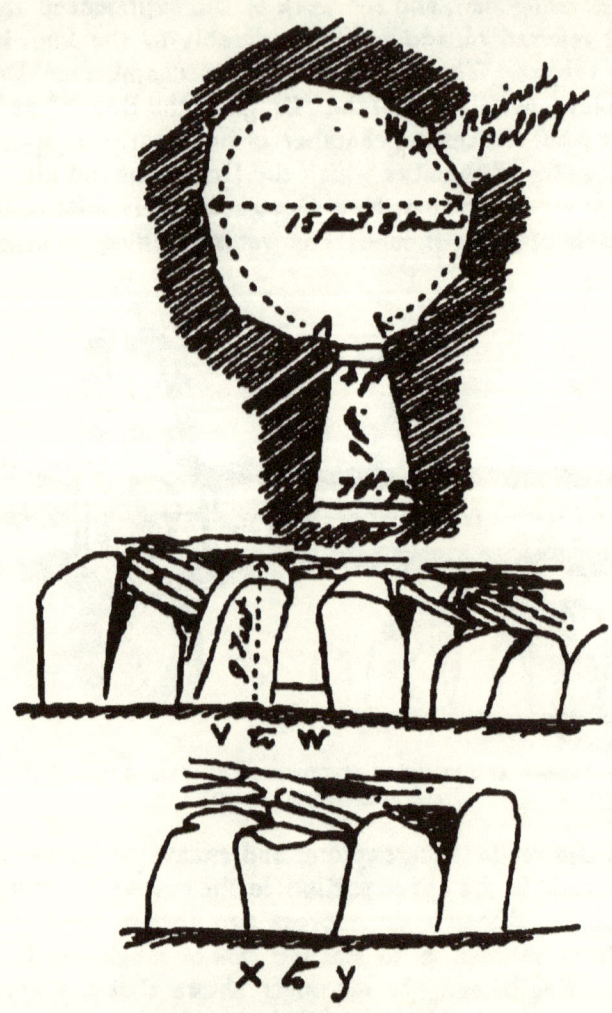

BEE-HIVE CHAMBER, DOWTH.

potent spells employed by the Fians and fairies for the concealment of their hidden treasures, the Danes, by their pagan magic and the diabolical power of their idols, were enabled to find them out." What was the "magic" of those ninth-century Danes, or of the order generally known as *Magi*, we only imperfectly know. But what is tolerably evident is that if those ninth-century Danes did not themselves rear similar structures (and Irish and Hebridean tradition says they did), they had among them those to whom such mound-dwellings were not "hidden" places; whether the entrances were uniformly made at one side of the mound, or were otherwise indicated to the initiated. In the case of "Knowth" there is less dubiety; as what appears to be the entrance to its interior is known to Irish archæologists. But local difficulties have hitherto stood in the way, and the mound is said never to have been entered since the ninth century; which, however, may be doubted. Dr. Molyneux, at any rate, in the tract quoted in Appendix A, states that he had then in his possession a stone urn which "was twelve years since (*i.e.* in 1713) discovered in a mount at *Knowth*, a place in the county of *Meath*, within four miles of *Drogheda*." He does not actually say that this urn, and the "square stone box, about five foot long and four foot broad" which contained it, were situated in an interior chamber of the mound. But very probably this is what he meant.[1]

[1] A more particular description of the Brugh of the Boyne will be found in Appendix A. These mounds are also described in "A Hand Book of Irish Antiquities," by William F. Wakeman, Dublin, 1848; in Wilde's "Beauties of the Boyne," Dublin, 1849, and two of them (Knowth and Dowth) by T. N. Deane, in the "Proceedings of the Royal Irish Academy," December, 1882.

CHAPTER XV.

SUCH barrows as these of the Boyne district belong to the largest class of these structures at present revealed to us. What may be taken as the average "fairy knowe" is very much smaller; therefore, when it is said that houses have, in all likelihood, been frequently built upon such artificial eminences, without the more modern builders being aware of their real nature, it is to be understood that the tumuli of the larger class are indicated. But, while it is probable that newer races very often built thus unconsciously upon the outer crust of the habitations of the mound-dwellers, it is still more likely that, in course of time, the central chamber of the mound became by slow degrees the dungeon of a fort or castle that had evolved itself from it. When a "how" of the larger class had been "broken" by invaders, and its inmates despoiled and killed or enslaved, their conquerors would quickly realize that this artificial mound, rising out of a level plain, formed an admirable site for a stronghold; and, indeed, that the only thing immediately necessary was to throw up a rampart round the top of the hill. To races who had no fancy for the subterranean manner of living, the strongholds of their predecessors would not suffice, although they would still prove very serviceable as cellars, or dungeons, or as forming a secret way of access to the castle which would eventually tower above them. Where the subject race was not exterminated, the former lord of the "broch" would still live on as the serf of his conqueror, and, on account of his physical peculiarities, he would be remembered as his master's "dwarf," or "brownie," while the women of his race, still claiming their inherited "supernatural" power, would be represented by the prophetic half-dreaded "banshee" (*ban-sithe*, or fairy-woman) that foretold the destinies of the house of her over-lord. It is a significant fact that the possession of a family "banshee" in Ireland is restricted to those families who trace their descent from the Milesians (Scots), the conquerers of the Cruithné or Pechts. And we are told that, at one time, in Shetland, where the Pechts became the subject race, "almost every family had a *brownie*.... which served them."¹ Innumerable references of this kind might be given. There is, for instance, the case of the "brownie" who was the attendant of Maclachlan of Stralachlan, in Argyllshire, and who is said to have "inhabited a vault in the dungeons of the castle" (Castle Lachlan), but who, like other "brownies," was accredited with prophetic powers!² Then there is the "little chap with a red cap on his head," referred to in a story told to the late J. F. Campbell;³ and this "little chap" is understood to occupy the cellar of a "haunted house"; which, as it was inhabited by "ladies and gentlemen," and must be assigned to the period when such "red caps" existed, was not unlikely a "house" of the same order as the castles just spoken of.

Such an example of a mediæval castle, the flower of a plant rooted in the interior of such a mound, may be recognized in Kenilworth. According to local tradition, the hill upon which Kenilworth Castle is built was once inhabited by fairies, who are remembered by the same characteristics as their kindred elsewhere. But the consideration of a Warwickshire mound might lead us too far away from the dwarfs more specially known as Picts or Pechts, and therefore it is better to continue as much as possible within the area already examined. It is enough to note that the Kenilworth dwarfs, in the days when their mound was merely a subterranean vault of the great castle overhead, and themselves nothing more than the "Redcaps" of the cellar, formed a marked contrast to the once dreaded "shag-boys" or mound-dwellers, as these are remembered in Lincolnshire tradition.⁴

---

¹ For such details see Scott's introduction to "The Monastery," etc., etc.; Bund's "Description of Zetland;" and Armstrong's "Gaelic Dictionary," s.v. "Uruisg."

² "Legends of Scottish Superstition," Edinburgh, 1848; "Maclachlan's Brownie."

³ "West Highland Tales," I., xlvii.

⁴ Although the dwarfs of central England may not rightly be considered under the name of Picts or Pechts, a chain connecting them with the people thus called is discernible. Scott says that, "according to romantic tradition," Kenilworth "had been first tenanted" by "three primitive Britons" who were "the soldiers of King Arthur" ("Kenilworth," ch. xxvi). Thus, the early inhabitants of Kenil-

However, if Kenilworth is too far south to be recognized as a home of the historical Pechts, Ancient Northumbria has not the same objection against it. And in East Lothian, which is a portion of that province, a certain Castle of Yester was once famous for its "Goblin Hall," which is thus described in the Appendix to "Marmion" (note 2 P):—

"*The Goblin Hall.*—A vaulted hall under the ancient castle of Gifford or Yester (for it bears either name indifferently), the construction of which has from a very remote period been ascribed to magic. . . . 'Upon a peninsula, formed by the water of Hopes on the east, and a large rivulet on the west, stands the ancient castle of Yester. Sir David Dalrymple, in his annals, relates that "Hugh Gifford de Yester died in 1267; that in his castle there was a capacious cavern, formed by magical art, and called in the country Bo-Hall, *i.e.*, Hobgoblin Hall." A stair of twenty-four steps led down to this apartment, which is a large and spacious hall, with an arched roof. . . . From the floor of this hall another stair of thirty-six steps leads down to a pit which hath a communication with Hopeswater. . . .'"

In this instance, the "pit" which communicated with the neighbouring stream was probably the original underground dwelling; and if the arch of the "vaulted hall" above it is not of the "Pelasgic" order, it is to be presumed that the "goblins" who built it had received fresh ideas from a race possessed of a more advanced civilization.

worth are equally "fairies" and "primitive Britons." Again, in Glamorganshire (according to Mr. Wirt Sikes, "British Goblins," pp. 6 and 392), there is "a certain steep and rugged crag" which bears "a distinctly awful reputation as a stronghold of the fairy tribe," and, in a secret cavern underneath this crag, "Arthur and his warriors" are believed to be sleeping. While an Edinburgh tradition, given by Dr. Daniel Wilson ("Memorials," vol. ii. ch. xix.), states that "King Arthur and the Pechts" have also withdrawn to a subterranean retreat in the hill which is still known as Arthur's Seat. Obviously, Arthur, if he ever lived, cannot have retired into all of these places, but there is, nevertheless, a vague agreement in these three traditions; and Kenilworth, Arthur's Seat, and Craig y Ddinas all testify to an identification of Arthur and his "primitive Britons," with the underground "fairies" and "Pechts." It may be objected that the tradition of Barbarossa, as in Ruckert's ballad, asleep in his underground castle, with his dwarf beside him, is evidently of the same origin as those just referred to. This is manifest. But, before attempting to reconcile Continental with British tradition, it is important to first demonstrate, if that may be done, that the British traditions here spoken of are *historical* and not *mythological*. (The story of the Kenilworth fairies will be found at p. 218 of "The Dialect of the English Gypsies," by B. C. Smart and H. T. Crofton, London, 1875.)

' It is impossible to refer here to the many terms used to denote what is really

The castle of Doune, in Perthshire, is another probable instance of the mediæval castle evolved from the primitive mound. What is nowadays known as the castle of "Doune," was formerly spoken of as "The Dùn (or Doon) of Menteith." "Doune (Dun, no doubt) had once, where its castle now stands, an ancient fortress; but the name is all that now remains to bespeak it," says a lady-writer on this subject.[1] It is very probable, therefore, that the original "Doon of Menteith" was the mound upon which the present building now stands; and that this was at one time the chief stronghold of the district of Menteith. One *doun,* which has apparently never advanced from its earliest stage, is that of Rothiemurchus, in the district of Badenoch (Inverness-shire). "A mound which has every appearance of having been used in ancient times for purposes of defence stands at the Doun of Rothiemurchus, and is properly the *Doun* or *Dun,*" says a modern historian of that district.[2] Such a structure as this seems to combine the dwelling and the fort; the "hollow hill" having presumably been so constructed as to render the "crater" on its summit a place of defence. That this Doon of Rothiemurchus was once inhabited seems clearly indicated. In speaking of the *ban-sithe,* or fairy woman, already referred to as the appanage of old Milesian families, Sir Walter Scott states that "most great families in the Highlands" were thus distinguished, and that "Grant of Rothiemurcus had an

one class of people; as these terms themselves show when analysed. But this term "goblin," although in recent centuries it has been surrounded with much that is unreal and fictitious, appears to have been once used in the most ordinary matter-of-fact way. This will be seen from the following reference quoted by Dr. Henry Rink ("Danish Greenland," 1877, p. 16), in the narrative of a Norse visit to Greenland in the eleventh century:—"One morning Thorgils went out by himself on the ice, and discovered the carcase of a whale in an opening, and beside two 'witches' (or 'goblins,' evidently Eskimo women), who were tying large bundles of flesh together. Thorgils instantly rushed upon one of them with his sword and cut off one of her hands, whereupon both of them took to their heels." In other words, the eleventh-century natives of Greenland, whom Dr. Rink believes were Eskimos, were at once classed by a Norwegian of that period in the same category as those whom he had been accustomed to call "goblins" in Europe.

[1] Miss C. MacLagan, "Proc. of Soc. of Ant. of Scot." (1st series), ix. 39.

[2] A. Mackintosh Shaw, "History of the Mackintoshes," 1880, vol. i. p. 24, *note.* This writer also points out that the word "Rothiemurcus" itself indicates a "fortified mound" or *Rath.*

attendant called *Bodach-an-dùin*";[1] in other words, "The Goblin of the Doon." And when Scott states, in the note immediately preceding that just quoted, that "a goblin, dressed in antique armour, and having one hand covered with blood, called from that circumstance *Lamh-dearg*, or Red-hand, is a tenant of the forests of Glenmore and Rothiemurcus," he indicates a tradition that seems to be connected with the "goblins" of the Doon of Rothiemurchus.[2]

However, although referred to in passing, the Rothiemurchus mound is not one of those on which a stone castle has been subsequently reared. But of the latter class an example is furnished by the "Castle Hill" of Clunie, in Perthshire. It is thus described in Sir John Sinclair's "Statistical Account":—

"On the western shore of the loch of Clunie stands the old castle-hill, a large, green mound, partly natural and partly artificial, on the top of which are the ruins of a very old building. Some aged persons still alive [in the end of last century] remember to have seen a small aperture, now invisible, at the edge of one of the fragments of the ruins, where, if a stone was thrown in, it was heard for some time, as if rolling down a staircase. From this it seems probable that were a section of the hill to be made, some curious discoveries might be the consequence."

Resembling Fierna's Hillock, near Limerick, in its having this "small aperture," communicating with an unexplored vault below, this Perthshire mound is also celebrated, like Knock-Fierna, for its association with the "fairies." The castle which once crowned its summit has more historical memories.

Of this castle, in which, it is said, King Edward I. of England passed a night, in the course of his triumphant progress through Scotland in 1296, almost nothing now remains. But a tradition relating to an earlier period asserts that this place was once a hunting-seat of Kenneth McAlpin, the ninth-century conqueror of the Picts (whose king he subsequently became). Although Kenneth, and his son after him, bore the title of "King of the Picts," it is tolerably clear that he was a Scot or Milesian by race, and it is certain that he broke up the power of the Pechts in Central Scotland. As he was

[1] Appendix to "The Lady of the Lake," Note 2 H.
[2] See also "West Highland Tales," II., 66, for a reference to this personage.

not one of this latter race himself, it is probable that any "hunting-seat" possessed by him at this place took the shape of an above-ground building, and that therefore the memories of the "supernatural" inhabitants of this mound date back to the time when it was still an unconquered stronghold of the Pechts. As, however, the suggested "section of the hill" has never yet been made, nothing definite is at present known regarding the interior of this mound.

One of the incidents relating to the "goblin" of Rothiemurchus is included by Mr. J. F. Campbell among the traditions obtained by him from the district of Badenoch, in Inverness-shire. "The Badenoch account of the fairies" is stated to be "much the same" as those from other parts of the Highlands, and they show "that according to popular belief, fairies commonly carried off men, women and children, who seemed to die, but really lived underground." A tale of this kind, "now commonly believed in Badenoch," is to this effect:—A man who, returning home after a short absence, found that his wife had disappeared and that another woman had taken her place, demanded from the latter, on pain of death, to tell him where his wife had been conveyed to. "She told him that his wife had been carried to Cnoc Fraing, a mountain on the borders of Badenoch and Strathdearn." "The man went to Cnoc Fraing. He was suspected before of having something supernatural about him; and he soon found the fairies, who told him his wife had been taken to Shiathan Mor, a neighbouring mountain. He went there and was sent to Tom na Shirich, near Inverness. There he went, and at the 'Fairy Knoll' found his wife and brought her back."[1]

Mr. Campbell adds that "the person who related this story pretended to have seen people who knew distant descendants of the woman"—but beyond indicating that the tradition is very old, this does not place these events in any particular century. The localities named, however, are full of suggestiveness. Of *Cnoc Fraing*, nothing is known to the present writer. But "Shiathan Mor," to which the woman is said to have been first taken, signifies "The Great Hill of the Fairies." Such a name is of very frequent occurrence

[1] "West Highland Tales," II., 67.

in the Highlands. One who is well versed in these matters says: "There is perhaps not a hamlet or township in the Highlands or Hebrides without its *sithan* or green fairy knoll so-called. Within half a mile of our own residence, for example, there is a *Sithean Beag* and a *Sithean Mor*, a Lesser and Greater Fairy Knoll."[1] In the Hebridean island of Colonsay, where Martin, the eighteenth-century traveller, found that "the natives have a tradition among them of a very little generation of people that lived once here, called Lusbirdan, the same with pigmies," one finds a "Sheean Mor" and a "Sheean Beg," along with many other traces of those people.[2] But it is unnecessary to multiply special instances. It was to a Great Knoll of the Fairies, then, that the woman was taken, and thereafter to "Tom na Shirich, near Inverness." This name also signifies "Hill of the Fairies." *Shirich*, more correctly *Sithreach*, is apparently a less common form, equivalent to Sidhfear, Duine Sith, etc., but it occurs more than once in the "West Highland Tales,"[3] both as a singular and a plural. When the initial "s" of *sithreach* or *sithrach*, becomes aspirated, after the common Gaelic fashion, the sibilant is no longer heard; and this is exemplified in the case of "Tom na Shirich," which is nowadays spelt as it is pronounced—*Tomnahurich* (or *Tomnaheurich*, etc.)[4] Of this Inverness hill much has been written.

It is sometimes called *Tommnan-hnrich*, and spoken of as a *tomman*, which connects it with the word *tulman* or *tolman*, already referred to. Hugh Miller, in speaking of "that Queen of Scottish tombans, the picturesque Tomnahuirich," employs both forms at the same time, which is contradictory. Pennant, who visited it last century, refers to it also as a

---

[1] Rev. Alex. Stewart, F.S.A. Scot., in "Nether Lochaber," Edin., 1883, p. 20.
He adds: "There is, besides, a *Glaice-af-Shithrin*, the Fairy Knoll Glade, *Tibearn-af-Shithrin*, the Fairy Knoll Well; and a deep chasm, through which a mountain torrent plunges dashing, called *Leum-an-f-Shithick*, the Fairy Leap."
[2] See "Proc. of Soc. of Antiq. of Scot." 1880-81, 113 *et sq*.
[3] See vol. ii. pp. 48 and 52. The latter page mentions a *Rudh na Sirach*, "the Fairies' Point," in the island of Kerrera, near Oban.
[4] Similarly, a "Fairy Loch" in Argyleshire is spelt *Loch an Hurich*, and a like example is that of *Glennahuirich*, in Nether Lochaber.

tomman. In his *Tour* he thus describes "the strange-shaped hill of Tomman heurich:"—

"The Tomman is of an oblong form, broad at the base, and sloping on all sides towards the top; so that it looks like a ship with its keel upwards.... It is perfectly detached from any other hill; and if it was not for its great size, might pass for a work of art." "Its length at top [is] about 300 yards; I neglected measuring the base or the height, which are both considerable; the breadth of the top [is] only twenty yards."

Captain Burt, in his "Letters from a Gentleman in the North of Scotland" (Letter XII.) speaks of it as follows:—

"About a mile westward from the town [Inverness] there rises, out of a perfect flat, a very regular hill; whether natural or artifical, I could never find by any tradition; the natives call it *tommanheurich*. It is almost in the shape of a Thames wherry, turned keel upwards, for which reason they sometimes call it Noah's Ark. The length of it is about four hundred yards, and the breadth at bottom about one hundred and fifty. From below, at every point of view, it seems to end at top in a narrow ridge; but when you are there, you find a plain large enough to draw up two or three battalions of men. Hither we sometimes retire on a summer's evening.... But this is not the only reason why I speak of this hill; it is the weak credulity with which it is attended, that led me to this detail; for as anything ever so little extraordinary, may serve as a foundation (to such as are ignorant, heedless, or interested) for ridiculous stories and imaginations, so the fairies within it are innumerable, and witches find it the most convenient place for their frolics and gambols in the night time."

Now, if this large hill, which "might pass for a work of art," was really, as tradition states, the residence of the little people known as dwarfs or Pechts, it was clearly an important seat of those people. And, on regarding them from the historian's point of view, one finds that this district was specially so distinguished. "When we can first venture to regard the list of the Pictish Kings preserved in the *Pictish Chronicle* as having some claim to a historical character, we find the king having his seat apparently in Forfarshire; but when the works of Adamnan and Bede place us upon firm ground, the monarch belonged to the race of the Northern Picts, and had his fortified residence near the mouth of the river Ness" [Inver-Ness]. And the same historian again observes:—"Adamnan, writing in the seventh century, tells us of the fortified residence of the king of the Picts on the banks of the river Ness, with its royal house and gates, of a village on the banks of a lake, and of the houses of the country people."[1]

Hitherto, the place which has been regarded as most likely the site of this seventh-century stronghold, is the vitrified fort which crowns the summit of Craig Patrick (or *Craig Phadraig*), a hill not far from Inverness. But the top of a hill more than four hundred feet high can scarcely be referred to as a situation "on the banks of the river Ness," from which river it is, moreover, two miles distant.[2] The situation of Tomnahurich, on the other hand, does exactly answer to the description given. And this "hill," whose peculiar appearance has attracted the attention of several travellers, is locally remembered as a celebrated home of the "Pechts." Nor is it necessary to confine oneself to the consideration of this hill alone. Adamnan speaks not only of a royal residence, but also of "the houses of the country people." "The country people" of whom he speaks were Pechts, and their "houses," of course, were "Pechts' houses"; "houses" such as the Fairy Knowe unearthed at Coldoch, near Doune, already referred to. In other words *sheans*. Now, when Hugh Miller speaks of "that Queen of Scottish tomhans, the picturesque Tomnahuirich," he states that it belongs to "a wonderful group" of similar mounds "in the immediate neighbourhood of Inverness." The "houses" of the mound-dwelling Pechts had one admirable characteristic; they were almost indestructible. If the King of the Dwarfs had his residence at Inverness during the seventh century, with "the houses of the country people," of the same race, scattered all through the immediate neighbourhood, their dwellings must be there still: and any one who wanted to localize them would naturally turn to such mounds as the "wonderful groups" of "tomhans" of which Hugh Miller speaks.[3]

[1] See Skene's "Celtic Scotland," i. 272; ii. 105-6; and iii. 10.
[2] This discrepancy is pointed out by Dr. Skene, who suggests "a gravelly ridge called Torvean," and also "the eminence east of Inverness, called the Crown," as more probable sites. ("Celtic Scotland," ii. 106, note.)
[3] Hugh Miller, although he confesses himself puzzled as to their origin, undoubtedly regarded these "tomhans" as entirely natural. And if it should appear that he was mistaken, there would, in that event, be a new question

Inverness, however, was not the only important centre of Pictish power. Among others, there was Abernethy, a few miles south-east of Perth. And at this place, says Small, in his "Roman Antiquities of Fife," the spot wherein the treasures of the Pictish king are believed to be hidden[1] was guarded by a *dronghy* (*droich* or *trow*) who fiercely assailed any invader. Of the Pechts in that neighbourhood there are many traditions.

A few miles to the west of Abernethy is Forteviot, where Kenneth MacAlpin, the conqueror and ruler of the Pechts, died in the latter part of the ninth century. Prior to the successful invasion of Kenneth's race, this district—like that of Abernethy and all the country north to Inverness—had been inhabited by Pechts: and Forteviot is stated to have been a seat of Pictish royalty. Some miles to the south-west of Forteviot there is a hill called Ternavie, which has characteristics similar to those of Tomnahuirich. "Ternavie has been pronounced 'the most remarkable spot in this parish or neighbourhood.' It is a hill or mound of earth of a very curious form, occupying, when the Old Statistical Account was written 'many acres of ground, covered with a fine sward of grass, and striking the eye at a distance of several miles. It resembles in shape the keel of a ship inverted.'" And local tradition asserts, says the writer quoted from,[2] that once upon a time, a countryman attempting to obtain turf on the side of this hill, was suddenly confronted by an old man who emerged from the hill, "and with an angry countenance and tone of voice asked the countryman why he was tirring (uncovering) his house over his head?" This story does not say that the mound-dweller was a dwarf, but here we have a hill whose appearance suggests

opened up; because of the peculiar characteristics of what he knew as "tomban."

It is an unfortunate circumstance that any practical attempt at testing the accuracy of the local tradition regarding Tomnahurich itself is out of the question, owing to the fact that for many years its exterior has been used as a burying ground—as more than one "hollow hill" is known to have been. But "the houses of the country people" would afford a sufficient test.

[1] A kettle of gold is specially mentioned, and in the "hidden places" of the fairies of White Cater Thun, near Brechin, a kettle of gold is also believed to be concealed.

[2] Dr. Marshall, "Historic Scenes in Perthshire," Edinburgh, 1880, p. 263.

that it is at least partly artificial, and local tradition alleges that it was once inhabited. And this in the heart of Pictavia, or the country of the Pechts.

In the same county, but farther to the west, there is a locality which is remembered, like the island on the Rossshire loch, as a gathering-place or rendezvous of the little people. It is situated in the valley of the Forth. The "Fairy Knowes" of Coldoch have already been spoken of. One of them, it was stated, has been opened, and its interior shows to the most sceptical that the tradition which told that it was a home of the dwarfs was absolutely correct. The other "knowe," some hundreds of yards distant, has not as yet been touched.[1] But that it, too, was a dwelling of the same "little people" is almost as certain as if the spade of the excavator had already done its work.

But the gathering-place referred to lies nearer the sources of the Forth than the "Fairy Knowe" of Coldoch and the Doune of Menteith. Like these places, it is situated in the district of Menteith, and beside the lake of that name, on its south-eastern shore. This hillock is known as *Cnoc nan Bocan*, or the Knowe of the Goblins, and we are told that it used to be "the headquarters of the fairies of the whole district of Menteith." These fairies, it is said, were employed as the drudges of a former Earl of Menteith, in making the small peninsula known as Arnmauk, which juts out from the southern shore of the lake towards the small island of Inchmahome. The earl, we are told, "in grateful acknowledgment of the work they had done in forming the peninsula, and wishing to be on good terms with them, made a grant to them of the north shoulder of Ben Venue; which is to this day called Coir-n'an-Uriskin, that is, the Cove of the Urisks or Fairies."[2] At this latter place, says another

---

[1] Owing, I believe, to the fact that it is on a different estate. The following remarks by M. T. N. Deane, in his paper on the "Hollow hills" of Knowth and Dowth, in the Boyne valley ("Proceedings of the Royal Irish Academy," Dec. 1888, p. 164), may be aptly quoted here :—"For many years it has been the desire of antiquaries to explore Knowth, but I regret to say the owner is unwilling to permit a search being made. I am in great hopes that when it is fully understood that the vesting of a monument does not involve an infringement of territorial rights the difficulty will be overcome, and monuments now neglected will be placed under supervision."

[2] Marshall's "Historic Scenes in Perthshire," pp. 383-84. Mr. Grant

writer,[1] "the solemn stated meetings of the order were regularly held"; presumably at a later date.

However, "the north shoulder of Ben Venue" ought probably to be regarded as the latest "reservation" accorded to these little people. For, among the many "knowes" in the district of Menteith which are claimed as their homes, there is one pre-eminently distinguished. Some miles to the west of the Lake of Menteith is the village of Aberfoyle, celebrated by Sir Walter Scott, who says of this locality: "The lakes and precipices amidst which the Avon Dhu [*Abhainn Dubh*; i.e., Black-Water], or River Forth, has its birth, are still, according to popular tradition, haunted by the Elfin people.... An eminently beautiful little conical hill, near the eastern extremity of the valley of Aberfoil, is supposed to be one of their peculiar haunts, and is the scene which awakens in Andrew Fairservice[2] the terror of their power." The passage in "Rob Roy" to which Scott here refers is as follows:—

"A beautiful eminence of the most regular round shape, and clothed with copsewood of hazels, mountain-ash, and dwarf-oak, intermixed with a few magnificent old trees, which, rising above the underwood, exposed their forked and bared branches to the silver moonshine, seemed to protect the sources from which the river sprung. If I could trust the tale of my companion, which, while professing to disbelieve every word of it, he told under his breath, and with an air of something like intimidation, this hill, so regularly formed, so richly verdant, and garlanded with such a beautiful variety of ancient trees and thriving copsewood, was held by the neighbourhood to contain, within its unseen caverns, the palaces of the fairies—a race of airy beings, who formed an intermediate class between men and demons, and who, if not positively malignant to humanity, were yet to be avoided and feared, on account of their capricious, vindictive, and irritable disposition."

Stewart, in his "Popular Superstitions" (as quoted in the *Scots Magazine*, 1803, vol. 15, p. 40), states that "the workmen of the great Michael Scott were all Fairies; and it is only in that way that it could be accounted for, that some stupendous bridges in the north country were built by him in the course of a single night." With this compare the above statement as to the Earl of Menteith's workmen, and all the foregoing references to "Pechs" and "Fairies" in similar circumstances; as also the "fierce tribe of Firbolgic origin, the Grasswroy," who are said to have built the earthworks of the Rath of Cruachan in a single day, working as the unwilling serfs of an apparently Gaelic lord.

[1] Dr. Graham, "Sketches of the Picturesque Scenery of Perthshire," Edinburgh, 1806, p. 19.

[2] A slip of Scott's for "Bailie Nicol Jarvie."

"'They ca' them,' said Mr. Jarvie, in a whisper, 'Daoine Schie—whilk signifies, as I understand, men of peace; meaning thereby to make their godewill. And we may e'en as weel ca' them that too, Mr. Osbaldistone, for there's nae gude in speaking ill o' the laird within his ain bounds.' But he added presently after, on seeing one or two lights which twinkled before us, 'It's deceits o' Satan, after a', and I fearna to say it —for we are near the manse now, and yonder are the lights in the clachan of Aberfoil.'"

To describe this as a "*little, conical* hill," as Scott does, is misleading. When viewed transversely, from the opposite bank of the Blackwater, it has a conical appearance, certainly, as the gable of a roof has. But when its true length is seen, as when viewed from the west, this Fairy Knowe of Aberfoyle reveals itself as of the "hog-back" order, or as was said of Tomnahcurich, like a "Thames wherry, turned keel upwards." And as for its height, neither Scott's "little" nor its local name of "Fairy *Knowe*" gives anything like a true idea of its dimensions. How much of this "knowe" is artificial, or whether any of it is, remains to be discovered. But if it and Tomnahcurich have truly had the origin that tradition assigns to them, then they belong to a class of "hollow hills" which are as much greater than New Grange ("The Brugh of the Boyne") as New Grange is greater than Maes-how, or Maes-how than the Broch of Coldoch. Such a mound as Maes-how may be held to represent the ordinary Pecht's House or Fairy Hillock; a structure which, though of artificial origin, may be correctly styled a hillock. But the Brugh of the Boyne is a "hill," rather than a "hillock." What limits the mound-builders set themselves is not known. But the people who were capable of the ideas and the labour implied in such a structure as "the Brugh of the Boyne" might as well have reared mounds that were two or three times its size.

This Fairy Knowe is not only known locally by that name, but also as the Doon,[2] or Doon Hill. If that implies that it was a fortification, the site was perfect. Protected on its north-eastern side by the river, and on the south-west by its

[1] See "Rob Roy," chap. xxviii., and Note o.
[2] This spelling is only tentative. On hearing it thus pronounced, a resident in that district corrected the pronunciation to *Doo'n*, or *Doo'an*, which may signify a quite different meaning from *Dûn*.

own almost precipitous rampart, the Doon of Aberfoyle stands like a sentinel at what is there called "The Gate of the Highlands." The little valley which it protects teems with traditions of the dwarfs who are said to have once dwelt there, and whose dwellings are yet pointed out. Even yet the old people have many a tale of how the ruling family of Graham won their possessions there; and one such tale is that which has just been spoken of, wherein a Graham (Earl of Menteith) appears as the overlord of the dwarfs. That this family, properly *de* Graeme, traces its origin to those Anglo-Normans, such as Bruce and his chief nobles, who were the founders of the Neo-Scottish kingdom, is quite compatible with the idea that De Graeme's dwarfish labourers were, historically, Picts; a race distinguished as the allies of the English and the enemies of Bruce.

Enough has now been said to illustrate what is really the test of the "realistic" theory of the fairy tales. Tradition has truly stated, during many generations, that such apparently-natural hillocks as Maes-how and Coldoch were inhabited by little people. All archaeologists are agreed that many artificial hillocks are at present standing with their secrets unrevealed. But if, by following the lead of tradition, we find it a reasonably safe[1] guide to those primitive habitations, then its statements must deserve a much fuller and more serious consideration than they have ever yet received. Either the "realistic theory" is a vain imagination (as it is believed to be by those who take the "mythological" view of such traditions), or else it is something of the very greatest importance; as others, of whom the present writer is one, believe it to be. Should this method of interpreting the past be proved a true one, the results which would flow from its acceptance would be far-reaching indeed. But tradition has yet to establish its right to be unquestionably regarded as a guide. It may be that every chambered mound already opened had long had its real nature foretold by the voice of

[1] One would like to regard tradition as infallible in this respect. But, unfortunately, the age of the "shean" is so far back, that the term may now be used to denote any "conical hill," by Gaelic-speaking persons. However, a strong and persistent local tradition would far outweigh this modern misuse of the term *sithean*, in its general application, if such *sithean* (of which the dictionaries give a hint) is really common.

local tradition. But the surest test of the authenticity of tradition lies in its future application. It is known to all archæologists in Western Europe that it is not necessary to go so far east as Mycenæ to find the chambered mound, with its dry-stone walls and "Pelasgic" arch. And tradition points to many a seeming "hillock,"[1] and says that it, too, is a "treasure-house of Atreus." The question to be decided is, How far is tradition to be trusted? And the answer can be very easily obtained.

[1] The Continental examples are, of course, very numerous. In Denmark alone, according to J. M. Thiele, tradition points out as chambered mounds "two hills, Mangelbierg and Gillesbierg, in the environs of Hirschholm, on Hösterklöb Mark"; "a hill called Wheel-hill, at Gudmandstrup, in the Lordship of Odd"; "a large knoll called Steensbierg, at Ourtie, near Joegerspriis"; "the high ridge on which the church stands, at Kyndebye, in the Bailiwick of Holbeck"; and, in the same bailiwick, at a place between the towns of Mamp and Asgerup, "near the Strand"; Galtebierg also supplies another to the list; while "between Jerslöse and Söbierg, lies Söbierg bank, which is the richest knoll in the land." (For similar references in this neighbourhood, see also Mr. W. G. Black's "Heligoland.") And Thorpe's "Northern Mythology" specifies many such mounds. M. Pol de Mont (in his Flemish "Volkskunde," ii. 5, pp. 89-90) points out an "Aschberg," at Casterlé, in the province of Antwerp, which is said to have held fifty Aergenoortjes, or hill-dwarfs. (With this may fitly be compared three Eskimo "mounds" at Hopedale, Labrador, which, though they are now deserted, "more than one hundred persons of both sexes and all ages are said to have inhabited.") But every Continental "Veensberg," into which men of the taller race were tempted by the attractions of the dwarf women, and every "berg" that is affirmed to have been the residence of a "berg-foe," comes under the same denomination as the special examples already cited.

CHAPTER XVI.

It is manifest that the traditions relating to "the little people" contain many statements which at the first sight seem to be irreconcilable with one another. In one aspect, the dwarf races appear as possessed of a higher culture than the race or races who were physically their superiors. They forge swords of "magic" temper, and armour of proof; beautifully-wrought goblets of gold and silver, silver-mounted bridles, garments of silk, and personal ornaments of precious metals and precious stones, are all associated with them. They are deeply versed in "magic" (a term generally held to denote the science of the Chaldæan Magi), and this renders them the teachers of the taller race, in religion, and in many forms of knowledge. In short, it is only in physical stature that they are below the latter people: in everything else they are above them. In another aspect, the positions are reversed. The dwarfs are the serfs and drudges of the taller race, to whom they are distinctly inferior in intellectual capacity. The articles associated with them, such as the primitive arrow-heads of flint, still spoken of as "elf-shot," are all indicative of the rudest savagery. They themselves are accustomed to go without clothes, which, when offered to them by their masters, they reject indignantly. As great a contrast is presented by their physique. In some tales, they are fair, and beautiful in feature, and yellow-haired; in others they are swarthy in complexion and hair; and again they are described as red-, or russet-haired. From such conflicting evidence what is one to infer?

Two or three solutions of this question may be offered. One that, as the Icelander Gudmund said of these people, they were "subject to poverty and wealth," like the members of any modern nation, which contains in itself the most violent contrasts. Or, again, that the fairy tales belong to various epochs, during a long stretch of time, in the course of which those tribes, like any others, underwent marked modifications. But what is probably the best solution is that the dwarf races of the past, like those of the present, were of various types. That as the South African Bushmen, the dwarfs of the Congo region, and the Ainos of Japan, though all included among the dwarf races, are really different from each other in many respects, so the dwarf races of the past were not one but many. That then, as now, there were black, yellow and white dwarfs; dissimilar in their history and characteristics; but all alike in one important respect. This last explanation, although the two others deserve consideration, is the one that to the present writer seems the most important.

To state even a few of the inferences to be drawn from the acceptance of these explanations, is more than can be attempted here. It is enough to continue as far as possible to confine these remarks within the limits already observed; and to keep specially in view that race which is known to British history as that of the "Picts." What, then, is the traditional idea of the outward appearance of these people, apart from their stature?

Scott's "Rob Roy," as he is described in the Glasgow prison, is said to have greatly resembled the Picts, as they are remembered in Northumbrian tradition. And when his appearance is again referred to in a later chapter (ch. xxxii.), one point of this resemblance is brought out; where it is stated that his legs were "covered with a fell of thick, short, red hair, especially around his knees, which resembled in this respect, as well as from their sinewy appearance of extreme strength, the limbs of a red-coloured Highland bull."

It matters little whether the historical "Robert MacGregor or Campbell," really answered to Scott's various descriptions of him. *Rob Ruadh*, or "Red Rob," may no doubt have been fitly applied to many a native of the British Islands, descended from the race of the Picts.[1] But this excessive hairiness of skin was one of the most marked characteristics

---

[1] There is a Rob Roy's Town in Lanarkshire, celebrated as the scene of Wallace's capture, and even if the name is no older than Harry the Minstrel (who uses it), it indicates a "Rob Roy" ante-dating Sir Walter Scott's by a couple of centuries.

of the Pechts, and forms indeed one of the most distinct clues to their ethnological position.

Whatever the man was like himself, however, "Rob Roy's country" contains, among its other features, that "shoulder of Ben Venue" which we have seen a former Earl of Menteith is said to have assigned to the dwarfs, and which is remembered in local tradition as a great resort of theirs. And a spot specially known as their gathering-place is called the Coire-nan-Uruisgean, which is rendered "the Corri, or Den, of the Wild or *Shaggy* men."[1] Now the same word here held to represent a "shaggy" man is also a synonym for a "brownie,"[2] and when we regard such a specimen of that class as the particular "brownie" that was an attendant of the chief of the Grants, we find her (for this was a *ban-sithe*, or fairy-woman) known as "May *Mollach*," which signifies "hairy May"; it being asserted by tradition that this May was distinguished for the hairiness of her arms.[3] The adjective *mollach* signifies "hairy,"[4] and, among other uses, it is appropriately given, as a name, to many a shaggy little "Scotch terrier." But in that part of Armstrong's "Dictionary"

---

[1] Scott, who gives this definition ("Lady of the Lake" Note 2 q), says it is the *literal* one. This, however, is not the *literal* meaning of "Uruisgean." But it is enough to know that the people so named were believed to be wild, "shaggy" men.

[2] Armstrong's "Gaelic Dictionary," s.v. *Uruisg*.

[3] See Note 2 n to "The Lady of the Lake." This May Mollach is well known in the legendary history of the Grants. Scott again refers to her in his Introduction to "The Monastery," where he asserts that she "condescended to mingle in ordinary sports, and even to direct the Chief how to play at draughts." With this may be compared Thorpe's statement ("Northern Mythology," I., 145) that the Scandinavian dwarfs, who were also hairy, used to "play at tables." There is also a story in the Island of Skye of a "brownie" who watched over and instructed one of the players in a game of "tables." (*See* Dafoe's "Duncan Campbell," London, 1896, p. 106.) "Tables" seems to have been a comprehensive name for draughts, chess, and other games played on a chess-board; and these remarks recall the set of chessmen, carved out of walrus tusk, already referred to as having been found in the Hebrides in 1856, and of which eleven are in the Museum of the Society of Antiquaries of Scotland. "Chess-playing was one of the favourite amusements of the Irish chieftains," says O'Donovan ("Book of Rights," Dublin, 1847, p. lxi), and he gives illustrations of an Irish chess-man, which he states is exactly similar, "as well in style as in material," to the Hebridean specimens just mentioned.

[4] It may be seen again in the name given in former times to a section of the Clan Mac-Ra, "Clann ic Rath *Mholaich*," or "Hairy Mac Raas." The surname *Mulloch* also represents the same word.

where this adjective is spelt *maildhanch* and *mailghanch* (of which the pronunciation is still *mäl'yack*), its meaning is defined as "having large shaggy eyebrows." And this, it will be seen, is specially a characteristic not only of the traditional dwarfs, but of a race known to ethnology. But it is probable that the general meaning of "hirsute" is signified when the derivative noun *mailleachan* is used as an equivalent of *brownie* or *urwisg*;[1] and that a *mailleachan* was a "hairy one." Similarly, a special brownie, known as *Peallaidh an spilit*, or "Peallaidh of the waterfall," once well known "at those congresses" "in a certain district of the Highlands,"[2] may be Englished into "The Shaggy One of the waterfall." Thus, although *urwisg* does not literally mean "a shaggy man" (as Scott says), yet there is nothing wrong in saying that *Coir-nan-Urwisgean*, on Loch Katrine, was "the Den of the Wild or Shaggy Men"; because various terms and descriptions applying to those *urwisgean* show that they were actually "shaggy men."[3]

No one had a better opportunity of imbibing the traditional idea of a brownie than the late Mr. J. F. Campbell; whose birth and upbringing, combined with his great studies in later life, gave him every chance of learning the various Highland traditions regarding the appearance of those people. And when, during his stay in Lapland, he saw a certain Lapp "of the old school," he speaks of him thus:—
"He was an old fellow with long, tangled elf-locks and a scanty beard, dressed in a deerskin shirt full of holes, and exceedingly mangy, for the hair had been worn off in patches all over. He realized my idea of a seedy Brownie, a gruagach [another synonym] with long hair on his head; an old wrinkled face, and his body covered with hair."[4] Of course,

---
[1] Armstrong's "Gaelic Dictionary," s.v. *Mailleachan*.
[2] *Ibid.* s.v. *Urwisg*.
[3] Scott says ("Letters on Demonology," London, John Murray, 1830, p. 115) that Rob Roy once gained a victory by disguising a part of his men, by means of goat-skins, as "eurisks," and so terrifying their opponents. But if that Rob Roy, or any section of his followers, presented the appearance which Scott himself portrays, or if any remnant of the ancient "Pechts" survived in that neighbourhood, it does not seem that any disguise was necessary to give them the appearance of "wild, or shaggy men."
[4] "West Highland Tales," II., 366.

it is not to be understood that the *Lapp's* body was "covered with hair." But the deerskin shirt, worn with the hair outwards, was one of the things that helped out the "brownie" appearance of the man; for Mr. Campbell's traditional brownie had *his* body covered with hair, like the other "shaggy men" we have just been speaking of. Again, the traditional *brollachan* or *fuath* of Sutherland is described as "rough and hairy."[1] Mr. Campbell also points out that the *glashan* of the Isle of Man[2] was the same as those "shaggy men" of the Scotch Highlands. " He wore no clothes, and was hairy; and, according to Train's history, Phynodderee, which means something hairy, was frightened away by a gift of clothes,—exactly as the Skipness long-haired Gruagach was frightened away by the offer of a coat and a cap. The Manks brownie and the Argyllshire one each repeated a rhyme over the clothes; but the rhymes are not the same, though they amount to the same thing."[3] In a certain story of South-Western Scotland, a brownie is described as a naked, hairy man; and in a Scotch "chap-book" of the eighteenth century, an old woman is made to state that the brownies are "a' rough but the mouth," and that they "seek nae claes" (do not wish any clothes).[4] The dwarfs of Northumbrian tradition, whether spoken of by that name or as " Picts," are hairy; and, as just mentioned, the Isle of Man contains similar evidence. The same thing is recorded in Wales. In his "British Goblins," Mr. Wirt Sikes not only describes the *coblynau* as hairy of skin, but he cites the well-known account of a sixteenth-century race of "Red Fairies" who "lived in dens in the ground," and bore several other resemblances to the Picts of Scotland. These "Red Fairies" have

[1] "West Highland Tales," II., 189-192. For further references to the *fuath*, or *duine fuathasach*, see pp. 97-101 of the same volume. It may be added that Armstrong simply defines *brollachan* as "a ragged person." Similarly, McAlpine states that in the West Highlands *urwig* signifies "a savage, ugly-looking fellow." Both of these definitions point to the *real* and matter-of-fact aspect of the traditional *urwig* or *brollachan*.

[2] Gaelic *glashan*, from *glas*, grey. Cf. the Shetland allusion to the dwarfs as "the grey women-stealers."

[3] "West Highland Tales," Introduction, pp. liv, lv.

[4] With the above use of "rough," as also in relation to the *brollachan*, compare the statement in Defoe's "Duncan Campbell" (London, 1895, p. 139) that the brownie "appeared like a rough man."

also been recently cited by Mr. G. L. Gomme, in the course of an article which points out the survival of savage customs and savage people, within the British Islands, during recent centuries.[1] The "Red Fairies" inhabited a certain part of Merionethshire, where it is said that people inheriting some of their blood are still pointed out. They are remembered as a race of much-dreaded marauders, their depredations being carried on in the night time, "and scythes were fixed in the chimneys of the nearest houses, to prevent the nocturnal descent of these plundering ruffians." The writer whose words have just been quoted, contributed an account of these people to the *Scots Magazine* of 1823,[2] and he states in this connection, that "scythes were to be seen in the chimney of a neighbouring farm-house about thirty years ago, but they have been since removed." After referring to their various characteristics, the same writer goes on:—"It appears that the enormities of the Gwylliaid Cochion Mowddwy [the Red Fairies, or Banditti,[3] of Mowddwy] had arrived at such a pitch as to render necessary the interposition of the most prompt and vigorous measures. To this end, a commission was granted to John Wynne ab Meredith, of Gwedir, and Lewis Owen, one of the Barons of the Welsh Exchequer, and Vice-Chamberlain of North Wales. These gentlemen raised a body of men, and, on Christmas Eve, 1554, succeeded in securing, after considerable resistance, nearly a hundred of the robbers, on whom they inflicted chastisement the most summary and effectual, hanging them on the spot, and, as their commission authorized, without any previous trial."[4]

A similar race to these "fairies" of Merionethshire seems to be suggested by the "gubbings" or "gubbins" of Dartmoor. Those people are described by Fuller, in his "Worthies

---

[1] *The Archaeological Review*, Jan. 1890, pp. 433, 434.
[2] *See* Vol. 13, pp. 424-6 (*Magna Cambrica*).
[3] It is to be noted that this writer renders "Gwylliaid" by "Banditti," and never refers to them as "goblins" or "fairies," though this is the usual meaning given to the word. There is no good reason for objecting to the less usual translation, except that, while it denotes one recognised characteristic of the dwarfs, after they had been cut up into small confederacies, it loses sight of other notable features of such "banditti."
[4] The difference between these people and the intangible "fairies" created by the imagination (but originating in reality) is nowhere brought out more strongly than in this passage. A hanged fairy would be quite a novelty in poetry.

of England," published in 1662. Readers of Kingsley's "Westward Ho!" will remember "how Salvation Yeo slew the King of the Gubbings," and the description given at that place. Mr. R. D. Blackmore seems also to have had the same race in view in his "Maid of Sker"; although that novel is placed in the eighteenth century. "Cannibal Jack," or "Jack Wildman," the most civilized of those Devon savages, is made to state:—" I was one of a race of naked people, living in holes of the earth at a place we did not know the name of. I now know that it was Nympton in Devonshire." As to the origin of the term "gubbing," Fuller confesses himself ignorant.[1] But those Devonshire gubbings were, like the Red Fairies of Wales and the Picts of Scotland, underground people, or earth-dwellers. It does not seem to be stated anywhere that the "gubbings" were hairy of skin; but both in Devon and in Cornwall the underground people otherwise designated are so described.[2] Altogether the savage "gubbins" of Dartmoor, as described by Kingsley and others, seem to be practically the same people as the cave-dwelling "pixies" of Dartmoor, whose occasional raids into the town of Tavistock are still remembered in local folklore.

This nakedness of the brownie is referred to again and again in the folk-lore of Scotland. The general belief seems to be that when he was offered clothes in return for his

[1] In her "Borders of the Tamar and the Tavy" (London, 1879, Vol. I., Letter xix.), Mrs. Bray speaks of these "gubbins," referring to the account given by Camden as well as Fuller. Halliwell also cites "Milles' MS." As for the derivation of the word itself, it seems clearly to be connected with Welsh *coblyn*, English *goblin* and *god*, and Italian *gobbo*—pigmy. Compare also *gubbas* (*anti*, p. 134); and note the etymology quoted by Fuller (*op. cit.*) "that such who did 'inhabitare montes gibberosos' were called Gubbings."

[2] See Mrs. Bray's work just cited, Vol. I., Letter 2.: also a reference to the goblin or "bucka" as hairy, in Mr. Whitley Stokes' "Owssem an Byn," pp. 124, 125.

In Mr. Hunt's "Popular Romances of the West of England" (London, J. C. Hotten, 2nd edit., pp. 217, 218), there is a weird story of a wrestling-match by night, at a certain cairn near Penzance. The wrestlers were believed by the two onlookers to be supernatural beings:—"They were men of great size and strength, with savage faces, rendered more terrible by the masses of uncombed hair which hung about them, and the colours with which they had painted their cheeks." They had appeared to issue out of the rocks of the cairn. Although the term "great size," if it denotes stature, does not include these men among dwarfs, yet they are represented as *Picts*; and as "supernatural," hirsute cave-dwellers.

labour he left the place where he had been working, in high dudgeon. Other accounts indicate that he accepted the clothes without demur. But the indications that the "shaggy men" were naked men, are numerous. And when Mr. Campbell says that "the Highlanders distinguish between the water and land or *dressed* fairies,"[1] he clearly infers that one section of the little people was remarkable for the entire absence of dress. Indeed, it was this peculiarity that, as the various stories show, offended the delicacy of the womenfolk at those farms where "brownies" worked, and so led to the offer of clothing, by way of wages. And, of course, the reason why their special hairiness of skin is so well remembered is because their own shaggy coats formed all their clothing; and probably answered the purpose very well.

Outside the British Islands there are plenty of similar traditional accounts. The Scandinavian trolls, or dwarfs, of the Eddas were hairy; and so was the German dwarf. The latter has one name, that of *Bilwis*, said to be derived from a word denoting matted hair; and we are told that "the Bilwiz shoots like the elf, and has shaggy or matted hair."[2] And he, there can be little doubt, is the same as the "little forest-man." For the same authority[3] states that "little forest-men, who have long worked in a mill, have been scared away by the miller's men leaving clothes and shoes for them." And if these nude and hairy "little people" were not of the same race as the hirsute brownies of Scotland, they were remarkably like them in several striking characteristics. With them also may be compared the shaggy dwarfs remembered in Brittany under the name of *villanous*, who are doubtless the same as the long-bearded *barbao* of the same province. (*See* M. Sébillot's list of such names in the "Revue des Traditions Populaires," Feb. 1890, pp. 101-104.)

The German traditional idea of the mound-dwelling, metal-working dwarf people, is nowhere more perfectly given than in the etching which is here reproduced, and which is the work of a German engraver. It forms the base of a title-

---

[1] "West Highland Tales," II., 64. (For a general reference to the nudity of those drudges see Ritson's "Fairies," London, 1831, p. 46.)

[2] Thorpe's "Northern Mythology," I., 244.

[3] Thorpe: *op. cit.* I., 252.

page, executed about thirty years ago,[1] consecrated to the memory of the great Barbarossa, whose figure occupies the centre of the title-page, and whose achievements are otherwise symbolically indicated. It is understood to be a facsimile of the base of Barbarossa's statue. The little gnomes, then, underneath him, are clearly meant to represent his companions in the "berg" where he and they are popularly believed to be still living—whether that be the Thuringian Kyffhäuser, or the Untersberg, near Salzburg. And the hairiness of skin, so characteristic of the Scottish *brownie* or *pecht*, is equally marked in this case. The term "shaggy men" could be applied to them with very great appropriateness. And if the artist has not made them as destitute of clothing as the "brownies" and "forest-men" are said to have been, yet what they do wear only serves to remind one of the red-cap of the traditional Lincolnshire dwarfs, and others of the same class, and of the "apron" so often mentioned in connection with the dwarfish builders of England and Scotland. It is not to be supposed that this picture represents in every detail the dwarfs of German or other traditions, nor is it to be supposed that any single account gives an absolutely correct idea of the appearance of those primitive races, but this will be generally recognised as being, on the whole,[2] a wonderfully good representation of the dwarfs of German folk-lore.

But this characteristic of the dwarfs of Scottish tradition and of the "Picts" of history does not tend to show that such people were *identical* with the modern Lapps. Nor, indeed, is this to be looked for. A race which was in its prime two thousand years ago may have many points in common with one or another of the modern races (presumably its own

---

[1] In Edinburgh, for the firm of Messrs. Schenck and McFarlane, lithographers.
[2] There is at least one detail overlooked in this picture by the artist. And another detail, which he has introduced, has not been referred to in these pages, viz., the miner's lamp worn by the dwarfs. In Cornwall, the earliest miners are understood to have been those "little people," whose subterranean habits would undoubtedly render them early acquainted with the use of metals. And the miner's lamp may reasonably be regarded as an inheritance from the dwarf races. It is noteworthy that the typical miner's dress, in seventeenth-century England, appears to have been "canvas breeches, red waistcoats and red caps," a garb closely in agreement with some versions of the dwarf attire. (See Hone's "Ancient Mysteries, p. 259.)

THE DWARFS OF GERMAN FOLK LORE.

descendants, in some measure); but absolute identity of type can hardly be expected, if one considers the crossing, re-crossing, and in some cases almost the extermination of the various races of Europe during that period. At any rate, this marked hairiness of skin, attributed to the Pict, or Pecht, or dwarf, is not a Mongoloid characteristic. It is certainly not *Mongolian;* and although some divisions of the Mongoloid group—such as the Eskimos of Labrador—are described as wearing moustaches and beards, this fact, even if it be not exceptional, goes a very little way towards suggesting an actually hirsute ancestor. Had there been less doubt about the matter, one might have supposed that the hairy skin-garments of those Northern races had been erroneously assumed in the traditional tales to be the natural skin of their owners; and, indeed, the pictures of the modern Eskimos in their winter dress of skins with the hair outside, gives quite the appearance of a race of hairy little men. But the nudity of the historical Picts, and certain sections of the traditional dwarfs, or brownies, is beyond all doubt. To the Latin writers, as to the housewives of legendary history, this was equally an unmistakable and objectionable fact.

There is, however, an existing race that offers itself as akin to those traditional dwarfs in this respect, as well as in some others; although the modern Lapps, in several of their characteristics, also suggest that a not insignificant line of their ancestry is traceable to the same origin. The race referred to is that of the "hairy Kuriles," or Ainos of Japan; included by ethnologists among the modern dwarf races.

"Twelve hundred years ago," says Mr. E. B. Tylor, "a Chinese historian stated that 'on the eastern frontiers of the land of Japan there is a barrier of great mountains, beyond which is the land of the Hairy Men.' These were the Aino, so named from the word in their own language signifying 'man.' Over most of the country of these rude and helpless indigenes the Japanese have long since spread, only a dwindling remnant of them still inhabiting the island of Yezo. Since the early days when a couple of them were sent as curiosities to the Emperor of China, their uncouth looks and habits have made them objects of interest to more civilized nations."[1]

[1] Introduction to "Aino Folk Tales," by Basil Hall Chamberlain, Professor

Of their own traditions, another writer states:—" To them the past is dead, yet, like other conquered and despised races, they cling to the idea that in some far-off age they were a great nation. They have no traditions of internecine strife, and the art of war seems to have been lost long ago. I asked Benri [a chief] about this matter, and he says that formerly Ainos fought with spears and knives, as well as with bows and arrows, but that Yoshitsuné, their hero god, forbade war for ever, and since then the two-edged spear, with a shaft nine feet long, has only been used in hunting bears."[1] Yoshitsuné, it may be explained, is stated (*op. cit. infra*, II. 94, *note*) to have been the brother of a Japanese general of the twelfth century, famous for his victories over "barbarians." This tradition, therefore, if accepted without reserve, would place the conquest of the Ainos by the Japanese, with the consequent disarming of the former, somewhere about the twelfth century. And the scene of this struggle may be placed south and west of their present home. "The inference from records and local names, worked out with great care by Professor Chamberlain, is 'that the Ainos were truly the predecessors of the Japanese all over the Archipelago. The dawn of history shows them to us living far to the south and west of their present haunts; and ever since then, century by century, we see them retreating eastwards and northwards, as steadily as the American Indian has retreated westwards under the pressure of the colonists from Europe.'"[2]

"As is well known, the hairiness of the Ainos marks them sharply off from the smooth-faced Japanese. No one can look at photographs of Ainos without admitting that the often-repeated comparison of them to bearded Russian peasants is much to the purpose. The likeness is much strengthened by the bold quasi-European features of the Aino contrasting extremely with the Japanese type of face."[3] "The expression of the face and the manner of showing courtesy are European rather than Asiatic," says Miss Bird, who has lived

of Philology at the Tōkyō University. [Privately printed for the Folk-Lore Society, 1888.)

[1] "Unbeaten Tracks in Japan," by Miss Isabella L. Bird. London, 1880, II., p. 103.
[2] Introduction to "Aino Folk Tales," vi.-vii.
[3] *Ibid.*, v.

among these people; and she again remarks, on a later page, "I am more and more convinced that the expression of their faces is European."[1]

"The men are about the middle height,[2] broad-chested, broad-shouldered, 'thick-set,' very strongly built, the arms and legs short thick, and muscular, the hands and feet large. The bodies, and specially the limbs, of many are covered with short bristly hair. I have seen two boys whose backs are covered with fur as fine and soft as that of a cat." "The 'ferocious savagery' of the appearance of the men is produced by a profusion of thick, soft, black hair, divided in the middle, and falling in heavy masses nearly to the shoulders. Out of doors it is kept from falling over the face by a fillet round the brow. The beards are equally profuse, quite magnificent, and generally wavy, and in the case of the old men they give a truly patriarchal and venerable aspect, in spite of the yellow tinge produced by smoke and want of cleanliness." "The beard, moustache, and eyebrows are very thick and full." "At a deep river called the Nopkobets," says the same writer, "we were ferried by an Aino completely covered with hair, which on his shoulders was wavy like that of a retriever, and rendered clothing quite needless either for covering or warmth. A wavy, black beard rippled nearly to his waist over his furry chest, and, with his black locks hanging in masses over his shoulders, he would have looked a thorough savage had it not been for the exceeding sweetness of his smile and eyes. The Volcano Bay Ainos are far more hairy than the mountain Ainos." Again—"These Lebungé Ainos differ considerably from those of the eastern villages, and I have again to notice the decided sound or *chick* of the *ts* at the beginning of many words. Their skins are as swarthy as those of Bedaween, their foreheads comparatively low [the Aino forehead being in general remarkably high], their eyes far more deeply set, their stature lower, their hair yet more abundant, the look of wistful melancholy more marked, and two, who were unclothed for hard work in fashioning a canoe, were almost entirely covered with short, black hair, specially thick on the shoulders and back, and so

---

[1] "Unbeaten Tracks in Japan," II., p. 107. (Also p. 75.)
[2] The writer here refers to a less pure type of Aino.

completely concealing the skin as to reconcile one to the lack of clothing I noticed an enormous breadth of chest, and a great development of the muscles of the arms and legs. All these Ainos shave their hair off for two inches above their brows, only allowing it there to attain the length of an inch." "Their voices were the lowest and most musical that I have heard, incongruous sounds to proceed from such hairy,

AN AINO PATRIARCH.

powerful-looking men. . . . These, like other Ainos, utter a short, screeching sound when they are not pleased, and then one recognizes the savage.'[1]

The picture of "An Aino Patriarch," which is here reproduced from Miss Bird's book,[2] does not enable one to fully

[1] See "Unbeaten Tracks in Japan," II., q. 75-6, 106, 118, 136-7, and 143-4.
[2] For the use of this block I am indebted to Mr. John Murray, Albemarle Street.

realize the purest type of Aino; partly owing to the fact that the figure is clothed, and partly because this man appears to have belonged to one of the more modified sections of the race. However, as he is, he is not a very bad representative of the bearded dwarf, with disproportionately large head, so familiar in tradition; and that he is one of the race of "shaggy men," we know without fuller evidence. His beard does not fall down to his waist, like that of his kinsman who figures as a ferryman in the foregoing quotation; but the heavy moustache and beard, and the shaggy eyebrows, strongly characterize this living race as well as the legendary dwarfs. The latter are again and again referred to as "little old[1] men, with long beards"; and, indeed, in one of Grimm's tales ("Snow-White and Rosy-Red"), a dwarf has a beard so long that it gets caught in the trunk of a tree that has been felled. The artist who drew the picture of Barbarossa's dwarfs has not forgotten this marked traditional feature.[2] Such dwarfs are all remembered as possessed of supernatural powers, enchanters, magicians, etc.; and, conversely, the magicians (Gaelic *druidhean*) of early Britain are famous for their flowing beards.

An earlier Aino than those pictured by Miss Bird is that which Baron Nordenskiöld gives in his "Voyage of the Vega." With regard to it he says:—"The drawing is taken from a Japanese work, whose title, when translated, runs thus—'A

---

[1] This adjective can be otherwise accounted for.

[2] One might multiply special instances without end. But it is appropriate to notice that the "Arabian Nights" tales are, in this respect, in keeping with those of the West. For example, Schaibar, the brother of the fairy Peri-Banou, is a powerful dwarf, possessing a tremendous beard and moustache (his strength, the smallness of his stature, and his beard are all vastly exaggerated, but they are all distinguishing features). And again, in the Third Voyage of Sindbad, his vessel approaches an island of which he says:—"The captain told us that this island was inhabited by hairy savages, who would come to attack us; and although they were only dwarfs, we must not attempt to make any resistance; for, as their number was inconceivable, if we should happen to kill one, they would pour upon us like locusts, and destroy us. No sooner had he said this than we saw coming towards us an innumerable multitude of hideous savages, entirely covered with red hair, and about two feet high. They threw themselves into the sea, and swam to the ship, which they soon completely encompassed. They spoke to us as they approached, but we could not understand their language. They began to climb the sides and ropes of the vessel with so much swiftness and agility, that their feet scarcely seemed to touch them, and soon reached the deck."

Journey to the North Part of Japan (Yezo), 1804.'" In this picture, which is here annexed, there are several notable features. Not only has this Aino of 1804 the short, thick-set figure, heavy beard, and "bull-necked" appearance of the traditional dwarf, but he is represented as driving a reindeer. Now, this seems at once to connect the Aino with the Samoyed and the Lapp. For, although the reindeer is hunted by the Eskimos of North America, these people have never domesticated it. Moreover, the Aino is standing on runners, which appear to be very similar to the "skies" of the Lapps. Both of these details are distinctive of the Aino and the Lapp (for although the "skies" are used to the south of Finmark, they are peculiarly associated with the Lapps,

AINO OF 1804.

who excel all other Norwegians in this accomplishment). "The deer-hide moccasins which they wear for winter hunting"[1] form another link of custom uniting the Aino to the Lapp and the Eskimo. So also does the harpoon and line which the Ainos use, or used, in seal-hunting, as is evidenced by two of Professor Chamberlain's tales.[2] Thus, although the Aino differs very much, in some respects, from the Eskimo type of man, he cannot be regarded as wholly different from him.[3] As regards stature, the two are

[1] "Unbeaten Tracks in Japan," II., 143.
[2] xxvii. and xxxiii. The harpoon tip is said, in one tale, to have been "made half of iron and half of bone."
[3] Miss Bird met with some Ainos of whom she says (II., 37):—"I thought

much alike; and several usages have just been cited that
distinctly unite the two. If one might discriminate, it might
be said that the relationship extends westward from the
Kurile Islands, rather than eastward into North America.
That the Aino should remind travellers so strongly of certain
European types, is very suggestive of a line of ancestry
which is shared by Europeans. Indeed, those hirsute qualities which distinguish the Aino exist, though in much more
modified forms (even in the instance of Russian peasants)
among the people of Europe; sufficiently to mark off the
average European from the races of other continents. That
one line of European ancestry should lead back to a race
strongly resembling the modern Ainos is therefore a belief
that the outward appearance of the modern European rather
tends to strengthen.

In speculating upon the appearance of the European
"cave-man" of the past, a writer in the "Cornhill"[1] (? Mr.
Grant Allen) states as his opinion that "at any rate, he was
distinctly hairy, like the Ainos, or aborigines of Japan, in
our own day, of whom Miss Isabella Bird has drawn so start-
ling and sensational a picture." Again, after remarking that
those cave-men "seem to have been in most essential particulars almost as advanced as the modern Eskimo, with whom
Professor Dawkins conjecturally identifies them," Mr. Grant
Allen goes on to say[2]—"But if Professor Dawkins means us
to understand that the cave-men were physically developed
to the same extent as the Eskimo, it is necessary to accept
his conclusion with great caution. It does not follow because
the Eskimo are the nearest modern parallels of the cave-men,
that the cave-men therefore resembled them closely in appearance. Several of the sketches of cave-men, cut by themselves
on horn and bone, certainly show (it seems to me) that they
were covered with hair over the whole body: and the hunter
in the antler from the Duruthy cave has a long pointed beard
and high crest of hair on the poll utterly unlike the Eskimo
type." And although Mr. Allen admits, on a later page, that

that they approached more nearly to the Eskimo type than to any other." This,
of course, was exceptional; but the remark is noteworthy.

[1] March, 1885. "A Very Old Master."
[2] *Fortnightly Review*, September, 1882, p. 312.

"it is possible enough that the cave-man was the direct ancestor of the Eskimo," yet he qualifies this admission by observing that "it does not at all follow that in physical appearance the earlier cave-men were the equals of the Eskimo, or, indeed, that the Eskimo are any more nearly related to them than ourselves."[1]

Of course, it is understood by the writer of these lines that the remarks upon "cave-men" just quoted, were made in the belief that all those cave-men lived at a period immensely removed from the present time. But the classification of man's history into so many "periods" and "ages" is admittedly vague. And the recognition of a visible relationship between certain races of living men, and those others who are called "pre-historic," is practically a recognition of the possibility that the not very remote ancestors of such races may be remembered with comparative clearness in the popular memory of those who are mainly descended from races of a higher type.

That this is really the case is what all the evidence adduced in these pages tends to show. And, indeed, the actual picture of a living Aino of about ninety years ago, reproduced above, is by no means remarkably different from the traditional figure given below, which represents the magician, or "good fairy," as he appears in the popular memory, when arriving from the far North, on Yule Eve, laden with gifts for his vassals. The annexed woodcut gives the idea of "Santa Claus," as he figures in the American fancy, and that, as the title given to him indicates, is really the German idea. The German idea, then, of this good magician is that he is a thick-set, bearded, little man, whose heavy furs denote that his home lies in the North, and whose reindeer team, harnessed to the sledge in which he has travelled, indicates that, like the Lapp and the Aino, he not only lives in a country where reindeer abound, but he has learned to tame them and make them serve his purposes. In this traditional figure one seems to see the type of a race that was even more like

---

[1] Opinions still more antagonistic to those of Professor Dawkins were expressed by Professor Flower, in commenting upon a paper read by Dr. John Rae at the Anthropological Institute, July 7th, 1886, wherein Dr. Rae had referred to this subject.

the Aino than the Lapp, or the Eskimo, although closely connected in various ways with all of these. Neither this figure, nor those of Barbarossa's dwarfs, need be regarded as absolutely correct; but in both we see that the popular

A "GOOD FAIRY" OF TRADITION.

memory is wonderfully faithful to what appears to be the actual truth.

The existence in Europe of such a race, neither Lapp nor Aino, though akin to both, seems indicated by as recent a geographer as Olaus Magnus. In his map of Northern Europe,[1] the extreme north of Norway is neither "Lappia" nor "Finmarchia" (although both of these are shown), but a country which borders them on the north, and which he calls "Scricfinnia." This name appears to have been otherwise spelt "Scritfinnia" or "Scridfinnia," and one writer states that its people, the "Scridfinni," "derived their name from the word *skrida*, which in the Danish and Swedish languages means to slide."[2] This refers to the snow-skates, or "skies," which they are described as using, but as Olaus Magnus pictures the people of "Lappia" as also using "skies," it does not seem that that usage was distinctive of the "Scridfinni." But what appears to be of much more importance than this etymological point is the fact that the gloss which Olaus Magnus places opposite "Scricfinnia" is to this effect :—"*Hic habitant Pygmei Vulgo Screlinger dicti.*" The earliest cited mention of the *Screlinger*, or *Skrælings*, occurs in the accounts of the Norse visits to North America, at the end of the tenth century; and the people thus referred to are generally identified with the Esquimaux. "The Northmen were used to call the Esquimaux Skrælinga, a term of contempt, meaning, says Crantz, 'chips, parings, *i.e.*, dwarfs.'" And the North American Skrælings of the tenth century, who are described as paddling about in skin-canoes, "skimming the surface of the water in their swift flight," are quite obviously either of the same race as the modern Eskimos, or else closely allied to them.[3] In the course of eight or nine centuries, the "Skrælings" may have become modified to some extent; and, indeed, modern travellers are wonderfully unanimous in remarking upon the effect that nineteenth-century intermixture has had upon Asiatic and Greenland Eskimos, and upon the Ainos. But whatever the exact appearance of the tenth-century "Skræling," the map of Olaus Magnus denotes that, five or six centuries later, the

---

[1] A reprint of which is appended to Mr. Elton's "Origins" (Plate IV).
[2] Brooke's "Travels in Lapland," London, 1827, p. 5.
[3] For these references see Appendix B and the "Antiquitates Americanæ" (Copenhagen, 1837), conveniently condensed in W. C. Bryant and S. H. Gay's "History of the United States," Chap. III.
[4] Such as Nordenskiöld, Cevensenn, Joest, &c.

extreme north of Norway was inhabited by a race of
"Skrælings"; and that these people were the same as the
"pygmies" of classical writers. It has already been pointed
out¹ that the Greenland "Skrælings" were also spoken of
as "goblins," and this again shows that that American type,
whether most akin to the modern Eskimo or to the Aino,
was not a *new* type to those European explorers,—whose
legendary history was already teeming with stories of en-
counters with "goblins."²

Whatever may have been the ethnical position of the tenth-
century "Skræling" of America, this sixteenth-century
map of North Europe certainly signifies that the "pigmies,"
"Screlinga," or "Scric-Finns" of the extreme north of Scandinavia were neither "Finns" nor "Lapps," but a race that
ultimately yielded place to these. There are similar indications
in the extreme north of Asia. The Chukches of Siberia undoubtedly connect the Lapp in the west with the Eskimo in
the east. But these Chukches have traditions of a race
called *Onkilon*, i.e., "sea-folk," whom the Chukches, moving
northward, displaced or annihilated. "Tradition relates that
upwards of two hundred years ago these Onkilon occupied
the whole of the Chukch coast, from Cape Chelagskoj to
Behring's Straits; and indeed we still find along the whole
of this stretch remains of their earth-huts, which must have
been very unlike the present dwellings of the Chukches;
they have the form of small mounds, are half sunk in the
ground and closed above with whale ribs, which are covered
with a thick layer of earth." Baron Nordenskiöld, who is
here quoting Wrangel's "Reise" (1835), gives himself a
representation of one of those Onkilon earth-dwellings, seen
by him at Cape North.³ In these now-extinct "Onkilon,"
then, we have a race of people who, like the Finns and sea-
trows of Shetland, were famed as "sea-folk," and who at the
same time were underground-people or mound-dwellers.

¹ *Ante*, p. 144, note.
² Further statements upon this point will be found in Appendix B.
³ "Voyage of the Vega," I. 443.

CHAPTER XVII.

THERE is yet another characteristic of the modern Aino which suggests the dwarf of the British Isles. "Mention must also be made of an anatomical peculiarity of the Aino skeleton, consisting of a remarkable flattening of the arm- and leg-bones."[1] This peculiarity, which is known scientifically as "platycnemism," forms a part of Herr von Siebold's "Ethnologische Studien uber die Aino, auf der Insel Yesso."[2] Much may be learned with regard to platycnemism in a paper "On the Discovery of Platycnemic Men in Denbighshire,"[3] by Professors Busk and Boyd Dawkins; and the subject of platycnemism generally has been very fully discussed in Dr. L. Manouvrier's "Mémoire sur la Platycnémie."[4] The question is full of interest; but what we are here concerned with is the fact that, characterising the dwarfish, hairy Ainos of the nineteenth century, this flattening of the leg-bones is also associated with the dwarfs of Britain. Those cave-dwelling, "platycnemic men" of Denbighshire, though not actually dwarfs, were of no greater height on an average than five feet, or a trifle over. Again, the skeletons found in the underground dwellings of Wiltshire, which have been so closely studied by General Pitt-Rivers, exhibit marked platycnemism in several instances, and of these the average height was 5 ft. 1·3 (among eleven males), and (among three females) 4 ft. 10.[5] In Wigtownshire, also, the bones of certain cavemen have yielded at least one tibia which has been pronounced to be "highly platycnemic." The locality where

[1] This statement, made by Professor Tylor in his Introduction to the "Aino Folk-Tales," is based upon the accounts of others; for a reference to one of which (Von Siebold's) I am indebted to Mr. Tylor.
[2] Berlin, 1881.
[3] Jour. Ethnol. Soc. of London, Jan. 1871.
[4] Paris, 1888.
[5] See General Pitt-Rivers' "Excavations in Cranborne Chase," 1887. (Privately Printed.) II., 206-7.

these remains were found has been spoken of on a previous page,[1] as a locality famed as the last refuge of the "Pechts," and, at the same time, as a home of the "fairies." These are a few special instances; but if once we recognize the probability that platycnemism was specially a characteristic of "the little people," then there will be small difficulty in accepting as true the forecast with which Mr. Boyd Dawkins concludes his remarks in the paper above mentioned:—" I have not the slightest doubt that platycnemism will be recognized in remains from chambered tombs in many parts of Britain, and that eventually the men found in Denbighshire will be proved to belong to a race that spread over Britain and Ireland, and a large area on the Continent."

The effect of this flattened tibia or leg-bone is to give to the "platycnemic man" an unusual degree of agility. Thus one reads that the Ainos who drew Miss Bird's *kuruma* raced "for a considerable distance" with some mounted Japanese, drawing the *kuruma*, of course, at the same time. Similarly, the mountain-ponies of the Picts "could hardly excel the speed of the troops on foot."[2] The traditional accounts of the "Fians" have much to say of their marvellous swiftness of foot. The same thing is noted of the Dartmoor *gubbins* of the sixteenth century: "Such their fleetness, they will outrun many horses."[3] And the earth-dwelling "Red Fairies" of Merionethshire "were also remarkable for their swiftness and agility."[4] There is a Scotch story of a brownie who successfully "herded" a hare; and the lightness of foot of the fairy in general is proverbial. From all these references, then, there is every reason for believing that the little people were "platycnemic men."

This identification of the traditional dwarfs with the Ainos on the one hand and the Eskimos on the other, amounts to an assumption that the dwarfs were not only hirsute like the first of these, and mound-dwellers like the second, but also that, like the extinct *Onkilon* of Siberia, they were in a distinct sense "sea-folk." In other words, that, while showing

[1] Page 99. See specially pp. 87-8 of the volume quoted (1885-86) of the Proc. of the Soc. of Antiq. of Scotland.
[2] Elton's "Origins," p. 169; quoted from Dion Cassius.
[3] Fuller, as quoted by Kingsley.
[4] *Scots Magazine*, 1823, Vol. 13, pp. 424-6.

a strong *affinity* with the two modern types chiefly referred to in these pages, they were nevertheless not *identical* with either. That they were the ancestors of both seems probable, bequeathing to each division some of the qualities and customs of the original stock; which might be described as Aino-Eskimo.

So far as tradition goes, there is every indication that the hairy dwarf was of a sea-faring race. The Gaelic *ur-uisg* was rightly called a "wild or *shaggy* man" by Sir Walter Scott, but literally he was a *water-man*"; which term has many equivalents, such as wasser-man, mer-man, and others. The Guernsey "King of the *Aurrisiers*," previously mentioned,[1] may also denote this identification of the *sea-water* with the "shaggy man"; unless the name *aurrisiers* bears a less obvious meaning than it appears to do. But no better illustration of this union can be found than the historical Picts. Tradition has told us of their shaggy skins, and the "small boats" which they used. And both of these are indicated by the sixth-century Gildas, in his account of the inroads of the Picts and Scots, after the withdrawal of the Romans, where he says:—" Itaque illis ad sua revertentibus, emergunt certatim de curicis, quibus sunt trans Cichicam[2] vallem vecti, quasi in alto Titane incalescenteque caumate de arctissimis foraminum cavernulis fusci vermiculorum cunei, tetri Scotorum Pictorumque greges, moribus ex parte dissidentes, sed una eademque sanguinis fundendi aviditate concordes, furciferosque magis vultus pilis, quam corporum pudenda, pudendisque proxima, vestibus tegentes."[3]

There is complete agreement among the commentators of Gildas that the word "curicis" is a Latinized form of the Celtic *curach*, a skin-boat. And the expression "de arctissimis foraminum cavernulis" is singularly confirmative of the

---

[1] Page 16.
[2] This is variously spelt "Aticam," "Scyticam," and "Tihicam" (Petrie's *Monumenta Historica Britannica*); and the solutions are as various as the spellings. If by "Tihican vallem" is denoted the valley of the River Teith, this variant appears preferable to any; and the district referred to would be the whole of the Teith or Forth basin, which at that period was probably a mixture of land and water,—a northern Bedford Level, or fen-country.
[3] Gildas' "De Excidio Britanniæ," Stevenson's edition, London, 1838, pp. 24-25.

assumption that the variety of skin-boat denoted was the narrow kayak with its small round man-hole, and covered "hold," out of which the invading Pict "eagerly emerged" in his haste to attack the Romanized and civilised people in the neighbourhood of the Wall. The reference to their appearance generally is, moreover, very much like the terms used by the Norse writers in speaking of the tenth-century "Skrælinga."

That the historical Picts were as "amphibious" as any other "sea-folk" of the kind here discussed, is further testified by such a statement as this:—"They passed their days in the water, swimming in the northern estuaries, or wading with the stream as high as the waist. Dion Cassius adds, with his characteristic vivacity, that they would hide in the 'mud for days together, with nothing but their heads out of the water."[1] Although the custom of hiding from an enemy in the fashion just described was practised quite recently by the "bog-trotters" in Ireland (see *Rahrby*, Note 2 R), it is doubtful how far these statements ought to be accepted literally. But at least they point to the Picts as a race as much at home on sea as on land; and the reference to their "wading" in the water waist-high is again suggestive of the traditional mer-man or Triton, and the actual Eskimo (as he appears at a distance).

Thus, although the dwarfs of Shetland tradition are separately remembered as "sea-trows" and "hill-trows" (otherwise "hill-people," or "hógfolk"), it seems quite evident that these two names simply refer to two different aspects of one race. The memory of them, in connection with their homes in chambered mounds ("hows," "hóga," or "pechts' houses"), has gradually become dissociated from the memory of them in their character of sea-rovers, when in their swift "sea-skins" they darted after and easily overtook the heavy wooden boats used by the rival race. Nevertheless, although popular tradition, in thus remembering them, has almost transformed them into an actually amphibious race, it yet asserts that these seafaring "Finns" "are reckoned among the Trows."

* * * * * *

[1] Rhys's "Origins," p. 169. The first sentence is from Herodian.

Such are some of the deductions to be drawn from a comparison of traditional accounts with those of history, taken in connection with the ethnical features and the customs of certain races of people. There are many more inferences which could be made, but these may reasonably be deferred until the true value of tradition has been tested. The way in which this can be done has been pointed out in the foregoing pages. Should tradition prove itself reliable as a guide to the dwellings of "the little people," then *all* its statements regarding them will merit the closest consideration.

APPENDIX A.

THE BRUGH OF THE BOYNE, NEW GRANGE.

The descriptions of the New Grange mound given by Llhwyd and Molyneux are of much importance, since they both belong to about the beginning of the eighteenth century; and as they are not very accessible to the general reader they may suitably be quoted here. The two writers do not altogether agree in their account of the appearance of the chamber, and their theories as to its origin are certainly different; but whatever may be the value of the latter, there can be no doubt that descriptions which were made at a time when the interior of this mound was fresher by two centuries than it now is have a value that is lacking in the descriptions of modern writers, however accurate. The following is

"*An Account of a large Cave nigh Drogheda, by Mr. Edward Llhwyd.*"[1]

"The most remarkable curiosity we saw by the way, was a stately mount at a place called *New Grange* near *Drogheda;* having a number of huge stones pitch'd on end round about it, and a single one on the top. The gentleman of the village (one Mr. *Charles Campbel*) observing that under the green turf this mount was wholly composed of stones, and having occasion for some, employ'd his servants to carry off a considerable parcel of them; till they came at last to a very broad flat stone, rudely carv'd, and placed edgewise at the bottom of the mount. This they discovered to be

---

[1] This paper forms the last of "A Collection of such Papers as were communicated to the *Royal Society*, Referring to some *Curiosities* in Ireland. *Dublin:* Printed by and for George Grierson, at the Two Bibles in Essex-Street, M,DCC,XXVI." (The "Collection" forms Part II. of "A Natural History of Ireland," issued from the same press.)

the door of the cave,[1] which had a long entry leading into it. At the first entering, we were forced to creep; but still as we went on, the pillars on each side of us were higher and higher; and coming into the cave, we found it about twenty foot high. In this cave, on each hand of us, was a cell or apartment, and another went on straight forward opposite to the entry. In those on each hand was a very broad, shallow bason of stone, situated at the edge. The bason in the right hand apartment stood in another; that on the left hand was single; and in the apartment straight forward there was none at all. We observed that water dropt into the right hand bason, tho' it had rain'd but little in many days; and suspected that the lower bason was intended to preserve the superfluous liquor of the upper, (whether this water were sacred, or whether it was for blood in sacrifice) that none might come to the ground. The great pillars round this cave, supporting the mount, were not at all hewn or wrought; but were such rude stones as those of *Abury* in *Wiltshire*, and rather more rude than those of *Stonehenge*: but those about the basons, and some elsewhere, had such barbarous sculpture (*viz.*, spiral like a snake, but without distinction of head and tail) as the forementioned stone at the entry of the cave. There was no flagging nor floor to this entry nor cave; but any sort of loose stones everywhere under feet. They found several bones in the cave, and part of a stag's (or else elk's) head, and some other things, which I omit, because the labourers differed in their account of them. A gold coin of the emperor *Valentinian*, being found near the top of this mount, might bespeak it *Roman*; but that the rude carving at the entry and in the cave seems to denote it a barbarous monument. So, the coin proving it ancienter than any invasion of the *Ostmen* (sic) or *Danes*, and the carving and rude sculpture, barbarous; it should follow, that it was some place of sacrifice or burial of the ancient *Irish*."

From the account given by Dr. Thomas Molyneux,[2] the following extracts may be taken:—

"'Tis situated in the county of *Meath* and barony of *Slaine*, within four miles of the town of *Drogheda;* from its largeness and make, from the time and labour it must needs have cost to erect so great a pile, we may easily gather 'twas raised in honour of some

---

[1] Either this describes a slab which was subsequently destroyed or carried away, or it relates to the carved slab fixed in the ground below the doorway (as portrayed by Mr. Wakeman, at p. 121, ante).

[2] In the volume already referred to as containing Lhwyd's description, and other papers.

mighty prince, or person of the greatest power and dignity in his time. I have not heard of any thing of this kind that equals it in *Ireland*: 'tis a thousand foot in the circumference at the bottom, and round the flat surface at the top measures three hundred foot, it rises in the perpendicular about a hundred and fifty foot; and is seated so advantagiously upon a rising ground, that it is seen from all parts round at a vast distance, and from its top yields a delightful prospect of all the adjacent country.

Round the bottom of the mount, at some distance from it, are raised in a circular order, huge unwrought stones, rudely expressing pyramids, fixt with their basis in the ground, now at unequal distances, because some I suppose have been removed in length of time, and others faln down; neither do they answer one another in height, some being eleven, others not four foot high; . . . .

The mount it self is composed of small round paving stones, heapt together so as to form a pyramid, within whose center lies a cave that's somewhat round in figure: to this you can only pass through a narrow hole placed on the north[1] side of the mount, so strait, it does allow an entrance but to one man, and that when on his hands and feet: it seems they industriously contrived this hole should lye concealed, for 'twas but lately discovered, and that by accident in removing part of the stones to make a pavement in the neighbourhood.

This strait entrance leads into a narrow gallery of 80 foot in length, 3 foot wide, gradually rising in height, still the further it advances from the narrow passage where you enter, there 'tis about 4 foot high, and from thence rises slowly till it is 10 foot in height: the differing heights in this gallery at several distances from the first entrance, must be occasioned by the passage suiting its figure to the outward conical shape of the mount, which obliged the contriver to make the gallery lower as it was nearer the outside of the pyramid, but the farther it advanced from thence allowed him still to raise its height more, and most of all about the middle of the mount.[2] The walls or sides of this strait gallery are made of large flag stones set broad-ways with their edges close to one another, not hewn or shaped by any tool, but rude and natural, as when they were at first dug from the quarry; they differ in their sizes

---

[1] A slip for "south."
[2] The writer has evidently overlooked his previously expressed belief that the whole "mount" was artificial; or else he has assumed that the builders *first* raised a solid "pyramid" of stones, and then burrowed into it; which is obviously absurd.

as the several heights of the gallery require, the top of which is covered over with the same flag stones laid along; some of those in the covering measure full nineteen foot in length.

The furthest end of this long narrow passage lets you into the dark hollow cave, of an irregular figure, nineteen or twenty foot high, and in the middle about ten foot broad. As you enter the vault, on each hand you have a hollow cell or nich, taken out of the sides of the cave, and a third straight before you; these three cells each are about five foot every way, and ten in height: the walls round the circumference of the cave, and of these side apartments are composed like those of the long gallery, of huge, mighty flag stones set end-ways in the ground, of seven or eight foot high; these upright stones support other broad stones that lay along or horizontally, jetting their ends beyond the upright stones; and over these again are placed another order of flat stones in the same level posture, advancing still their edges towards the center of the cave, further than those they rest upon, and so one course above another approaching nearer towards the middle, form all together a rude kind of arch, by way of roof, over the vault below; this arch is closed at top by one large stone that covers the center, and keeps all fast and compact together: for through the whole work appears no sign of morter, clay, or other cement, to join or make its parts lye firm and close, but where a crevise happens, or an interstice, they are filled up with thin flat stones, split and wedged in, on purpose with that design.

The bottom of the cave and entry is a rude sort of pavement, made of the same stones of which the mount is composed, not beaten or joined together, but loosely cast upon the ground only to cover it. Along the middle of the cave, a slender quarrey-stone, five or six foot long, lies on the floor, shaped like a pyramid, that once, as I imagine, stood upright, perhaps a central stone to those placed round the outside of the mount; but now 'tis fallen down.
. . . . .

When first the cave was opened, the bones of two dead bodies entire, not burnt, were found upon the floor. . . . .

In each of the three cells was placed upon the ground a broad and shallow cistern, somewhat round, but rudely formed out of a kind of free-stone; they all were rounded a little at the bottom so as to be convex, and at the top were slightly hollowed, but their cavities contained but little; some of their brims or edges were sinuated or scolopt, the diameter of these cisterns was more than two foot wide, and in their height they measured about eighteen inches from the floor.

The cell that lay upon the right hand was larger, and seemed more regular and finish'd than the rest; for rude as it was, it shewed the workman had spent more of his wild art and pains upon it, than the other two: the cistern it contained was better shaped, and in the middle of it was placed another smaller cistern, better wrought, and of a more curious make; and still, for greater ornament, the stone that lay along as lintal, o'er the entrance of this cell, was cut with many spiral, circular, and waved lines, that with their rude and shallow traces, covered the surface of the stone. This barbarous kind of carving I observed in many other places of this cave, promiscuously disposed of here and there, without the least rule or order; but it was express no where with so much industry and profuseness, as on the stones belonging to this cell: yet tho' they were so lavish of their art, not the least footsteps of writing, or any thing like characters were found in the whole work. . . . .

* * * * *

But the true genuine figure of the cave, and the description of the niches in its sides, and the long entry leading to it, will be far better understood by a plan which Mr. *Samuel Molyneux*, a young gentleman of the college of *Dublin*, delineated with care and accuracy, upon the place, last summer.[1]

A is the entrance, from *A* to *B* the long narrow gallery or passage, eighty foot in length, leading to the cave *C*. *D D D D D* the great flag-stones that make the sides or wall both of the cave and entrance. *E E E* the three cells or apartments let into the sides of the cave, for the convenient reception of the three altars or shallow cisterns, *F F F*. *G* a second altar, raised upon the lower altar in the right hand cell. *H* a pyramid stone now fallen, but formerly set up erect in the middle of the cave. The situation of the cave, as to its length, stands north and south, its entrance lies directly south; but whether this position may be observed in laying out the caves, and passages that lead to them, in other *Danish*

[1] This tract was published in 1725. The "young gentleman's" illustrations have been re-produced in the present volume, in the plates facing pp. 124 and 126.

[2] Dr. Molyneux assumes throughout that such "mounts" were erected by the Danes; and this origin is very often ascribed to them by Irish and Hebridean tradition. But Lady Ferguson's observation that the "Danes" and the "Danaans" or "Tuatha De Danann," are evidently confounded in the popular memory, is worth considering here. It is clear, at any rate, that the "Danes" of the year 861 who plundered those Boyne mounds cannot have been the people who reared them.

mounts, and so may be some mark or direction to find out the hidden entrance, to other sepulchres of this kind, further enquiry may inform us.

Figure the 7th [reproduced p. 126, *ante*] shows more particularly the manner and contrivance of the altar in the right hand cell, ... expressing all the rudeness of its work. *a a a a* the upright flag-stones that compose the side-walls. *b b b* the lintal-stone that's laid a-cross over the entrance of the cell; upon the surface of this stone, the artist has exprest abundance of rude barbarous sort of sculpture. *c c* a lower altar serving us a basis to *d*, another lesser altar raised upon it."

Dr. Molyneux also describes " two *Roman* golden coins " (Llhwyd only mentions *one*) which " about ten or twelve years since " were found " near the surface," on the exterior of the mound; but these have practically as little to do with the structure itself as if they had been found in the neighbouring meadow.

In comparing these two eighteenth-century accounts, one observes a few points calling for observation. But, before referring particularly to these, it may be convenient to add some of the statements made by Col. Forbes-Leslie with regard to the same mound. This writer, in his " Early Races of Scotland " (Edin., 1866, Vol. II., pp. 331-341), makes several interesting remarks upon the mound of New Grange, and others of a similar nature, and among his illustrations are two of New Grange, drawn by himself. These, however, do not supply any additional information. On the subject of this and similar mounds, Colonel Leslie remarks thus:—

" Neither historical evidence, nor that derived from an examination of these monuments, appears sufficient warrant for the decision that all these chambers were exclusively intended for places of sepulture. Certainly in some of these chambers the massive materials used in their construction have apparently been designed and employed for other purposes. The following questions are suggested by peculiarities in these specimens of chambered tumuli—Were they intended to be occupied by the living, or as sepulchres for the dead? Were they originally used as temples, and afterwards turned into tombs? Or, on the contrary, although raised for tombs, were they afterwards used as habitations? . . . .

" An examination of the remarkable tumuli above mentioned gives rise to the above questions, and they are not answered by any theories or explanations regarding these monuments which have yet been offered to the public. It may be admitted, although it cannot be proved, that all or most of these monuments have at some period been used as sepulchres, and that the mound of stones or earth in which they are enveloped is sepulchral." But, in a foot-note, Col. Leslie adds: "There is no authentic record of human remains having been discovered either in New Grange, in the tumulus of Gavr-Innis [Brittany], or in that of Maeshow."

* * * * *

"What are usually called sarcophagi in the chamber at New Grange may more correctly be designated as very shallow trays of a circular or rather oval form. In the eastern recess there are two— one placed above another of somewhat larger dimensions, the uppermost being 3 feet long. The position and appearance of all of them are very unlike anything intended for the reception of sepulchral deposits."

. . . . "New Grange cairn is about 70 feet in height, and is said to cover an area nearly two acres in extent. Composed of loose stones, slightly covered with earth and partly overgrown with trees, this mound formerly had little appearance of being artificial, except that at a few yards' distance it was encircled by a line of single stones of great size fixed upright in the ground. The entrance to the chamber in this mound was accidentally discovered in 1699 by labourers who were removing stones to repair a neighbouring road." . . .

"In each of the three recesses of the chamber were the shallow trays already mentioned, which by different writers have been variously designated as 'basins,' 'rude bowls,' 'urns,' 'typical urns,' 'sarcophagi.'¹ There was one in the northern and one in the western recess, but the most remarkable are two in the eastern recess. The uppermost of these is somewhat oval in shape, slightly concave on its surface, and 3 feet in length: in it are two small artificial cavities. This tray lies on another, which is rather larger and less concave than that which rests on it. The tray in the western recess, although but slightly hollowed, has a well-defined rim on the edge of the upper surface. . . .

"New Grange was first described by Edward Lhuyd the antiquary, who, writing in 1699, makes no mention of any human remains being found in it, but notes 'a great many bones of beasts and some pieces of deers' horns' lying under foot."

¹ Of all these terms the "shallow tray" (or "saucer," if a new one may be added) is the most appropriate. From the plan of the Dowth mound (*ante*, p. 138) it will be seen that the central chamber there also has one of those large stone "trays." No satisfactory solution has yet been offered of the purposes for which these "trays" were made.

It will be seen that these accounts vary in several respects. One curious discrepancy is that relating to the shallow stone "trays" in the recesses of the central chamber. Dr. Molyneux states that the northern recess contained one of these, and his young namesake shows such a "tray" in his plan; and yet Llhwyd, writing twenty-five years earlier, distinctly says that "in the apartment straight forward there was none at all." That this is the case at the present day will be seen from the plan by Mr. W. F. Wakeman. It is noteworthy that Colonel Leslie also gives the number as three; but he speaks in the past tense when referring to the north recess, and he probably only echoes Molyneux. But Llhwyd's statement is so distinct that, considering his priority of date, his version must be accepted as the true one, in spite of the fact that young Molyneux (who, although he is stated to have drawn his plan "on the place," may have supplemented it from memory) represents the inner "apartment" as occupied by one of those "trays."

As for the theories of the two earlier writers, on the subject of the origin and purpose of this "mount," it will be observed they differ widely. Molyneux has no doubt about its being the work of the ninth-century Danes, while Llhwyd, arguing from the discovery of Roman coins on the outer crust, infers that it was erected by "the ancient Irish." Although the coins cannot be held to constitute a strong reason for accepting Llhwyd's conclusions, other good grounds for doing so are obvious to every reader of the foregoing pages.

Again, while Molyneux states very definitely that "when first the cave was opened, the bones of two dead bodies entire, not burnt, were found upon the floor," Llhwyd merely remarks that "they found several bones in the cave, and part of a stag's (or else elk's) head, and some other things," and Forbes-Leslie asserts that "there is no authentic record of human remains having been discovered" in this chambered mound.

All of the writers quoted differ also as to the uses to which this structure was put. It was "some place of sacrifice or burial," according to Llhwyd; Molyneux is sure that it was a "sepulchre"; and Forbes-Leslie regards the whole matter as undecided. But, though the last-named writer is of opinion that this, and similar mounds, may have been dwellings, he nevertheless admits that undoubtedly many of them, if not all, have also been used as places of burial. And these two beliefs are quite reconcilable, if one accepts what Professor Boyd Dawkins refers to as "the hypothesis of the origin of chambered tombs invented by Prof.

Nilsson." "Chambered tombs, according to that great authority, were originally the subterranean houses in which the deceased lived, and there the dead were laid literally each 'in his own house.'" Whether human skeletons were really found in "the Brugh of the Boyne" or not, it seems clear that the mound at Dowth was ultimately, at any rate, a place of sepulture. "The most remarkable difference" between it and its more famous neighbour was, says Colonel Leslie, "that in Dowth fragments of burned human bones were discovered." And it is to be noted that tradition speaks of this place as "the cave (or 'weem') of the grave of Bodan, above Dowth:" (*Uaimh Fairt Bodan os Dubath*). Dowth, or Dubath, may have denoted the mound itself; in which case the word signifying "above" or "upon" might refer to an exterior burial, in the "crust" of the mound, of which there are many examples. For instance, although tradition speaks of the Inverness *Tomnahurich* as an inhabited "brugh," yet its exterior was used as a place of burial at a very early date, as is testified by the discovery, a few years ago, of a stone "kist," containing a human skeleton, buried some feet below the surface of the mound.¹ However, the word *Dubath* (conjectured on a previous page to have signified *dubh-ath*, "the black ford") probably did not originally denote the mound itself, and *if* therefore was "above Dubath," and the central chamber of the mound constituted "the weem of the grave of Bodan," who was presumably the owner of the "burned human bones" referred to by Colonel Leslie.

But, while a description of the "Brugh of the Boyne" would be very imperfect without a reference to the subject of burial in chambered mounds, the various traditions which have been collected in these pages (themselves a minute fraction of the whole) show that such mounds, whatever their secondary use, are pre-eminently distinguished in the memory of the people as the *dwelling-places* of a certain peculiar "underground" race.

¹ Described in the Edinburgh *Courant* of January 6, 1886.

APPENDIX B.

THE SKRÆLINGS.

THERE are many references to the North American Skrælings in Rafn's great work entitled "Antiquitates Americanæ: sive Scriptores Septentrionales Rerum Ante-Columbianarum in America," published under the auspices of the Royal Society of Northern Antiquaries (Copenhagen, 1837). This is a collection of the accounts in the old Northern chronicles, relating to the Northmen's (*gamle Nordbœrs*) voyages of discovery to America, between the tenth and fourteenth centuries. And from these accounts it is seen that the tribes then inhabiting the territories on either side of the Gulf of St. Lawrence, and as far south as Massachusetts, were the Skrælings; with whom the Northmen occasionally fought, and at other times traded, giving them pieces of red cloth in exchange for furs.

That the term by which they are chiefly known to modern writers was not the only one given to them by the Northmen is seen from a remark made by one of the chroniclers of Thorfinn Karlsefne, who states that "these people are called Lappa in some books (*thar thjódhir halla sumir hakr Lappa*)."[1] On the other hand, the map of Olaus Magnus, referred to in the foregoing pages, shows that the northern corner of Norway was then inhabited by a race of *Scri-Finni*, "commonly called 'Screlings,'" who at least were the neighbours of Lappa.

In connection with the North American "Lappa" or "Skrælings," the editor of *Antiquitates Americanæ* supplies the following note (p. 45):—"Skrælingos appellatos autumat Busæus ob humilem staturam; quam ob rem et interdum ab Islandis *Smælingjer* (homunculi) audiunt. Hæc vero communis appellationis ratio vix esse potest. Arnas Magnæus in collectaneis ad novam editionem

[1] *Antiq. Amer.* p. 182 n.

Schedarum Arii polyhistoris, vocem *Skrælingier* interpretatur erronea, incertum qua ratione, cum ipse nullam attulerit. Suhmius (*Kjöbnhavnske Selskabs Skrifter*, VIII., pag. 81) eos ita propter vilem armaturam appellatos putat. Nonne potius nomen istud ob ora macilenta adepti sunt, ab *at skrælu*, arefacere? Nota, Petrum Clausenium Undalinum, in descriptione Norvegiæ, ed. Hafn. 1632, pag. 375-6, hoc nomen scribere *Skregklinge* et *Skreglinge*, qu. a *skrælja*, clamare, ejulare, cfr. Partic. de Karlsefnio, cap. 10 infra."

Whatever may be the etymology of this word (which in some of its forms approaches the "*Skris-*Finni" of Norway), it is quite clear from the *Antiquitates Americanæ* that those tenth-century natives of what is now New England and New Brunswick strongly resembled the modern Eskimos. "Hæc descriptio Skrællingorum accurate quadrat in hodiernos Grænlandos sive Eskimoos," is the observation made by the editor (p. 149, *n.*) on a description of some of those people encountered by the Northmen. And, similarly, the note relative to their skin-canoes, or kayaks, is as follows: [1]— "*Hûdhkeipr*, species navigii, acatium coriaceum vel corio contextum, quo usi sunt indigenæ, ut etiamnunc Grænlandi ex genere Eskimoorum; itaque per carabum redditum, qui secundum Isidorum Hispal. in Orig. Libr. 19, cap. 1. est 'parva scapha ex vimine facta, qui contexta crudo corio genus navigii præbet.'—Vocem illustrat vir doctissimus Gunnar Pauli, *l.* in annotationibus, insertis indici vocum *Orkneyinga saga*: '*Hûdhkeipr*, navis sutilis, vel, si mavis, corio obducta vel circumdata. Nam phocarum ad hanc usum pelles adhibere Grænlandos notum est, quorum naves *hûdhkeipr* nostratibus olim sunt appellatæ.'"

In these references there is much that is suggestive. One would like to know the occasions on which the Latin term "acatium" was used; and also the circumstances which induced an editor of the *Orkneyinga Saga* to enlarge upon the appearance of the *hûdhkeipr*. Taken in connection with the existence of kayak-using Finnmen, in the Orkney Isles, less than two centuries ago, this latter allusion is very striking. Similarly, an explanation of the term "Skregklinge" or "Skreglinge," occurring in a description of *Norway*, of the year 1632 (above referred to), arouses equal interest in that work.

That the Skrælings, wherever situated, were "pigmies," is evident from the testimony of Olaus Magnus,—and the accounts of the eleventh-century Northmen fully corroborate this. One of their references is as follows: "They were small, ugly men, with horrible

[1] P. 43, note *a.*

heads of hair, great eyes, and broad cheek-bones: (*Their voru nadir menn ok illiligir, ok illt höfdu their hár á höfdhi, eygdhir voru their mjök ok breidhir í kinnunum*)."[1] Another description occurs in the *Saga of Thorfinn Karlsefni* which relates how, in the year 1011 A.D. (three years after his first encounter with the American Skrælings), he and his people arrived at Markland,—a country identified with the modern New Brunswick and other lands lying round the Gulf of St. Lawrence. Here they encountered five Skrælings, one man, two women and two boys: ("... *ok funnu thar Skrælingja 5, ok var einn skeggiadhr ; konur voru 2, ok börn tvö ;*" in which passage it may be noted that the man was distinguished by the term "bearded," —*skeggiadhr*). They captured the two boys, "but the others escaped, and sank beneath the ground:" ("*Verisimile est, Skrælingos in cavernas subterraneas se abdidisse,*" is the explanation given by the commentator in *Antiquitates Americanæ*).[2] Karlsefne's people took the boys away with them, had them baptized, and taught them Icelandic. These stated that their father and mother (no doubt, the "bearded one" and one of the two women, then lamenting them in their underground dwelling) were respectively named Uvægo and Vethillda;[3] and that their people had no houses, but lived in dens and caves: ["*I hellum edha holum*"]. The country of the Skrælings, they said, was governed by two kings or chiefs, one named Avalldamon (or Avalldunon) and the other Valldi-dida."

It will be seen from these references that although those Skrælings of nine centuries ago are rightly regarded as probable progenitors of modern Eskimos, there were some differences between the two. The term "shaggy" or "bearded," used to distinguish the man from his two female companions, certainly does not indicate that the latter were themselves hirsute. But the previous reference to the "ugly" or "horrible" heads of hair, and the description of their eyes as very large, are two points that seem to denote a race not wholly identical with modern Eski-

---

[1] Pages 180-1. It ought to be added that the version which is given on p. 149 has *svartir* ("swarthy" or "black") instead of *nadir*. But whichever of these versions has the correct word, the small stature of the Skrællings is beyond dispute.

[2] Page 162, note a. The account above referred to is given at pp. 161-2, and again at pp. 182-3.

[3] According to the version on p. 162. That of p. 182 makes both names feminine, and indicates that the boys were not sons of one mother. A footnote on p. 162 gives many variants of these names, *e.g.*, Ægi, Ovægi, etc., Wethlildi, Vehbildi, etc.

mos. Moreover, the rapid disappearance of the adults underground, on the occasion when the two boys were captured, is more suggestive of the dwarfs of tradition (such as those who similarly escaped from Snafurlami when he attempted to smite them with his magic sword), than of the Greenlanders of to-day.

Although the accounts of the two boy prisoners might be held to denote that the manners they described were new to the Northmen, yet an incident of earlier date shows clearly that the latter quite understood the subterranean ideas of those North American "Lapps." The incident referred to is this: In the year 1004, Thorwald Ericson and his followers had surprised a small party of nine Skrælings at the entrance to Plymouth Harbour, on the coast of Massachusetts,[1] and of these they killed eight. The ninth sped away in his skin-canoe to the inner end of the bay, out of which there presently emerged an infuriated swarm of kayakkers. But before they appeared, the Northmen had had time to note a group of "hillocks" on the beach (apparently on the interior curve of the promontory terminating in the modern "Gurnet Point,") and these "hillocks" they assumed to be the abodes of the Skrælings.[2] This was seven years before the capture of the boys by Karlsefne's party, and the inference clearly is that they were accustomed to regard kayak-using dwarfs as mound-dwellers. Indeed, the very fact that they styled the natives "Lapps" and "goblins,"[3] as well as Skrælings, shows that they regarded them as belonging to the same race as similar people well known to them in Europe.

[1] That, at any rate, is the locality agreed upon by those who have traced the routes of the Northmen.
[2] *Op. cit.*, p. 43.
[3] See p. 144n., *ante*.

INDEX.

Aagerup, Denmark: reputed chambered mound near, 155.
Aberfoyle, Perthshire: reputed chambered hill at, 152-3.
Abernethy, Perthshire: Round Tower of, said to have been built by Pechts, 67, 86. A. district a former territory of the Pechts, 190.
Ainos. A dwarfish race, 163; their past history, 163-6; their characteristic hairiness, 166-170; their platycnemism, 170; their speed, 171; their "short, screeching" cry, 168; A's. make use of reindeer, moccasins, "ships," and harpoons, all of which show affinity of custom, if not of blood, with Eskimo families, 169-171.
Alaskan, or Aleutian Eskimos, 90, 22.
All-Hallows. (See Halloween.)
Almhain or Allen, Hill of, Kildare: Finn's dwelling at, 56.
Almhain or Almond, Glen, West Perthshire: resort of Finn, 77.
Ardmore, Waterford: Round Tower of, said to have been built in the manner ascribed to the Pechts, 71n.
Argyleshire. (See under Mounds.)
Arthur, and "primitive Britons" or "Pechts," 142-3n.
Arthur's Seat, Edinburgh, 143n.
Aschberg, Castarld, province of Antwerp. A reputed chambered mound, 86-7, 155.

Ashbury, Berkshire. A chambered mound, 132n.
Auverimiers of Guernsey tradition, 16, 17n.

Baie Thaqgardell, Island of Barra: story of a chambered mound near, San, 115.
Ballindalloch (near), Banffshire: reputed chambered mound, 117.
Bantby, Lincolnshire: tradition of dwarfs wearing red caps, 107n.
Battle. A Flan dale, 94. A Fairy dale, 98.
Ben-cnock, Islay: reputed chambered mound, 114.
Ben Muich Dhui, Aberdeenshire: Dwarfs of, 97.
Bergen, Norway: a celebrated resort of the Shetland Finns, 5. 13: suzerainty of B. over N.E. Scotland, 37. The Strith of B., 7n.
Birnes, Aberdeenshire: reputed chambered mound, 117.
Blackwater, Leinster, 92.
Blackwater, Munster, 92, 127.
Blackwater, East Perthshire, 94-5.
Blackwater, West Perthshire, 152.
Bolg. (See Fir-Bolg.)
Bondorup, Sylt: the Pudelal at, 87.
Brechin, Forfarshire: Round Tower at B. said to have been built by the Pechts, 72.
Brittany: church in B. said to have been built by Fairies, 85-6; Frais or Fians of B., 85.
Broch, Brug, etc., 43n, 61, 77-79.

Brugh of Crichoch, Perthshire: a chambered mound, 119, 149-151, 153.

Brownies, 80, 141-2, 158-164. (See also Fairies, etc.)

Brugh of the Boyne, County Meath, 84, 111, 119-133, 153.

Bugle, Buffalo, or Urus, 80-81n, 93.

Buildings said to have been reared in a single night: Abernethy Tower, 85-6; Chapels in Brittany, 85; Castle of the Gypsiesses, 86.

Burray, Orkney. Finnman's boat once preserved there, 6. All trace of it now lost, 17n.

Canoe. (See Skin-Boat.) "Dug-out," 31.

Cassiterides. (See Oestrymnic Isles.)

Caser Thun, Forfarshire: said to be Pictish, 73, 76, 86, 99; alleged to have been built by a witch, and inhabited by Fairies, 99-100: a kettle of gold believed to be hidden there, 150n.

Cathair Mhor } Cairbach, Ross-shire: Cathair Bheag } fairy residences, 118.

"Castell" in S. of Scotland, said to have been built by Pechts, 67.

Cave-Men: in Uist, Hebrides, during 17th century, 29.

"Cavern" at Yester, or Gifford, East Lothian, 143.

Chambered Mounds. (See Mounds.)

Chessmen of Walrus Ivory, found in Hebrides, 32, 158n.

Chroie, Perthshire, Castle Hill of: reputed chambered mound, 145-146.

Clydesdale. Pecht's house in C., 66; Glasgow cathedral said to have been built by Pechts, 72; traditional description of dwarf of C., 97.

Cnock-donn, Islay: reputed chambered mound, 114.

Cnoc Fraing, Inverness-shire: a house of fairies, 146.

Coir-nan-Uruisgean, Perthshire, 151-152.

Cuilloch beard, Perthshire, 119, 149-151, 153.

Colonsay, island of: Macphail of C. and his (?) Finn lover, 15-16; tradition of dwarfs living in C., 147: Sith, an Mor and Stidhean Rag, 147.

Connaught, Fians of, 76, 93.

Corrywrekin, Argyleshire: The (?) Finn woman of C. and her Colonsay lover, 15-16.

Corstorphine Church, near Edinburgh; said to have been built by the "Hornemen," 70-71.

Craig Patrick, Inverness-shire, 148.

Craig y Dinas, Glamorganshire, 149n.

Crocan Corr, Kilbrannon, Argyleshire: reputed chambered mound, 114.

Cromar, Aberdeenshire: underground gallery at, 101.

Crown, Inverness, 149n.

Cruachan rath: re-built by a servile race, 68n, 135n, 136, 152n; "a party of smiths at work" in its interior, 158.

Cruithne. (See also Picts, etc.) Were pre-Milesian, 51. Were connected with the "Lochlin" territory, 51. Their connection with Feens and Fairies, 128-9.

Cusligan: Finn's fort on, 75-76.

"Cyclopean" character of Pictish buildings, 73.

Danaans (Tuatha De Danaan): classed with the Cruithne as of "Continental origin," and "pre-Milesian" in settling in British Isles; and consequently to be classed with the Fians, 51. Known also as the Fir Sìth or Fairies, 126; account of their rivalry with the Milesians, 124-127; description of the dwelling assigned to the King of the Danaans, 129-130 and Appendix A.

Danes; their ravages in the Boyne Valley in 861, when they plundered the underground chambers of the "Fians and Fairies," 83-84.

Danish ballad of dwarfs and submarine,
  105-6.
Dartmoor; Pixyhouses and pixies, 161-2.
Davis Straits. Conjectured by some
  to be the home of the Orkney
  Finnmen, 7. Kakau of D. S. at
  Leith in 1816, 8, 12
Deer. (See also Reindeer and Elk.)
  Hunted in Ulenshire, East Peeb-
  shire, by the Finns, 94-5; "great-
  horned" D., 95; D. milked and
  used as beasts of burthen, 96.
Denghoog; chambered mound in Sylt,
  87, 112-113, 122.
Denmark. (See also Lochlin.) Eck-
  walls church said to have been
  built by a "hill-man," 85-86n.
  (See also "Mounds reputed to be
  chambered.")
Devonshire, 161-2.
Dig-à; an equivalent for sidhean, 79n.
Donegal. Skin-boats used by natives
  of "The Rosses," 28; Finn Town,
  D., 83.
Doon, or Doo's, of Aherfoyle, 153-154.
Dunn of Mentethh, 144.
Doon of Kullmunnogshan, 144-145.
Dornoch Firth; Natives ferried them-
  selves across D. F. in "cockle-
  shells," 17, 32.
Dowth, or Dubath; chambered mound,
  80, 111, 119, 152-3, 157.
Drimirch, or Trimirch, a Gaelic term
  applied to the Picts, signifying
  "labourers," 71-72.
Druigan. Crusches each re-built by
  an ancestral race, 68n, 125n, 136,
  152n. Similar references, 68-74,
  151-2, Cypiudara, 88.
Druids, 135-157.
Dunnan, in Galloway; a fairy fort, 99.
Dunstanborough Castle, Northumberland, said to have been built by
  the Picts, 67.
Dwarfs. (See also Pechts or Picts.)
  D's of Shetland tradition, otherwise Finns, 56; also 59.
  D's of Scottish tradition generally,
  otherwise Pechts, 58-60; D's
  of Highland tradition, 57, 97;
  D's of Clydesdale, 97.

Dwarfs: D's of Northumberland, 67,
  80, 86, 99.
  D's of Yorkshire, 100.
  D's of Lincolnshire, 107n.
  D's of Wales, 160-2.
  D's of Cornwall, 162.
  D's of Devon, 161-2.
  Finn of the Fians a D., 55-56.
  D's of Brittany (Finns, etc.), 85.
  D's of Antwerp, 86-87.
  D's of the Netherlands, 86.
  D's of Denmark and Danish tradi-
    tion, 85-86n, 105-106.
  D's of Sylt, 87, 112-113.
  D's of Scandinavia, 91.
  D's of Germany, 163-4, 172-3.
  D's of Greenland and North
    America, 63.
  D's of Japan, 157, 165 et seq.
  D's of Africa, 157.
  Great bodily strength ascribed to
    the Scotch Pechts, 72-73; to
    the Northumbrian Picts, 67,
    72-3; to the dwarfs of Tiamen,
    in the Netherlands, 86.
  D's at war with each other, and
    with men, 99n.
  Coom the colour of the D's, 97.
  Tribute exacted by the D's, 97.
  Magic of the D's, 108.
  Hidden treasures of the D's, 107n,
    139n, 150n.
  D's as serfs or drudges, 151-2.
  D's in one aspect civilised, in
    another savage, 196-7.
  Hairiness of skin of D's, 157-164,
    169n.

Eamhain, or Eamhna, 49, 133-4.
Eckwalt, Denmark; residence of a
  "hill-man" seen, 85n.
Eday, Orkney; Finnmen seen there in
  1682, 5.
Edinburgh. Finnman's skull preserved
  there 6; Corstorphine church
  said to have been built by the
  "Flauntunts," 70-71; Pecht-lands
  near E., 68-71; King Arthur and
  the Pechts believed to have entered
  a subterranean chamber at Arthur's
  Seat, 141n.

Eilean Suthainn, Loch Maree; a fairy resort, 118.
Elk. Hunted in East Perthshire by the Finns, 94-95; horns of E. found there, 95; *lus-Mablann* "birch elk," 95.
Erribol, Sutherlandshire: Worm, Pecht's House, or Fairy Hall at, 101.
Eskimos.
    Compared with Shetland Finns, 7-8; with Pechts, 53, 77-78; with Finns and Lapps, 53; with "Skraelings," Appendix B; with Ainos, 169-171.
    E. or Skraeling chambered mounds in Greenland, Labrador, and Massachusetts, 60-4, 77-78, 155, and Appendix B.
    Kayaks: their speed, 8; feat of overturning kayak, 12.
    Kayakker, at some distance, resembles triton or mer-man, 13.
    Open skin-boats of E., 52.
    Dwarfish stature of E., 63.
    E's of Alaska, 92, of Greenland, 12-13n, 53, 60-4, 142n.
    E. magicians believe they can control the winds, 53, 69.
    An E. type in modern Britain, 37-8.
Ew, island, Ross-shire; a haunt of 17th c. "pirates," 29.
Evie, Orkney; reputed chambered mounds at, 112n.

Fairies. (See Danaans, Finns, Pechts, Dwarfs, &c.)
    F's inhabited the *brugh*, sidh-bhrugh or *sheen*, otherwise the "Pecht's house," 79.
    F's associated with Pechts, 80; with Finns, 81-84; with Finns, 85.
    As Danaans (q. v.) F's associated with Cruithne, 51, 127-129.
    Builders of a church in Brittany in circumstances suggestive of the Pechts, 85.
    Inhabitants of the White Cater Thun, an alleged stronghold of the Pechts, 99-100.

Fairies:
    "Dancing and making merry" in the Orkneys, c. 1700 (cf. Shetland Finns, 31, 14, 112n.
    Frequently seen at Fairy Hill, Westray, at same period, 33.
    "Fairy Ha'" in Shetland, 104.
    "In armour" in Orkney, 14; at war with each other in Ireland, 93.
    Tithes due to F., 97.
    "Good" F's of christenings, etc., 81-8; "Christian" F's, 85.
    F's of Clydesdale, 97.
    F's as tarfs or drudges, 131-2.
Fairy Knowe of Aberfoyle, 132-4.
Fairy Knowe beside Broch of Cahluch (itself a sidh-bhrugh Fairy Knowe), 119, 148, 151.
Fearna, Worm of, 136-7.
Fern Fiord, Bergen, 70.
Finns, or Feens, or Feinne of Gaelic lore:
    The Land of the F's, 45.
    The Well of the F's, 43.
    The Hillock of the F's, 130.
    Other F. localities, 48, 49, 51, 52.
    Dr. Skene's belief as to the historical position of the F's, 46.
    F's preceded the Milesians in Ireland, 46, 51.
    F. Confederacy not restricted to Ireland, but included the following divisions:—F's of England and Wales; of Northern and Central Scotland; and of Lochlin, understood to be the Rhine-Elbe region, 47-51.
    Irish F's divisible into:—F's of Connaught and West; F's of Leinster; and F's of Eastern Ulster, 78, 93.
    F's referred to in Scotland in Perthshire (Glenlyon, Glenmailie-with-Glenshee, and Glenshee or Blackwater) 77, 94-95. Outer Hebrides and part of West Highlands specially the Land of the F., 45. (?) Referred to in Ayrshire, 85.

Finns:
  F's exacted tribute from Irish kings, 47.
  Their ancient rights of hunting and of free-quarters, 94.
  Overthrow of F's at Battle of Gawra, 47.
  Vanished glory of the F's, 75-76, 110.
  Fin, their chief, court dwarf to the king of the "big men," 56.
  F's as the drudges and serfs of another race, 75.
  F's inhabited "Pechts' houses," 76-77.
  F's as builders of stone forts, 75-76.
  F's regarded as dwarfs, 65.
  F's associated with Danaans, Fir Sidhe, or Fairies, 51, 81-84.
  F's regarded as Cruithne or Picts, 51-2, 54.
  Their assumed identity with historical and traditional Finns, 44-50, 54-5, 65.
  Their magic identified with that of the Finns, 54.
  Their "great-antlered deer," 95.
  Their darts, 54-5.
  Their swiftness of foot, 177.
  A descendant of the F., 46.
Fierna, or Fieria, King of the Sidhe of Munster, 93, 127.
  His "hillock" near Limerick, 93, 145.
Fin, Finn, or Fionn, a chief of the Feens of Gaelic tradition:
  Grandson of a Finland woman, 49-50.
  Described as going in his skin-boat to the Kingdom of the Big Men, where he became the court dwarf, 55-6.
  A dwarf in a Scotch poem of said race, styled a grandson of F., 65.
  His stone fort on Coolgan, 75-6, 93.
  His "castles" in Glenlyon, Perthshire, 77.
Finland. Alleged to be the home of the Orkney Finnmen (6), of the grandmother of "Fin" (49-50), of the Fomorians (50n).
Finn, a chief of the dwarfs of Sylt tradition, 87, 112-113.
  Chambered mound of Denghoog said to have been his dwelling, 87, 112-113.
Finnmen of Orkney:
  Used to fish in Orkney waters in 17th century, 5-6.
  Their seal-skin boats described, 6.
  The great speed of these skin-boats, 5-6.
  Specimens of their boats at Burray and Edinburgh, 6, 10, 11n, 87n.
  F's said to have come from Finland, 6.
  Regarded as "barbarous men" by Edinburgh physicians of 1694, 10, 30-31.
  "The Dart he makes use of for killing fish," 6.
Finns of Shetland tradition:
  Their "sun-skins or seal-skins," 5.
  The great speed of these "skins," 4-5.
  F's said to have come from Norway, and also from "Shool Skerry," 3-4.
  Sea-rovers or pirates, 3, 34-35.
  Magicians, soothsayers, and doctors, 1-5.
  Inter-married with Shetlanders, 1-6, 34-35.
  Descendants of such marriages "lucky," and proud of their descent, 1, 2, 5.
  Cattle of the F's, 4.
  F's regarded as death, 56, 92.
  Dancing on the sands "every ninth night," 3 (cf. Fairies, 14, 111n.)
  Identified with Ferns, 43-44, 54, 65.
Finns and Lapps:
  Their territory formerly greater than now, 35.
  Inter-marriages with non-Finnish races, 37-42.

Finns and Lapps:
　A semi-Finn race of Orkney, 40-41.
　F. or L. type in modern Britain, 37-38.
　F's of Lofoten neighbourhood in 13th century, 31, 39.
　Boats made by them, 31. Skiffs of modern L's, 29n.
　Swedish-F. settlement in Pennsylvania, U.S. in 17th century, 36-37.
　"Lapp" natives of North America in 11th century, Appendix B.
　F's or L's as magicians, "selling winds," etc., 16, 41, 53, 91-92. Identified with Fairies, 96-97; with Feens, 30; with Dwarfs, 129n and Appendix B.
Finns, etc. on the Continent:
　Finns of Brittany (dwarfs who lived with the fairies), 85. Feins, 84n.
Fir-Bolg, or Firbolgs. Canadian raid re-built by a race of F., 68n, 135n, 136, 152n.
Fitty Hill, Westray. (See Westray.)
Fortevict, Perthshire, 69.
Forth, River. Chambered mounds of Forth valley, ascertained and reputed, 114, 119, 151-154.

Gabhra, or Gowra, Battle of, 47-50.
Gaels. (See Milesians.)
Gairloch, Ross-shire. Toachuidhe Ghearrloch, 112; Big and Little "Cathairs" of G., 113; Sidhnean Dubha, 113.
Galloway: probable Finns in G., 35; Picts commonly called "Galloway-men," 69-70n; last stronghold of Picts in G., 99; stronghold of Fairies in G., 99.
Garbhriach.—translated as "the rough bounds," and defined as the country between Loch Linnhe and the Hebrides, formed a portion of the "Land of the Feens," 45. Called also Garbh-chriocha, 112.
Germany. (See under Lochlin.)

Gillenbierg, Denmark: reputed chambered mound, 155n.
Glac-an-t-Shithein, Nether Lochaber, 147n.
Glasgow Cathedral, said to have been built by the Pechts, 72.
Glenlyon, Perthshire, a home of the Feens, 77.
Glen Odhar, Sutherlandshire: its fairy herds believed to have been reindeer, 97.
Glenshee and Glen Almain, West Perthshire, a home of the Feens, 77.
Glenshee, East Perthshire, a favourite hunting-ground of the Feens, 94.
Glen-na-Shirich, Nether Lochaber, a glen of the Fairies, 147n.
Gobban, Goblin, Gabhlan, etc., 113, 144n, 162n.
Gobban Saor (The Noble Smith), 84, 152-3; his chambered mound, 152.
Goblin Ha', East Lothian, 143.
Goblin Knowe (Cnoc nan Boran), Perthshire, 151-152.
Goblins of Greenland, 144n.
Gomarees. An enslaved tribe of Firbolgic origin, 68n, 135n, 136, 152n.
Green, the colour of the Fairies or Dwarfs, 97; of the Feens, 97-8; of the Pechts, 99.
Grudie, near Lairg, Sutherlandshire: reputed chambered mound at, 116-117.
Gruinard, Ross-shire: resort of 17th-century pirates, 30.
Gubbins of Dartmoor, 161-2; their swiftness of foot, 177.
Gulstbierg, Denmark: a reputed chambered mound, 155n.
Gurnett Point, Massachusetts: reputed chambered mound near, Appendix B.
Gwyddaid Cochion Mawddwy, an underground race in Wales, 180-1; "their swiftness and agility," 177.
Gyppiners, or Dwarf-women of the Netherlands, 86.

Hadeland, Norway, raided by a semi-
   Finn, 40-42.
Hadrian's Wall said to have been built
   by the Picts, 67.
Hairy Men. (See Shaggy Men, Ainos,
   etc.)
Halfdan Haleg, a semi-Finn noble:
   was lord of Orkney for some
   months: slain at North Ronald-
   shay, 40-41.
Hallowmas. A Fenn date, 94. A
   Fairy date, 98.
Hebrides:
   Outer H. regarded as part of the
      "Land of the Fenns," 45.
   Some parts of H. thickly wooded
      in 16th century, 105n.
   Raids made by Lewismen on
      Orkney and Shetland in 15th
      century, 33-35.
   Certain Hebrideans not properly
      subjects of British monarch in
      1608, 26-32.
   Some of the Hebrideans styled
      "savages" by James I. (28),
      and by Skyemen (29); and
      these, or others, referred to as
      "robbers" or "pirates" by a
      17th-century writer (29-30).
   Chessmen of walrus ivory found
      in H., 32, 158n.
   Wigwams of Jura islanders in
      1772, 34.
   "The Harridan physiognomy"
      and stature, 24.
Hill-men, how-folk, Argreammunter,
   hog-boys, shag-boys, etc., 83n,
   107, 111-113.
"Houtmen," builders of Canterphine
   church, 70.

Iberians: used skin-boats, 19-20;
   Iberian type in modern Britain,
   32.
Inverness, 146-149.

Jura, Island of; wigwams of islanders,
   34.

Kaempe Vises, 105.
Kayaks. (See Skin-boats.)

Kaempies or Champions, 43.
Kenilworth, Warwickshire; underground dwarf of, 142-3.
Kettlester, Shetland; remembered as
   a dwarf abode, 50.
Kildrummy, Aberdeenshire; group
   of Weems, Pechts' Houses, or
   Fairy Halls at K., 101.
Kirkcudbright: "in terra Pictorum,"
   69n. (See also Galloway.)
Knowth (Cnoghbha), County Meath;
   chambered mound, 84, 152-4,
   157, 149, 151n.
Kundehye, Denmark; reputed chambered mound at, 155n.

Lapps. (See Finns and Lapps.)
Leinster: Fenns of, 81-2; Fairies of,
   81-2, 92.
Leam-na-Shidhein, 147n.
Limerick: Knockfeerin, 93, 145.
Lincolnshire; shag-boys, fairies and
   red-capps in, 107n.
Lochlin or Lochlan; believed to denote
   the territory between the Rhine
   and the Elbe, but also applied to
   Scandinavia, 49.
Lofoten; Finns or Lapps of L. neigh-
   bourhood in 12th century, 81, 39.

Maes-how, Orkney. (See Mounds.)
Magic: of the Shetland Finns, 1-5,
   14; of the Norwegian Finns or
   Lapps, 16, 41, 53; of Mana
   women, 18; of Picts, 53; of
   Eskimos, 53, 65; of traditional
   dwarfs, 91, 106.
Man, Isle of: Inter-marriages of land-
   folk and sea-folk, 15; witches
   selling winds to sailors, 16; tradi-
   tional description of departure of
   fairies, 17.
Mandans of Upper Missouri; skin-
   boats of, 18.
Mangekbjerg, Denmark. (See Mounds.)
Mer-men and Mer-women. (See Sea-
   Folk.)
Migvie, Aberdeenshire; Weem,
   Pecht's House, or Fairy Hall
   at, 101.

Milesians: A name given to the Gaelic-speaking race, 46, 51; conquered the "Cruithne" or "Pechts" of Scotland in the ninth century, 51; conquered the "Danaans" of Ireland at an earlier period, as described in tradition, 125-126; the possession of a dwarf restricted in Ireland and Gaelic-Scotland to families of Milesian descent, 141-142, 144.

Mounds. Chambered M's of the Pechts described, 61-2, 64; of the Eskimos, 62-3; of both, 77-8. The *mdhus*, *sithidh ag*, etc., 78-79. The "Pelasgic arch" of the chambered mound, 60, 78n.

Mounds ascertained to be chambered:
 Brugh of the Boyne, county Meath, 84, 111, 119-125, 153.
 Dowth mound, County Meath, 84, 111, 119, 132-3, 137.
 Mae-how, Orkney, 106-616, 113, 114, 131, 153.
 Maund on Wideford Hill, Orkney, 62.
 Caldoch "broch," Perthshire, 119, 149-151, 153.
 Ashbury, Berkshire, 132n.
 Dunghong, Syk. 87, 110-112, 132.
 Eskimo Mounds in Lobrador and Greenland, 62-4, 155.
 Mycenæ "treasure house," 153.

Mounds reputed to be chambered:
 In the British Isles:—
  "Some small hillocks" in Evie, Orkney, 111n.
  "Tomhan" near Laing, Sutherlandshire, 116-117.
  Tomhaidh Ghuerrich, Ross-shire, 113, 114.
  Sithsenan Dubh, Gairloch, Ross-shire, 118.
  Specimens of the "Cathair Mhor" and the "Cathair Bheag" in the district of Gairloch, Ross-shire, 118.
  Tomnahurich, Inverness-shire, 146-149, 153.
  Cnor Bradg, Inverness-shire, (? "mountain"), 146.

Mounds reputed to be chambered:
 In the British Isles:—
  Shithan Mor, Inverness-shire, (? "mountain"), 146.
  Dows of Rothiemurchus, Inverness-shire, 144-5.
  Sithean in Corrie-Vinnean, Nether Lochaber, Inverness-shire, 118.
  Sithean Mor and *Sithean Rvag*, in Nether Lochaber, Inverness-shire, 147.
  "Tulman" near Balle Thangusdall, Barra, Inverness-shire, 115.
  At Ballindalloch, Banffshire, 117.
  Hosea, Aberdeenshire, 117.
  Sithean Mor and *Sithean Rvag*, in island of Colonsay, Argyleshire, 147.
  "Dign" at Borra-chuill, an island of Islay, Argyleshire (? the "Dign mōr Thallama" of MacAlpine's Dictionary), 79n.
  Sro-cnock, Island of Islay, Argyleshire, 114.
  Cnoc-donn, (?) island of Islay, Argyleshire, 114.
  Cross Glen, Kilbrennian, Lorn, Argyleshire, 114.
  "Hill" at Mochairn, Argyleshire, 114.
  "Fairy Knowe" or "Dorn" of Aberfoyle, Perthshire, 152-154.
  "Liobhn Kanve" (*Cnoc nan Sheven*), Montalih, Perthshire, 151.
  "Fairy Knowe" beside Broch of Caldoch, Perthshire, 119, 149, 151.
  Ternavie, Perthshire, 150-151.
  "Castle Hill" at Clunie, Perthshire, 145-146.
  Kenilworth, Warwickshire, 142-143.
  Knowth (Cnoghbha), County Meath, 132-140, 151n.
  Slich Nerula, or Hill of Carbury, (? its summit), W. Meath, 89n.
  Knockfierin, County Limerick, 93, 143.

Mounds reputed to be chambered:
  In Denmark:—
    Mangelsbierg, Hirschholm, Hosterkiob Mark, 155n.
    Gilbrebierg, Hirschholm, Hösterkiob Mark, 155n.
    Wheel-hill, Gurlmachtrap, Lordship of Odd, 155v.
    Steenbierg, Ourou, Jaegerspriis, 155v.
    Kundebye, Holbaek, 155n.
    Oukebierg, 155n.
    Söbierg, 155n.
    Mound (or underground gallery) between Augerup and Kamp, 155n.
    The residence of a certain " hill-man " near Edswadt, 85n.
  In Belgium:—
    Aschberg, Casterlé, province of Antwerp, 86-7, 155n.
  In North America:—
    Group of " hillocks " situated, it is believed, on the southern side of Plymouth Harbour, assumed to be the residences of tenth-century " Skraelings " or " Larps " of America, Appendix H.
Mounds, and other localities, referred to as homes or resorts of dwarfs, fairies, Feens, gobblins, etc.:—
  Norwick, Shetland, 107a.
  Uist, Shetland, 106.
  Villenshaw, (?) Orkney, 105, 116.
  Ællean Suthainn, Loch Maree, 112.
  Tobar na Volann, 43.
  Tobar an f Shithrin, Nether Lochaber, 147a.
  Glac an f Shithrin, Nether Lochaber, 147n.
  Lenos an f Shithirbs, Nether Lochaber, 147n.
  Cive-na-Shirird, Nether Lochaber, 147a.
  Knudd na Sitard, Kerrera, 107n.
  White Cater Thun, Forfarshire, 99, 190n.
  Abernethy, Perthshire, 190.
  Glenshee (?) and Glen Almond, Perthshire, 77, 94-5.

Mounds, and other localities, referred to as homes or resorts of dwarfs, &c.:—
  Coir-nan-Uriaguan, Perthshire, 151-2.
  " Cavers " at Yester, 143.
  Hill-country of Galloway, 115-6.
  Thorpe, Lincolnshire, 107n.
  Beesby, Lincolnshire, 107n.
  Mowddwy, Merionethshire, 160-1.
  Craig y Ddinas, Glamorganshire, 143n.
  Nymptom, Devonshire, 162.
  Dartmoor, Devonshire, 162.
  Penzance, Cornwall, 162n.
  Sith Ramhna, Armagh, 133-4.
  Cruachan rath, Connaught, 68n, 135n, 136, 152n.
  Tienen, The Netherlands, 86.
  (See also " Underground Galleries.")
Mulgrave Castle, Yorkshire, 86, 100.
Munster. Fairies of M., 93.

Netherlands. Resemblance of Tienen dwarfs to Scotch and Northumbrian Picts, 86.
Nine. Shetland Finns held festival every ninth night, 3.
" Nine men " apparently the smallest division of a Feenan army, 48.
Norns identified with dwarfs, 91.
Northumberland. Traditional ideas regarding the Picts, 67, 157.
Norway. Finns from N., 3-5; Arrival of N., 37; Lofoten Finns, 31, 39; Ringeriki, Hadeland, and Thoten governed by semi-Finns, 40-42.

Ostryæsic Isles; skin-boats used by natives of, 19-20.
Oisin, 73-77.
Orkney. Picts were early inhabitants of O., 104; O. governed by a semi-Finn in tenth century, 41. (See also Burray, Eday, Evie, Fiaraso, Marr-how, Ronaldshay, Stronsay, Westray.)
Oscar of Emhala, 49.

204 Index

Pabbay, Hebrides, a haunt of 17th-
century pirates, 29.
"Pelasgic arch" of chambered mound,
6a, 78v, 103, 110-111.
Pickering Castle, Yorkshire, 86, 100.
Picts, Piks, Pechs, Pechts, etc. (See
also Crutihne.)
P's said to have been first settlers
in Orkney and Shetland, 59,
104.
Their small boats, 59, 178-179.
Their dwarfish stature, 58-60, 65.
Their great strength, 60, 66-7,
74.
Their mounds or underground
houses, 58-66, 77-78.
Their method of building, 69.
White Caterthun, Brochs
Tower, Abernethy Tower, Glasgow Cathedral, Dunstanburgh
Castle, the Catrail, the Wall of
Hadrian, and many old castles,
popularly believed to have been
built by P's, 67-74, 99-100.
Their last stronghold in Galloway,
99.
P's, or Galloway-men, at the
Battle of the Standard, 69-70.
P's popularity regarded as magicians and supernatural beings,
53, 79-80, 99.
P's associated with Fauns, 53,
64-5; with Fions, Feins, and
Fairies of Brittany, 85; and
with a Danish "hill-man,"
85-6.
P's as serfs or drudges, 67-74, 76.
P's identified by J. F. Campbell
with Lapps and Finlobs, 96.
P's and King Arthur, 143n.
Hairiness of P's, 157-8.
Their swiftness of foot, 177.
Pict or Pechs-land, 52, 68-73.
Pixies of Cornwall and Devon, 162.
"Puchs" of Sylt, 87.

Red-caps in Sylt, 87. In Lincolnshire, 107n. (See also 129n. and
142.)
Reindeer in Scotland, 96-97.
Ringerike, Norway, 90-2.

Rona, Hebrides, and its "pirates," 29.
Ronaldshay (North), 41.
Ross-shire; in 17th century, 29-30,
45; a legendary mound in, 112.

Samoyede. Bergen Strids conjectural
to have linguistic affinity with S.,
71. Skin-boats of N., 18.
Sarogs:
Orkney Fishermen spoken of as S.,
10, 30-31.
Certain Hebrideans referred to as
S., 28, 29, 31.
Strathnaver people in 1658 "barbarous," 30.
Term "Houremen" applied to
traditional builders in Mid-
Lothian, 71.
Sea-Folk. Their inter-marriages with
land-folk:—In Shetland, 1-5, 15;
in Hebrides, 15; in Ireland, 2,
15; in Isle of Man, 15; in Wales,
8, 15. Mer-women as wives and
mothers of land-folk, 1-5, 13, 15.
Mer-men and father-s-ives, 1-5, 13,
15, 154, 31n.
Seal's coat, The, 97.
Setter, Shetland and its "trow's
door," 58.
Shag-boys, Bag-boys, or how-dull, 107.
Shaggy Men. Pechts, 157-8; Traditional dwarf generally, 158-162;
Ainos of Japan, 166 et sq.
Shormen or Sithramen. (See Morasks.)
Shetland. Dwarf abodes in S., 99,
102-3, 106. Plan early inhabitants of S., 104. (See also Finns
of S.)
Shoul Skerry, or Sule Skerry, 3, 34n.
Suibe-folk. (See also Fairies.) Siddhe
and Tsland, 89-90. Hobil-men,
90-91. Worship of S., 92, n.
of North of Ireland and Munster,
93. Identified with Damnonii,
126. Associated with Feens,
158-9. Former high rank, 132.
Skin-boats :
"Sea-skin or seal-skin" of Shetland Finns, 1-5, 8.
Kayaks of Orkney Finnmen,
5-11, 18-19.

Skin-boats :
   Skin-boats of Iberians, Hebrideans, Irish, Welsh, Scotch, Samoyeds, Skraelings, Eskimos, Mandans, 8, 12, 13, 18, 22.
   Fish-skin-boat, 55-6.
   Skin-boat of Picts, 178-9.
   Skin-boat of North American "Lapps" or "Skraelings," 7, Appendix R.
Skraelings, 7, Appendix R.
Smiths, Underground: The "Noble Smith" and his chambered mound, 132-4 ; Wayland Smith's chambered mound, 132n. ; Smiths working in "cave" of Cruachan, 136 ; German traditional idea of such people, 163-4.
Stromay, Orkney. Finnmen seen there about year 1700, 6.

Troith valley. Mounds of, 114. Assumed to be the "raths" referred to by Cichles, as retreated by the Picts, 178n.
Thorps, Lincolnshire ; shag-boys at, 107n.
Thrum, Norway, 40-2.
Tiakhavnal, Norway, 38.
Tionen, Netherlands, dwarfs of, 84.
Tomhuddic Chaorriach ; a reputed chambered mound, 112.
Trow, Troll, or Trollman. (See Dwarfs.)
Tskuda by-go.

Ugrians. (See Finns, Lapps, Skraelings, etc.)

Uist, Hebrides, 29.
Ulster. Forms of, 76, 93 ; Cruithne or Picts of, 93 ; skin-boats of, 18. (See also Raakain.)
Underground Chambers. (See also Mounds.) Indications, apart from those of tradition, that these were dwelling-places, 101-2, 113 (see plans).
Underground galleries, not having mounds over them, 101-4.
Unst, Shetland, 108.
Ur-sing, or Water-men, 142n, 158-164, 178-9.
Urns. (See Bugle.)

Vates, or Volvas, 90-2.
Villemshaw : (?) a locality in Orkney, 105.

Walpurgis Night. (See Beltin.)
Weems. (See Mounds and Underground galleries.)
Westray, Orkney. Finnmen seen near W. circa 1700, 5, 6, 33-4 ; Fairies said to be seen at Fitty Hill circa 1700, 33 ; defeat of Hebrideans at Fitty Hill, 33.
Wideford Hill, Orkney ; chambered mound at, 60.
Witchcraft. (See Magic.)

Yorkshire tradition as to "supernatural" labourers at Mulgrave and Pickering Castles, 86, 102.

Zee-Wemen. (See Sea-Folk.)

www.ingramcontent.com/pod-product-compliance
Lightning Source LLC
Chambersburg PA
CBHW031820230426
43669CB00009B/1201